P9-DBO-964

TOWARD THE

LIVABLE CITY

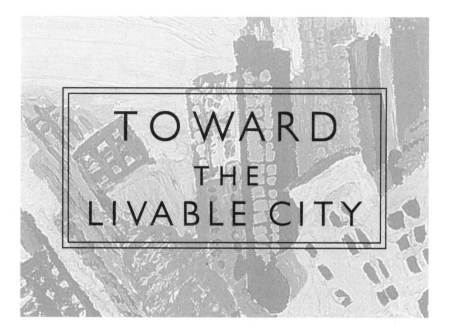

TOWARD
THE
LIVABLE CITY

EDITED BY
EMILIE BUCHWALD

MILKWEED EDITIONS

© 2003, Selection, arrangement, and introduction by Emilie Buchwald.

Individual contributions to *Toward the Livable City,* essays and visual art alike, are protected by copyright and gratefully printed with permission from the creator of each contribution, except when noted otherwise, below.

"Food for the City, from the City," © 2003 by the Food Project, reprinted with permission from the Food Project and the author.

Emily Hiestand is deeply grateful to the editors of the *Atlantic Monthly* and *Bostonia,* in which parts of "The Backside of Civility" first appeared as "Real Places" (*Atlantic Monthly,* August 2001) and "Promised Landscape" (*Bostonia,* Fall 2002).

An earlier version of Tony Hiss's "A Burden, a Blessing," titled "Man About Towns," was published in *Sierra* 86, no. 6 (Nov./Dec. 2001): 62–65, 84–86.

The *Roadkill Bill* character descriptions on pp. 41–42 are reprinted with permission from Randy Ghent.

"New York Sunshine" copyright Ralph Steadman, www.ralphsteadman.com.

All rights reserved. Except for brief quotations in critical articles or reviews, no part of this book may be reproduced in any manner without prior written permission from the publisher: Milkweed Editions, 1011 Washington Avenue South, Suite 300, Minneapolis, Minnesota 55415. (800) 520-6455 / www.milkweed.org / www.worldashome.org

Published 2003 by Milkweed Editions
Printed in the United States of America
Cover and interior design by Christian Fünfhausen
Front cover painting, "The Fountain at Nicollet Park, oil on canvas, and back cover painting, "New York New York I," oil on canvas, by Gladys Beltran.
The text of this book is set in Granjon.
03 04 05 06 07   5 4 3 2 1
First Edition

Milkweed Editions, a nonprofit publisher, gratefully acknowledges support from the Jerome Foundation for the publication of this book and its *Toward the Livable City* web component at www.worldashome.org.

Library of Congress Cataloging-in-Publication Data

Toward the livable city / edited by Emilie Buchwald.—1st ed.
       p.   cm.
    Includes index.
    ISBN 1-57131-271-4 (pbk. : alk. paper)
    1. City planning. 2. Architecture—Human factors. 3. Architecture and society.
 I. Buchwald, Emilie.
    NA9053.H76T69 2003
    307.3'416—dc21

                                                                    2003010374

This book is printed on acid-free, recycled paper.

TO MY GRANDCHILDREN'S GENERATION.
MAY YOUR CITIES BE A TESTAMENT TO YOUR VALUES.

TOWARD THE LIVABLE CITY

ACKNOWLEDGMENTS

I would like to add my applause and thanks to America's civic pioneers and today's civic advocates for their vital involvement in creating and strengthening the vigor of our cities and communities.

Sincere thanks to William Morrish and the late Catherine Brown for leading the Design Center for American Urban Landscape to national prominence and for its work in promoting the recognition that neighborhood, city, suburb, and region are inextricably connected.

I salute Barbara Flanagan for thirty-eight years as a public voice for urban improvement through her newspaper column, urging, cajoling, and admonishing Minneapolis city fathers and mothers to do right by their town.

A world of thanks to each of the writers who interrupted hectic schedules and graciously agreed to write an original essay or to use previous research to write a new essay for this book.

I am deeply indebted to Lynn Marasco for a thoroughly expert copyedit that corrected and sharpened the text. I gratefully acknowledge: the meticulous work of Ben Barnhart on each new iteration of the manuscript; the talent of Christian Fünfhausen, who designed the book and searched for just the right artwork; and the invariable competence and consummate diligence of Laurie Buss in perfecting the whole.

FINDING COMMON GROUND

AN INTRODUCTION

A city with a skyline of memorable buildings or a commanding location is immediately appealing. But livability is more than skin deep, and a crucial factor in assessing it is the quality of one's daily experience. Ask yourself: Do I feel safe on my city's streets and in the parks? Can I avoid gridlock when I commute? Could I, if I so desired, take a bus or light rail to my home or my city destination? Does my city have a car-free area in the center of town for pedestrian use? Is housing available at different price ranges, for rent as well as for sale? Do I have ample choice in places to shop, dine, and find entertainment? Is my city supplied with and supportive of theaters, libraries, and museums? Has nature been incorporated as an essential part of the city environment in the form of parks, greenways, and sports fields?

If the answer to most of these questions is "yes," then you and your city are the fortunate beneficiaries of wise, comprehensive long-range planning. Such a legacy is generated through ongoing effort and involvement by a coalition of urban planners, elected officials from city, county, and region, and individual citizens.

How to achieve such a legacy is explored in *Planning to Stay* (Milkweed Editions, 1994 and 2000), a practical and inspirational book for those interested in revitalizing their neighborhood. Editors

William Morrish and Catherine Brown, cofounders of the Design Center for American Urban Landscape, point out that planning a neighborhood is a participatory act of community membership and an expression of belief about the future of one's community. They suggest that the first questions people should ask when they decide that they want to stay in a neighborhood are: What is it about this place that draws us here? What could we add to this place that will keep us here?

In creating *Toward the Livable City,* we decided to address these same questions on the civic level: What is it about our city or community that we care about? What should we keep? And, what should we change to make living here consonant with our values and our desire to live a good life in this place? We asked the contributors to this book for their definitions of a livable city and for strategies and tactics they believe might be helpful in achieving one.

The resulting essays are lively, varied, and opinionated. No one can accuse these writers of waffling! The authors of the two initial essays speak to what appeals and what repels about urban life; a few writers offer theories and suggest policies, while others present case studies, including practical suggestions for creating positive community change. Innovative thinkers on urban issues discuss topics such as smart growth, the New Urbanism, regional planning, waterfront redevelopment, infrastructure, opportunity-based housing, and the importance of including nature in the urban fabric. For an admittedly one-sided look at the influence of the automobile on urban life, there's the distinctive social commentary of cartoonist and writer Ken Avidor. James Howard Kunstler throws the wild card, predicting profound changes for our cities when we come to the end of the cheap oil that runs our present commuter society. A reading list, as well as a list of organizations working for urban progress, is included.

As you'll observe when you scan the reading list, a great many books about urban planning are intended for an audience of professionals in the field. *Toward the Livable City* is something else—a book for those who would like their home base to be vital and sustainable, whether that place is a large city, a small town, or a suburb. Our intent is to offer you information and insights about some of the most challenging issues facing cities; our hope is to whet your appetite for becoming involved in the life of your community.

The operative word in the title of this book is *toward*—for good reason. Cities are, as Jane Jacobs says in her classic *The Death and Life of Great American Cities* (1961), "a problem in organized complexity." In recent urban development parlance, a "livable city" includes a central core of mixed-use housing and commerce easily accessible to pedestrians, job and housing opportunities available to all socioeconomic groups, diverse cultural offerings, and a "green" agenda. That's a tough prescription to fill, but the literature suggests that cities are making serious efforts to move *toward* the realization of these goals and, definitely, to improve upon the status quo.

Most Americans are faced every day with some variant of urban or suburban problems and frustrations. In the 1990s, 76 percent of Americans lived in cities and suburbs, with a growing percentage heading for the suburbs. In the face of this concentration of our populace, land-use issues have grown both more urgent and more complex. In my own Twin Cities community, 75 percent of people in the seven-county metro area live outside Minneapolis and St. Paul. As land development hurtles forward, citizens are hard-pressed to counter effectively the massive economic, political, and social forces that shape our lives.

Transportation and Regional Growth, the March 2003 report of a five-year study by the Minnesota Department of Transportation and the Metropolitan Council, addresses the state's transportation and land-development issues. The study points out the great need for honest pricing, "which exposes the true costs of transportation and land development—most of which are currently hidden in state aids to local governments, local property taxes and motor-vehicle registration taxes." The report states that the single greatest factor contributing to the Twin Cities' current traffic dilemma arises from state and regional policy that encourages low-density, sprawling development; another key finding is that congestion on the roads is but a symptom of the larger transportation and regional growth issues that encourage spread-out growth coupled with nearly complete dependence on personal vehicles. Although the authors of the report acknowledge that at this point in time mass transit has a limited impact in relieving congestion, they comment that such transit effectively serves common destinations—such as the downtown areas and the University of Minnesota—regardless of where transit users live. The report also verifies the fact that present development patterns have negative environmental impacts, including endangering water resources.

Studies such as this one should point the way to future reforms in urban policy that take into account environmental issues, such as pollution of soil, water, and air, and the disappearance of farmland and species, all of them integrally linked to urban sprawl. Urban issues cannot be separated from the skein of regional, national, and planetary degradation.

Neighborhood activists, conservationists, conservation groups, and professionals in land-use and water planning and management have been working for decades on policies that both protect the natural world around cities and include nature inside the urban boundary. But in every community those of us who "plan to stay" will make a difference if we are involved in a remedial plan for whole-earth systems in the city. Including and caring for nature in our cities ensures a richer life for everyone. Robert Michael Pyle eloquently writes in *The Thunder Tree* (1993):

> The city, the suburbs, and the countryside must be viewed
> as a single, evolving system within nature, as must every
> individual park and building within that larger whole. The
> social value of nature must be recognized and its power

harnessed, rather than resisted. Nature in the city must be cultivated, like a garden, rather than ignored or subdued.

I find it hopeful that in November 2000 not only were there 240 state/local initiatives on the ballot for the purpose of preserving open space or managing growth, but that 173 (72 percent) of them passed, indicating that a majority of voters are concerned.

▶ ▶ ▶

We want the communities we live in to be safe, visually attractive, and culturally diverse and stimulating, not to mention convenient to the places everyday activities take us. The unfortunate truth is that few of us would be willing to apply all of those adjectives to our own city or suburb. City dwellers who live near entertainment and cultural centers might agree that their neighborhoods are not as safe or as clean—or as green—as they would like. Suburbanites who take pleasure in their lawns and gardens might equably agree that their home base isn't culturally exciting, and that their lifestyle involves them in hours of driving from mall to mall, or delivering their kids to a roster of activities. Most of us would be quick to concede that commuting between city and suburb is tedious as well as a major source of pollution, not to mention a waste of time, our most precious asset.

Cities of all sizes are attempting to incorporate the desires of their citizens into their plans for the future. Anyone who has attended a city planning commission meeting—and I have attended more than a few—will attest to the passion of citizens who are either for or against any new scheme for development. Everyone has an opinion about land, those who own it and those who don't. The opportunity for profit guarantees that a proposal for changing land use quickly becomes politicized. Planning proposals pit those who would gain from the new use, or the new zoning, or the community expenditure, against those, the NIMBYs ("not in my back yard"), who believe that their neighborhood or community stands to lose something significant if the measure is approved. The same tug-of-war takes place at the legislature, where highway bills are pitted against transit expenditures. There are rich financial rewards for the winners of these contests, indicated by the intensity of lobbying efforts.

The news media report daily on local clashes between developers and citizen groups, or on highway enthusiasts criticizing proposals for public transit systems. Proponents of an unrestricted free-market system believe that the system must be allowed to work in the planning and building of communities. The free market, they assert, brings to the fore innovative responses to the sprawl that unplanned development brought into being. Supporters believe that the marketplace will evolve new ideas to deal with land development issues and will introduce market solutions to relieve the nightmare of gridlock, practices such as peak-period road pricing on highways, and privatized transit, now in effect in some communities.

Those who favor planned development urge the adoption of a regional approach to housing, jobs, and transportation, arguing that only by circumventing the rivalry of individual communities at the regional level can planning be effective and achieve rewards for central cities as well as for outlying communities. Urban planner and advocate john powell [sic] forcefully argues in his essay that regional planning is the basis for encouraging "economic growth while at the same time channeling it to those areas of the state where infrastructure and services are already in place to support it," creating better housing and educational opportunities for all citizens.

The concept that the region is the fundamental economic unit for effective planning has become increasingly influential. Regionalism has been embraced by the Congress for the New Urbanism, organized in 1993 as a coalition of architects, urban designers, planners, engineers, journalists, public servants, and concerned citizens. The group espouses policies that have been called neotraditionalist, a term used to define whatever works and looks best and is the most environmentally sensitive, socially responsible, and economically sustainable. Their policies promote the mixed-use model based on the neighborhood and the village, in which a community comprises a variety of housing types, including apartments, condominiums, town houses, and single-family dwellings, as well as a variety of businesses and green spaces. The Charter of the New Urbanism is included at the conclusion of this book so that readers can judge for themselves the merits of these policies.

I find it promising that even those who disagree about free-market versus planned development recognize that strengthening our central cities is imperative; study after study has shown that without the presence of dynamic core cities, surrounding communities do not thrive.

Civic debate on issues such as these promotes public interest and involvement. A February 2003 urban design column by Herbert Muschamp in the *New York Times* cites the planning process for rebuilding Ground Zero in New York City for its heated discussion: "New York has been awakened to more enlightened concepts of urbanism that have been embraced by other cities of its class," he writes, asserting that this conflict of ideas was responsible for making an "upward readjustment in New York's architectural aspirations." He concludes by stating that "conflict is the most important cultural product that a great city puts out. It is the fuel that drives everything else." It may seem ironic that the positive change we want for our cities often seems to emerge out of the crucible of conflict, but as Jane Holtz Kay puts it in her essay, "without the will to do better, and, of course, to do well in the most brazen financial manner, cities would not grow."

Happily, conflict is not the only road to more livable communities. To resolve issues with *civility,* one of the words that grows out of the Latin word for city, is well worth attempting. Collaborations and partnerships form viable alliances for creating necessary change. In the Twin Cities, I have witnessed extraordinary stewardship of

urban resources through a variety of partnerships among unlike organizations coming together for mutual benefit. One such example,
described in Judith Martin's essay, is the long-term public-private
partnerships that succeeded in revitalizing and repopulating the
Mississippi riverfront. An example close to home was the collaboration of three dissimilar Minneapolis literary nonprofits that needed
a permanent home. Through the combined efforts of their stakeholders, Milkweed Editions, the Loft, and the Minnesota Center for
Book Arts bought, renovated, and now manage a thriving center
for literature and book arts called Open Book. Many other examples
could be cited from cities around the country where a collaborative
model has been successful. To struggle together for a common goal
builds bonds of trust among those involved, the trust that is essential
in resolving thorny issues in community building.

At the conclusion of *Planning to Stay,* a manifesto for citizens
reads, in part, "We declare our stewardship of this legacy and pledge
our efforts to ensure safe neighborhoods, stable schools, affordable
housing, amenable streets, resourceful development, equitable access to goods, services, and jobs, and an integration of the natural
environment. Let our acts not diminish this gift, but leave it greater,
better, and more beautiful than it was given to us. This ground—our
common ground—is a good place to start."

As citizens we will experience economic and social conditions
that we cannot accurately predict, yet we can embrace our common
ground to build our common good. To do so will mean that our cities
will conform more closely to our best hopes.

Emilie Buchwald
Minneapolis, 2003

TOWARD THE

LIVABLE CITY

THE LIVED-IN CITY/
THE SIREN SUBURBS

WHY LIVE IN A CITY? WHY MOVE TO THE SUBURBS?
Both Jane Holtz Kay and Lynda Morgenroth extol the
pleasures afforded by Boston, admiring its variety and
its rich, readily accessible cultural offerings. But Lynda
Morgenroth flees the city for reasons that have motivated multitudes—escape from ceaseless noise, pervasive
dirt, and stressful neighbors.

▶ A VIEW OF THE CUSTOM HOUSE DOWN STATE STREET IN BOSTON. PHOTOGRAPH BY FREDERICA MATERA.

THE LIVED-IN CITY
A PLACE IN TIME

JANE HOLTZ KAY

Author Jane Holtz Kay maintains that above all (if oxymoronically), "livable cities" are lived-in cities, cities that have worn well over time, as this historian, critic, and author writes. Boston, the quintessential walking city, known for its diversity in time and place, suffers the assaults of our carbound, overconsumptive era but survives as a spry symbol of the urbanity essential to global survival.

Robert, or rather Robairrrrrr, as even our monolingual lunchgoers managed to say, rolling his French forename with the same care he devoted to our sandwiches, was the host of our lunch hour. Endowed with the memory to recall three preferences while slicing and dicing a fourth, he was the maître d' of our neighborhood. ("So are you turkey rollup today or . . ." he would prompt one customer as he minced onions for a second while joshing along yet a third.) Time after time, he would jive us geographic provincials with a really bad joke about a trip he had just taken to his native Haiti . . . to play hockey, enlisting the assembled flock in his riff as the lines grew longer.

Now, our spirited chef, our slicer-dicer, our Haitian-born master of ceremonies has left, was let go: axed with the speed of his dancing sandwich knife, it seemed. In a day, the deli counter at the 24-store where he worked was swiftly sanitized, all signs of unwrapped food-stuffs swept away. The gleaming silver counter was gone, the food trays vanished. Just a shelf of neon-toned bottles, snapplekracklepop drinks parading behind the vacant cook 'n' serve space. And the Oasis 24-store was on to slicker things.

In his stead, the next day, strangers handed out free sandwiches with every drink purchase, plastic-wrapped fare, thin and meager next to Robert's oozing composite sandwiches, customized for our daytime neighborhood. And the neighborhood he created missed more than the food. More than the eating, the absence was in the serving, the rock 'n' rolling repartee—the power to unite us odd-lot Bostonians: more folks of color, more mix in income than any other eatery around this downtown edge, from stiff-jawed suits to slackers jiving with idle chatter. More nodding and smiling customers than I had found before, or would again in its sanitized reincarnation. And the absence went beyond the loss and lack within our strange but powerful semi-demi neighborhood of city life. For what was lacking in the aftermath was what defines cities: the everyday urbanity that exists nowhere else.

▶ ▶ ▶

So it ended, one day in late June, and, by now, the bustling "before" has become a sterile "after," as empty of life as the lost memory of our casual comrades in line those many months. Well, not quite comrades. For the urbanity that this corner collage boasted was based on the anonymity that defines a city. Oasis, unlike Cheers, was actually the place where *nobody* knows your name. And that was just fine, thank you. We knew one another's faces, the banter, the menu, of course, but not much beyond. And as a city lover, delighting in the absentminded but congenial anonymity that is downtown's hallmark, I say thank God for that: sing a hymn for the hammering, clambering nonring of the city's impersonal connections. Casual discourse, casual multiracial, mixed-income elbowing of our neighbors is at a zero in most suburbs (and, admittedly, in parts of this town). So is walking, even talking. Here, we mingled and moved, rubbed elbows casually, not nervously, in anonymous urbanity. And that was fine, too. For the strange permanence of the city's everyday, predictable flux was the very definition of the serious city: mixing ephemeral ease in everlasting surroundings, the lived-in city shares space as it does the centuries.

Need I stress, then, that lived-in cities like Boston are not the place "where everybody knows your name"? That, in fact, they can be proud fortresses of *not* knowing your name? Only real cities can teach us the meaning of place and time that is the opposite of television's "have-a-good-day" nonplaces like Cheers, which is now a tourist shop of T-shirts and trinkets tucked into the ground floor of an otherwise elegant Beacon Hill row house—a faux tourist place, more faux than even television.

Is this the comment of a tourist xenophobe? Yes, I confess, but also of a partisan of the city, a visceral and intellectual city lover possessed of the conviction that cities, eternal cities, are, indeed—well—too grown up, too historically genuine to turn a blind eye to Disney-style pastiche inflated along the street.

Not all American cities are the inheritors of four centuries of comings and goings as Boston is, of course, but they have time on their side. Serious time. And it is that sense of permanence and flux, growth and instability, tolerance and suspicion visible on their worn streets and sidewalks that lends character.

Diversity in place and time is just one of many partnerships in the city, of course. City life is the sharing of space with absentminded courtesy—the chance encounters of strangers and neighbors. (Check the subways to see how we suffer crowds politely, if not happily. Check the city, but not the suburbs, for acceptance of the Other, cheek to jowl, backpack to briefcase.) Urbanity is about mingling and hanging back, about civility and bellicosity, quirkiness and constancy. Above all, serious cities actively decline uniformity despite the Gaps—in both senses—that mar our streets: their flanks and facades offer an eclectic mingling that stands in contrast to the uniformity of the malls and supermalls that bloat the landscape in our new suburbs and outburbs.

Suburbanity, so to speak, is about another kind of civility, I concede: the civility of good schools and good roads, of manicured lawns and well-groomed street trees. It is, alas, about how the lopsided subsidies of our federal government have fed urban flight, promoting the pattern of settlement that breeds suburban wealth and urban poverty as Washington subsidized the highway exodus from downtown and dug our nation's Great Divide—urban versus suburban—and maintained it for a half century or more. Doubt it? Think, then: no one has yet to strive "toward a livable *suburb.*"

Strangely, even those who struggle for a livable planet, intermingling the built and natural environments in these days of global malaise and environmental activism, have yet to turn to the lived-in city to ally the green and the grid—the country and the city—as did our ancestors. Few follow the 150-year-old tradition of Frederick Law Olmsted's masterworks of naturalizing the city and urbanizing the planet's biological systems; fewer peruse the more recent classics *Design with Nature* and *Granite Garden,* invoking the need for whole earth systems in our urban zones. Is the city cacophonous? Irritating? Disrupted? Yes. Is the glass half full? Half empty? Yes, of course, both, and at the same time. Name it what you will, but add one thing: it is also this fragile planet's last, best hope—the only alternative to settling on the ever-contracting fringes, consuming the last chance landscape, extinguishing resources and species. If we are ever to become ecofluent, as the green warriors put it, the strengthening of our lived-in cities is where it must take place.

▶ ▶ ▶

To be sure, our livable cities tally wins along with losses; some big-box blanders along with a legion of local activists battle the most invasive attack of the chains in our nation's history. Meanwhile, an ethnic flavor continues to spice the eateries, and even the chains, in our quasi-cosmopolitan downtown and urban neighborhoods. Muslim women, their heads swathed in scarves, serve at Dunkin' Donuts. Newcomers from Afghanistan, El Salvador, and Algeria chat up customers at Bean and Leaf Café, as do two generations of Greeks under the Grecian blue letters of the Odysseus restaurant, inscribing their diversity in the architecture as it always has been: five centuries' worth—from the Union Oyster House, solid as its colonial bricks, to the upscale anyplaces of contemporary cuisine, the newcomer Irish bars and after-work scenes.

And yet, the Anyplace USA establishments proliferate more rapidly than ever before: in the Franco-fake Bon Pain, the Starbucks and Wendy's, undercutting diversity, destroying vivacity, while neighborhood by neighborhood we fight the good fight. Since Staples superstore came downtown, stationery stores have dwindled. A month-at-a-glance pocket calendar is nowhere to be found, nor the chance to buy *one* pen, *one* pad of paper, *one* anything, it sometimes seems. In the Back Bay row house world where I live, empty store-fronts have succumbed to soap and cell phone shops as rents rise and the economy slides. An eyeglass shop papered over with neon images stares like empty eyes. Chain stores sit in the old Prince School while the nearby Exeter Theatre, once the Spiritualist Temple, has fallen from grace over the years: a Friday's sits on one of its corners, an Internet company in the space above. And every site seems tentative.

Perhaps they always have. In the time line of the historic city, change is the constant. Yet the loss of flavor and the larger-scaled ano-nymity seem more rampant these days . . . the pace faster, bigger . . . the city planners more laissez-faire, the renters greedier here now, as across the country. A Shakespeare and Company bookstore bowing to a New York Barnes & Noble has its counterparts, and, across the ocean, cities in "Old" Europe and old everyplace fail to ward off the monopolies in our sprawling, ever-globalizing world.

Change, as history teaches us, can be good and bad alike. The grand design of Paris by its great builder, Baron Von Haussmann, caused the ferocious leveling of its medieval, quirky, charming streets for the grand boulevards, which we also love. So, too, the filling of Boston's murky Back Bay following Von Haussmann's lead in splendid avenues would never pass an environmental impact statement. Yet the planners who filled the bay with pilings to create the mile-long stretch of streets shaped splendid structures on the French model, as they had created English housing modes atop Beacon Hill. Again, is the cup of city change half full or half empty? One must always ask.

Today, truth be told, the cup seems overflowing. The pace has quickened, and change—rightfully—alarms us. The props for greedy growth are strong, the planning weak, the scale of building grandiose. For all the landmark legislation and historic cache that make these surroundings livable, neither neighbors nor activists can ward off the construction booms that turn land to unminted gold and money to "serious money" for serious building—building too serious to fret about architecture's ease and accommodation with its surroundings. As pernicious as any suburban subdivider, today's city builders focus on the bottom line, caring little for proper fit and public process in a city where planning is a lost art and politicians pay back the piper. And so a new generation builds. Chunky, pricey postmodern buildings rise, stage sets of history for architectural appeasement flourish, and the tall towers for the rich rise above the church steeples where the homeless take an icy night's winter sleep beneath timeless porticoes.

▶ ▶ ▶

In the lived-in, not always livable city, such issues become visible. That is the joy, and trial, of their heft and density. The city, as always, reflects "the times that try men's souls," and in these times of terror and increasing economic inequality, social malaise is manifest on its streets. The newly refurbished Bulfinch State House, with its 1789 golden dome and rolling front lawn, partakes of troubled times as they hide the security cameras that pry into passing sounds and sights. The fear of terrorist attack combines with privatism to virtually bar access to the landmark Custom House tower whose once-public balcony offered a splendid view of the city's wraparound world of water.

Downtown, the alliance of politics and money dictates, and the city skyline soars. Towers break through barriers to appropriate the sky. Human scale is lost while the winds they churn affront walkers. Blank-walled facades squeeze out shops below and rising property values threaten old ethnic neighborhoods like Chinatown with high-rise holdouts for the rich. The hot spot seaport sites in South Boston are being sliced and diced to serve the upper income, not the long-time artists.

And yet, the paradox of urban life defies its shortcomings as restored buildings enliven main streets and bustling neighborhoods thrive with new ethnic vitality. The city survives with a novelty and energy that baffle expectations. For all our days deploring slapdash change, a visit to the area once dubbed the Combat Zone offers a new/old downtown in a new after-hours world. Plunging through the streets of the newly named Ladder Blocks, we seek a meal in Restaurant Land's new digs and find one: FELT (so-called) dazzles our eyes. Across from old Washington Street's decay, we enter a black, cavernous space, dazzled by designer lights and silver mirrors. Lofty ceilings rise high, offering images of James Bond to the Great God of Retro Chic . . . and good food. On the second and third floors above, billiard tables explain the "felt" nomenclature and more glitz offers the decor du jour. Soon, the floor above will echo to dancing bands. The crowd's average age is not much beyond the twenties.

A minimiracle. How did this hip factor return again to the tired streets of the moribund picture palace world that headlined "Banned in Boston"? The endless city will survive a new generation, and surprise an old one.

▶ ALONG NEWBURY STREET IN THE BACK BAY NEIGHBORHOOD OF BOSTON. PHOTOGRAPH BY FREDERICA MATERA.

▶ ▶ ▶

Robert will survive, as well. His Oasis stand-ins say he has found work. In fact, from time to time, I have seen him in the Back Bay, driving by the Clarendon Street Baptist Church with his family, one of many immigrant and ethnic parishioners who have rescued this old Yankee edifice. In the shifting, lived-in city, the Back Bay's volume of nineteenth-century churches is a loose-leaf scrapbook of change. Its "proper Bostonian" members drifted off to the suburbs long ago, leaving fraying carpets, crumbling brownstone facades, and shrinking budgets. Today's urban influx brings a fascinating miscellany of new members—secular condo dwellers, social do-gooders, and a colorful congregation of immigrants. Five earlier incarnations of the Baptist assemblage and more than 300 years stand between the first Clarendon Street Church and its ethnic rainbow of newcomers who fill the chambers on Sundays and celebrate their weddings in spring and summer as the celebratory stretch limos line the block and flower-strewn brides in white gowns reflect the world's outposts, from Haiti to Vietnam.

To me, a sometime historian of this evanescent city, the city is a tale to be twice or thrice told, depending on willing audiences, and this peripatetic church that finally lit here in 1872 is one of my favorites. The very early work of two geniuses, Henry Hobbs Richardson and Frédéric Auguste Bartholdi, its design is decidedly the best of neither. Richardson, the great architect of nineteenth-century America, launched his career here, and the marginal and not altogether pleasing proportions of the church show his unsure hand. Ah, that lumbering campanile. Bartoldi, too, better known (and better accomplished elsewhere) at the Statue of Liberty, arrived in 1871 and created the sculpture adorning its peak with dubious success. Alike, the Richardson building and the Bartoldi figure tooting its horn in an ungainly pose caused the locals to dub the structure the Church of the Holy Beanblower. The name stuck.

The New Land above the Back Bay pilings was a city of churches reflecting the flux of population from downtown to the burgeoning new town, and, though their congregations have fallen off, the new members reflect history's ever-constant vigor and diversity as the new gallery of worshippers offer music events and instill art galleries to pay the bills in myriad ways, adding new life to the old neighborhood. And more. The Unitarian-Universalist Arlington Street Church a few blocks from the Clarendon Street congregation continues the open-minded political policies demonstrated by its basement horde of Sandista papers exploded by counter-radicals a few decades ago. On a cold winter day, the front stairs are packed with singers bundled against the chill, and "If I Had a Hammer," the song of sixties activism, wafts from the front steps of the church—a countercry to the president's State of the Union call to invade Iraq. The spiritual and the political ally visibly here. Internet activism has an alternative in the city's public streets. "Life is not about speed," said the church signboard, quoting Gandhi as its members prayed for peace and paid for restoring its Tiffany windows.

▶ ▶ ▶

Still, God loses out to Mammon, that Syrian deity, in the embattled city, and even ecclesiastical masterpieces are not safe from his claims. In fact, a soaring twentieth-century version dedicated to the monetary diety—the one-hundred-story-high glass John Hancock tower—famously just about undid that bastion of the former, Trinity Church. Designed by Richardson, who, by a mathematical irony, began creating his masterpiece there in 1872, exactly a century before the insurance company did, the tower suffered assaults from the new building from the start. The glass rhomboid cresting upward seemed hellbound from the beginning, despite (because of?) its proud and prestigious architect, I. M. Pei. As a young architecture critic for the *Boston Globe,* I deplored (still do) the overweening height of the sixty-two-story structure looming over Copley Square, whiplashing its famous public space, creating hostile wind tunnels for pedestrians, and diminishing surrounding architectural marvels including the magnificent Boston Public Library by McKim, Mead and White.

What ego! What arrogance, I thought, to break the barrier of this low-rise landscape, to create this antisocial climate change. And more, for suddenly it seemed that the sky-breaking building had

▶ IN BOSTON'S FINANCIAL DISTRICT. PHOTOGRAPH BY
FREDERICA MATERA.

caused yet another phenomenon: the sun reflected in its mirror-glass walls was glaring at Mass. Turnpike drivers from miles away, blinding them. A hue. A stew. A cry. An article. But first, of course, a call to the public relations staff about what the new "sunset" was doing to the accident rate. Did a building have the right? I asked. "Would you ask God to stop the sunsets?" came the reply. Not even the *Fountainhead* school of ego architecture had prepared me for the conceit of someone equating an act of the Almighty with an insurance company's phallic gesture. It was a first but not a last.

Worse luck, the glass windows began to pop, and wooden panels replaced them. A strange patchwork indeed. "The U.S. Plywood Building," they called it, as lawyers scrapped and engineers hemmed and hawed and failed for a long time, a very long time, to fix it. Worse still, the wooden foundations that secured the adjacent Trinity Church's foundations in solid soil below its watery bed began to quiver from the insurance company's construction work while the elegant Copley Plaza hotel, on the other side, next door, was wobbling . . . and . . .

To cut to the chase: they did it with dollars. You can say that a city is where everything has a price and nothing has a value, where everything is negotiated, not planned, but this was remarkable even in the annals of urban myths. After suits and a newspaper splash nationally, the Hancock's wealthy insurance folks bought the Copley to salve the suit and forked out the funds to fix up the church. But not quickly. Only now, decades later, has the church opened its basement to reveal the repaired foundations and take tourists through the site . . . just in time, it seems, for the flagging insurance folks to put their failing business up for sale in—ahhh, the indignity of it!—a package with other relatively dwarfed buildings they owned totaling perhaps a billion dollars.

Ego rises, ego falls . . . likewise architecture in the lived-in city. Is it that nothing is sacred in the striving city? Or, more positively, that the city is—happily and by definition—a striving city: the place of all places where we try . . . and try . . . to get it right? Incredibly, too, the square where these structures sit has also gone through three lives in the same time span. The square's nineteenth-century shape, an erratic and triangular landscape in early postcards, became a subterranean plaza in the 1970s, which, in turn, became the local subterranean "needle park," which was, then, more positively, raised and fountained and tree-filled and paved with a potpourri of brick patterns, statuary, and grass. And, yet again in the restless, lived-in city, as summer nears, the square is being enlarged. A portion of a road that straddles its western side will expand the space. With any luck, we could live through still more evolutions by folks who think they've really, finally, definitely, absolutely got it right this time, in the endlessly striving, endlessly lived-in city.

And why not? Belief in striving for the New New Thing could be the city's most important product. Not just here, though, but everywhere. Our oldest, best, and brightest cities—San Francisco, Chicago, New York, you know them—grew because they were built by some folks with nothing left to lose and some folks with a lot to gain. (They are also best, of course, because they are oldest and bound by preindustrial, "natural" laws of craftsmanship and gravity and kinship to that nature.) Without the will to do better, and, of course, to do well in the most brazen financial manner, cities would not grow. Without cities we would not have the coming together, the sense of history, the outrage that keeps us on edge. Only cities can teach us both the permanence and the impermanence of human handiwork. There is stability and its opposite, beauty and its lack, but always history in the midst of assault, creativity in the midst of destruction, and, for me, always stories to see and tell in the life and death, the liveliness and torpor, the wealth and poverty of their ever-shifting landscapes.

In the early morning hours, I hear a tinny rattle in the alley five flights below my bedroom window. A man with very white sneakers beneath a ragtag outfit and a silver shopping bag dangling from his hand has hit the heap of trash in the parking space beneath the ailanthus. It is very, very cold and as I watch him make his way through our rejects, I calculate the rentals for such alley parking lots. The premium to rent this paved plot is three hundred dollars a month, about the same sum to bed and board this trash picker shuffling below the weed tree; the price to buy it is an astounding $129,000 — offensive: "profane," as the sixties had it.

The city throws such inequities before public eyes, but not the suburbs. Is that why the deepest inhumanity, the inhumanity of indifference, lies in the isolated homes behind the greenest lawns in those affluent outposts? You can run but you can't hide in the lived-in city. There is color as well as sorrow here, I think as I survey the sad scene amid the beauty and the affluence. For even the weed trees shade the brick buildings in the summer and blush their alleys with bounteous red berries in the fall.

Yet cities themselves rise and fall in time, on the small scale — the loss of Robert to the neighborhood, I think — and on the large as well, I muse, contemplating the rising sea levels that could wash over my neighborhood on its watery pilings. The city's sunrise is over in a minute in the long span of planetary life. Still, ephemeral or not, I cling to the belief that cities are the finest record of human will and human creativity. In flux, yes, and flawed, but lived-in, they link their living neighbors and long-gone ancestors in a way that confirms our sense of community and the genius of humanity to create art from habitat.

JANE HOLTZ KAY is the author of several books concerning the built environment and planning, including *Asphalt Nation: How the Automobile Took Over America and How We Can Take It Back, Preserving New England,* and the recently revised *Lost Boston.* She is also architecture critic for the *Nation* and writes regularly on the art and politics of the built and natural environments for national newspapers and publications. A collection of her articles and speeches can be found on her website, www.janeholtzkay.com. Kay is currently writing *Last Chance Landscape.*

▶ "NEW YORK SUNSHINE." CARTOON BY RALPH STEADMAN.

DIVORCING THE CITY

LYNDA MORGENROTH

Cities resemble lovers, offering allure, annoyance, and late-night avail-ability. Still, in spite of their power, even the most inveterate urbanite may eventually, even if temporarily, be driven away. In "Divorcing the City," Boston writer Lynda Morgenroth describes her long relationship with, and attachment to, Boston and Cambridge and her perhaps not ir-revocable decision to move to the suburbs. The essay delineates what is lov-able, thrilling, and irresistible about culturally rich cities, and also what became too high a price for one urbanite to pay. Morgenroth describes her sorrowful but also watchful and enlivening transition, catalogs what is lost and found in suburbia, and allows for the possibility of return.

Like a woman who divorces and later remarries her former husband, I may have made a mistake that can only be corrected by public reversal. I feel abashed and silly. It is not only that I have caused myself and others distress and upheaval—though bringing joy to mortgage lenders and real estate brokers—it is that I will not be able to clean up my mess discreetly. Everyone will know I prover-bially divorced and remarried the same guy.

Six months ago, I sold my Cambridge condominium—a cozy first-floor flat in a hundred-year-old house near Harvard Square—and bought a place in the suburbs. I did so without reason of matrimony, maternity, or professional intention to open a kennel.

Financially, I traded a condo for a house, gaining porch, yard, attic, and garage—the first off-the-street parking of my adult life—and a lovely front room with an alcove of five windows to use as a library.

Sociologically, I traded life in Massachusetts's cultural hub—the nexus of Boston's and Cambridge's museums, bookstores, concert halls, cinemas, and libraries, and over a dozen local ethnic neighborhoods rich with people and their diverse customs, including their restaurants, groceries, and bakeries—for a pretty, pleasant town without a movie theater, museum, art gallery, or wine or liquor store. (A place to browse in dusty wine bins, preferably with an eccentric proprietor and a few store cats, would have gone a long way toward quenching my thirsts, especially in the early months.)

My decision to leave the city was not formed abstractly, but actively, as one runs from an assailant. I had lived for three years in a cacophony of noise, dirt, and literal upheaval. In 1998 a huge, rambling, double rooming house next door was gut-rehabbed over a fourteen-month period, including two long, stultifying summers when my windows could never be opened. A narrow path, not quite wide enough for a well-fed cat to sprawl on, separated my condo, located in a three-story house, from the construction site. My office faced the turmoil. For over a year, I tried to work and live in an atmosphere where teams of hard-hatted men worked all day, tearing down the house (but maintaining the footprint to qualify for a rehab permit), excavating to make an underground parking garage, and using hammers and power tools to reframe, construct walls, lay floors, and install tiles, fixtures, and appliances. A frequently used portable toilet was located outside my bedroom window. Workmen from Bosnia, Albania, Dominican Republic, and El Salvador would sometimes sing (not in unison) as they slammed the toilet door, their folk songs one of the few enjoyable aspects of the rehab.

I have asthma and migraines, which multiplied in the urban trap of airborne particles and ground-churning vibration. But it was more the relentless sounds—hammering, jackhammers, and high-speed drills—the psychological effect of their jagged sharpness, ear-piercing volume, and nauseating inescapability that did me in.

In the spring of 1999, the muddy trenches around the former rooming house—which had become three luxury condos—were filled in and smoothed down, and verdant sod was layered around the now unrecognizable property, as odd-looking on our street as the one woman in a group of old friends who has had a face-lift. Amazing to me and to other (unlifted) neighbors, buyers quickly materialized for the million-dollar condos the rehab had yielded. For a few precious weeks (it felt like peace after war, recovery after illness, soft breezes after a hurricane), calm descended on our quarter. I opened the windows, started to restore the garden, washed down the porch, and put out my wicker chair.

Then, like an episode in a farce, a major public works project that was to last almost two years began directly outside my house, on the opposite side of my condo, for the sake of variety, perhaps. The city of Cambridge had embarked on a massive sewer separation project, to be conducted neighborhood by neighborhood over a ten-year period, to replace the ancient system. The infrastructure of cable, gas, and electrical delivery and telephone service were part and parcel of engineering maneuvers. This was a massively disruptive undertaking: sidewalks and roads were ripped up, and deep trenches were cut into the street. Day after day, week after week, month after month, the inescapable noise, filth, and inconvenience of major road construction ground down the pleasure I had always felt living in the city. When friends came by they would stand stunned in my foyer, absorbing the effect of the construction from inside my home. "It's in your *living room,* Lynda," more than one observed. It was also in my bedroom, bathroom, kitchen, dining room, and office. Framed prints fell off the wall. Pots and dinnerware inside cabinets had to be washed before use. And when I went outside, it was louder, dirtier, the landscape dominated by massive, moving construction equipment.

My car was enrobed in clayish dust and grit, which eventually got inside the car, impregnating the upholstery. On the worst days, when I started the ignition, a cloud would come up from the gear shift, as in a cartoon.

The public works department tried to do right by the neighborhood, staging community meetings and keeping residents informed about the process. Block captains were appointed. Color-coded updates (about water shutoffs, or parking bans, or tree removal, or construction schedule changes) were hand-delivered to our doors. Diligent and sympathetic police officers rang our doorbells early in the morning to try to keep cars from being towed. Provisions were made for elderly neighbors and disabled people whose driveways and walkways were blocked. Over the months I learned most of the workmen's names, how many children they had, and where they lived. But the sound of the trucks and the digging never stopped, nor did the water-torture repetition of the backing-up beep necessary for the safety of pedestrians, motorists, and construction crews.

Huge, deep sections of the street were excavated to accommodate water holding tanks and pumping equipment—sections almost the size of dwellings, akin in appearance to archaeological digs, with mounds of dirt and clay built up like earthworks in front of people's houses. Cats and dogs were kept inside. According to city ordinance, work was not permitted before seven in the morning. But the construction workers—great guys, many of them apologetic about the havoc they were hired to create—would arrive at six to beat the Boston traffic and sit in their diesel trucks with heaters (or a.c.) and blaring radios for an hour. As I lived in a corner house, two, sometimes three hulking diesel vehicles would be pumping exhaust through my dining-room and living-room bay windows.

How profoundly weird to live in a visually serene but environmentally unbearable apartment for almost three years! I wore earplugs most of the day, went through three 1,000-tab bottles of aspirin over the course of ten months, and reacquired an inhaler. As a freelance

journalist who had always worked from a home office, I had to find
alternative settings in which I could conduct phone interviews. I lost
months of productive time because of the disruption, and, harder
to quantify, lost the peace of mind, refreshment, and haven at the
end of the day that home in a middle-class American neighborhood
generally provides.

To complete this urban farce of one small citizen craving peace
in an urban village, there were also domestic disturbances. Inside my
house were two other condo owners, neither of whom did anything
much to contribute to the maintenance of the 100-year-old house.
This may seem like yuppie carping (if only I were young or wealthy
enough to qualify for the description), but over time it became an
affront to care for a property that was supposed to be maintained as
a common enterprise. After scores of requests, entreaties, maneuvers,
and threats, all of which failed to elicit cooperation, I gave up and
ran the household, as though I were its landlord, which most neighbors assumed I was. For eleven years, I not only physically maintained the place—making minor repairs myself, arranging for and
supervising all others; sweeping walks and porches; planting and
maintaining the garden and grounds; shoveling snow—I also kept
the books and represented the household at community meetings.

The time it required to care for "our house" was a concern; I am
self-employed and time is money, among other things, to me. The
responsibility of taking care of the old wooden behemoth—as devoted
as I was to it—also weighed on me. But above all, it was the unfair-
ness. Caring for the house as a community of three owners wasn't
just a sentimental notion, it was part of the condo bylaws.

One of my condo mates was a lovely young woman who didn't
have time to participate in home maintenance, as she earnestly put
it, and so conveniently ignored much of what was going on. While
we lived together she attended medical school and became a child
psychiatrist—entirely without benefit of ever raking leaves or dealing
with floods in the basement. But she was a decent person who would

periodically express appreciation, which goes a long way in my book. The other occupant was a pathologically selfish piece of work who did as she pleased. She refused to attend condo meetings so she could operate on her own. One day I came home and found that she had ripped out the garden I had planted and long cared for, the product of six years' devotion, because she preferred grass. When she wanted to use the shared laundry facilities in the basement, she would interrupt the wash or dry cycle of whomever and insert her own clothing. When I asked her to try not to slam the porch door, located adjacent to my bedroom, late at night, she said, "That's not an adjustment I can make. We have different lifestyles."

My Manhattan sister, skillful in matters of war-with-assholes, as she delicately puts it, told me to put my face right up to that of the miscreant and say, "I will hurt you." And on another day, or upon a summer's eve, perhaps, to warn, "You are going to get cut." And when a longer sentence seemed appropriate, to get unsuitably close—hoping one's breath had become steamy and hot as a mad dog's—and intone, "When you look in the mirror tonight, say good-bye to your face. Loser."

I wasn't afraid to say these things, and threats might indeed have worked on the little monster. Nor am I squeamish about delivering a well-deserved blow. I admire the characterizations of Robert De Niro. But I didn't want to live in an atmosphere where threats became a condition of maintaining domestic peace. Once you are spending time conjuring up horrible things to say, and practicing your delivery, and rubbing your palms together anticipating how the evil ones will respond, the harmony you hoped for is long gone. You have become a little monster, too.

When you live in proximity to people who refuse to be reasonable, cooperative, and polite, you are not only trapped in a series of daily compromises and confrontations, your faith in community is damaged. When people in your close community refuse to be responsible, feelings of isolation and resentment grow. Not to sound more delicate than I am, but years of bad behavior by condo mates and neighbors eroded my faith in community. The social contract can take only so many violations.

To be urbane is not only to be sophisticated, but also to be civil. I have lived in cities almost all my adult life and have come to feel that bad behavior, even monstrous behavior, is more widespread in these tight quarters. It is not that urban and suburban citizens are different. The rate of monsters per thousand is probably the same. But populations are denser in cities. Life is stressful, conditions crowded. The resulting interdependence is an ideal opportunity to build community, or to suffer unbearable disharmony.

During the last several years, the combination of assault from within and without plain tuckered me out. Cambridge, in spite of its increasing discomforts to me, had become more fashionable—more crowded, more expensive, and less diverse. Rent control ended. Many of the big old houses were sold, divided, and turned into condos. Harvard University bought up more and more real estate and built large-scale buildings and parking garages.

A decade ago, my street—three city blocks long, a funky side street of Massachusetts Avenue—was populated by foreign students, elderly people, townies living in the houses they were born in, and people in their thirties and forties: writers, artists, filmmakers, and educators. By the end of the decade, it had become dominated by young, wealthy computer people, workers in the financial industry, and lawyers.

As in the eerie, troubling months before a divorce, I continued to hang on—walking to friends' houses for potluck suppers while carrying casseroles that arrived still warm; buying groceries, wine, and crusty loaves without ever using a car; choosing from Mexican, Thai, Indian, Korean, Chinese, and Italian restaurants a few blocks away; and making sudden decisions to go to movies and being in Harvard Square ten minutes later, at one of three theaters.

But I craved quiet, privacy, and serenity. I stopped using the common spaces in my condo—especially the sun-dappled porch and garden where I used to spend so much time—and avoided the basement laundry facility. My nerves were jangled. I no longer enjoyed the lively street life, and I started to notice how often people walking in the other direction would crowd me and my walking companions off the sidewalk. I wanted more space, in every way, including the freedom to choose what and whom I took care of. When the sewer project was entering its final stages (the street, curbs, and sidewalks had been put back; trees were plugged into holes in the sidewalk), Harvard announced plans to build a major facility in the heart of our neighborhood. This was like finding lipstick on your husband's collar, or innocently accepting home deliveries from Victoria's Secret that never become gifts to you. I decided to find a house of my own.

In the spring of 2001, I started to look, vigorously and intensively. Sometimes with brokers, but generally on my own, using newspaper listings, I saw over 270 houses in over a dozen communities; beginning with "near neighborhoods" of Cambridge such as Somerville, Arlington, and Watertown; then in Boston neighborhoods such as Jamaica Plain, Roslindale, and West Roxbury; and then heading farther and farther out, even making forays to southern New Hampshire and western Massachusetts. This was a sorry, desperate time. In the city, decrepit wood frame houses with sagging floors, pitted linoleum, kitchen counters mottled by cigarette burns, and forty-year-old furnaces the size of small rooms cost over half a million dollars. I all but closed down my business as a freelance writer; almost every day, for eight months, I lowered myself into my car with a geographically organized list of properties, and street maps, and directions, and would locate several houses per morning. Those that appeared to be standing, square, not too ugly (at least on the outside), and not next to a highway, gas station, or tombstone vendor, I would arrange to see.

As a veteran freelance newspaper writer, I thought I knew eastern Massachusetts pretty well. Nevertheless, I had never been to the town I eventually moved to, Melrose, north of Boston. One day, sitting next to a Cambridge real estate broker in his office, "looking" at properties in my price range on the Internet, I saw a pretty colonial with a porch for around the value of my condo. It wasn't the house I wound up with, but the lead brought me to Melrose. It seemed open and friendly, not that far from Cambridge and Boston, a place where I could resettle and find peace.

The circumstances of my eventual home selection are a disturbing tale, as they are for most buyers of limited means, especially those who need to sell their home to buy another, and most especially for those who finally sell their home and then can't find another. For present purposes I will decorously limit myself to saying I eventually bought an 1890s Victorian house in vastly imperfect condition, but structurally sound and with potential.

I would trade a lot, and I did, for waking up in a clean, spacious, quiet room overlooking a statuesque maple tree. Today, I no longer feel cramped, or imprisoned, or under siege in my home. The "noise" I hear is children playing, dogs barking, and, during rush hour, cars. I love walking through various neighborhoods in my new town, examining house styles and landscaping—and revisiting specimen trees—and I hope to become brave enough to hike alone in the 2,500-acre Middlesex Fells Reservation, which includes magnificent outcroppings of rock, sparkling ponds, and all manner of plants, ranging from mosses and ferns to sassafras (the mitten shrub), maple, and oak.

But the embarrassing truth is, after six months I haven't gotten used to the absence of culture as I knew it; and the warmth and liveliness of juxtaposed, varied ways of life; and the continual, alienating reliance on my car.

The city I left is not a normal city, it needs to be said. Cambridge is small, quirky, with an academic orientation. It's closely linked to Boston, just across the Charles River—within actual walking distance. The suburb I moved to is not a suburb in the sprawling, sterile, mall-defined sense (though there is a mall in the next town, but Cambridge has one, too). Melrose, named for a place in Scotland, is a pleasant, pretty, family-centered town—technically a city— seven-miles north of Boston. It is just five miles square, with lots of Victorian houses, and a main street with grand municipal buildings, a pond with mallards and swans, and many handsome storefronts. The library is an elegant stone building with a reading room like a living room—including upholstered chairs with individual lamps— and a lower-level children's library with fanciful, original, hand- painted murals that are changed seasonally.

I feel affection for the town, though it is not yet a relationship. (Perhaps relating to cities, which offer so many access points of involvement, is easier. Relating to a town requires one to respond to fewer and more subtle aspects.) Melrose is a sweet place, with its own weekly newspaper, an annual Victorian Fair, and a Unitarian church with a right-on, inclusive congregation. The people I've met have been kind. But there is less of everything that spoiled city people expect, and what there is, is watered down. The pizza crusts are soft, the gift stores show pretty things, but nothing with edge, and the yoga classes are for runners who want a little stretch—not searchers who want a little reach. The one bookstore, a feisty, friendly inde- pendent, closed for lack of customers not long after I arrived. For movies, good bread, wine, cooking supplies, a "girl's gym," and eth- nic restaurants, I need to drive into the city. And I do. But especially in the beginning, every car trip away emphasized what I had lost.

My neighbors are friendly, decent, and polite. Their children are engaging, wholesome, secure, beloved, and adorable. I have never seen so many good, patient, attentive parents in my life. A ten-year- old girl I like a lot—she is gangly, has freckles, and bursts with en- thusiasm (and punctuates sentences with cartwheels)—brought me a handmade card when I moved in, and a package of marigold seeds because she had been told I liked to garden. She appeared at my door with her mom on a chill February evening, brimming over with excitement and holding her enchanting construction-paper card. The two little boys next door, one six, one eight, show me wild animals (spiders, mainly) they've captured in jars. The children across the street shyly ask me if I will watch them perform gymnastics routines. The elderly widower whose lawn they perform on—he seems not to mind—shows me his little garden; we talk about layering different kinds of fruit into a crock to make brandied fruit. Last weekend I bought pickling cucumbers at a farmstand in New Hampshire—I am closer to New Hampshire now—and will perhaps make bread and butter pickles, and give him some.

▶ ▶ ▶

I moved to Melrose during a cold, grim passage between late winter and invisible spring. I felt ripped asunder from everything I held dear, except nature. Fortunately, Melrose has wonderful century-old trees, and a collection of small sanctuaries and parks, and borders the Middlesex Fells Reservation. But the amenities of urban life were gone and I was quite alone in my house, surrounded by neighbors with families who wondered why a single, childless woman had moved to a house recently occupied by a family with three young children. I was very quiet—not wanting to alarm my family, my friends, and myself—about my shocked sense of loss, which felt much deeper than getting used to a new place. I felt silly and ashamed. I, a self-supporting woman of modest means, had managed to swing the purchase of a house, a pretty Victorian with a fair number of alcoves and crevices; I should have felt celebratory, grateful, and proud. Instead I felt scared and unmoored. I had hoped to make a good-natured adjustment, and to feel like a pioneer. I had been put off by the parochial responses of friends who learned I was leaving Cambridge and Boston. "Where will you go?" they said, and, "How could you ever leave Cambridge?" When a neighbor asked, "Where else could you live?" I had thought, defiantly, "Plenty of places."

For my first three months, I mainly washed, scrubbed, and
unpacked boxes, day and night, seeing no one, shielded from the
recognition of how far I'd moved from what I'd known. Once the
house was fairly clean, I spent hours filling holes in walls with joint
compound, and holes in cabinets, drawers, and doors with plastic
wood; and constructing shims for bookcases and chests. I think I was
trying to smooth and balance my world.

A move is its own kind of misery; its crazy-making chaos and ex-
haustion would have been the same had I been able to afford a house
in Cambridge, Brookline, or Boston. But there were no little restaurants to duck into and regale myself, no cultural activities to escape
to, not even a bakery with good crusty bread and a wine store. There
were no friends nearby, though at least I had been prepared for that.
I did find a good hardware store within walking distance with a full-
figured cat named Frederica who slept in shelving near the register.
Sometimes it is a small thing—a new neighbor's gesture, a glimpse of
a cardinal, a potted plant in a window—that can provide the boost of
assurance we need.

Occasionally, I would leave the mess and disconnect of my new,
uncertain life and return to Boston. I would have strange, enraptured
experiences in which I would fling myself into her arms like those
of a clandestine lover. One early Sunday afternoon I went to a movie
in Davis Square, Somerville, visited an antiquarian bookstore, and
ate most of a sixteen-inch eggplant pizza and drank two glasses of
red wine at two in the afternoon. On a hot summer morning, I went
to the Museum of Fine Arts and visited the Buddhas, who had not
moved from their tawny, embracing sandalwood world; browsed the
museum shop and tried on necklaces; and lingered in the Fenway
rose garden where still lifes come to real life. I loved these excursions,
felt alive and connected while I was there, then disjointed and regret-
ful when I returned home. I did not know how to live in two places.

Once the house had become habitable, I established a routine of
driving into Cambridge four times a week—to go to the familiar and

comforting "girl's gym," to see friends for dinner or lunch, to go to movies. On good days it took just twenty or twenty-five minutes to drive the eight miles; during rush hour it took an hour, an exasperating hour of inching along just two exits of Route 93, then snaking through Medford and Somerville to Porter Square, in the northern part of Cambridge.

I had the same stunned, disbelieving, unremarkable response to commuting that all new suburbanites have. I was amazed by how boring, frustrating, and unproductive it was, alarmed that so many people considered it a normal way of life. No doubt, the other people in their cars, vans, and SUVs commuting into Boston and Cambridge were far better informed about what they were getting themselves into than I had been as I searched for a home. And there they were, millions of motorists, having normalized a pathology. And there I was, no longer walking.

I was in a permanent state of jet lag; a floating but airless feeling because of the more open landscape in my new community, and because I was in the car so much; so little grounded. Now, after six months, I am getting used to it, but I still find the amount of time in the car odd. All the years of using my feet and moving through an urban landscape, with intense sensation and bodily involvement, kept a primitive part of me alive. Driving destroys the connection between places, a frustration of our primate's need to recognize and register territory in a down-to-earth, sensory, kinesthetic way.

▶ ▶ ▶

The division between city and suburb is physically defined by the car commute; commuting exacerbates the psychological division, as well. Instead of being in one community where we live and work, we are traveling mindlessly over gray space between home and work. We don't care about it and don't think of it as a place. We are alone in our cars, in semi-daze, neither in community nor in conversation.

Herein, as though in direct response, lies the amazing power of public transportation, a tool for psychological integration as well as its more practical attributes. When we are able to travel on the train, or better still, I think, the subway (it's grittier and more linked to the urban infrastructure), city and town are more closely related, to each other and to us. It is not just the convenience of the subway—the speed and direct connections—it's the different kinds of people on board and our participation in the public realm, which necessitates response and interaction.

Melrose has a commuter train that goes into Boston's North Station, which connects, though not directly, to the MBTA, the subway, known as the T. Malden, the town just south of Melrose, and closer to Boston, is a more interesting transportation hub, with the last stop on the Orange Line, the actual MBTA. Since my house is in the southern part of Melrose, I can walk to Oak Grove in Malden in about thirty minutes. (There is also a local bus to Oak Grove, but it doesn't run very often, nor on weekends, and necessitates an annoying additional connection.)

One fine day I walked to Oak Grove, took the T to Ruggles behind Northeastern University, and spent an excellent morning at Boston's Museum of Fine Arts looking at Dutch landscapes. Meticulous depictions of people, animals, and objects in atmospheres, they were wondrous to behold, and the artists' decisions about what to paint, what to emphasize helped me to consider the relevance of surroundings, those we find and those we create. Another day, I took the T to Chinatown and spent the afternoon in Vietnamese markets, watched Asian men looking through girlie magazines with pictures of breast-enhanced Asian women (this at the back of a traditional-style Chinese apothecary), bought a sky-blue paper lantern for my bathroom, and had spicy eggplant on a heavy, hot, restaurant-china plate for lunch. On the T ride home, ladies in saris and young women in head scarves were on the train, and a middle-aged Asian couple who stayed on till the last stop. We

were both carrying shopping bags from Chinatown, and were the
only people still on the train. "Bye, bye," I said to them. They nodded
and smiled big smiles.

▶ ▶ ▶

Last summer I admitted to myself, and shortly afterward, whispering
on the telephone, to my Manhattan sister, that it was possible I had
made a mistake and might have to move back to the city. For reasons
I do not know, the admission was a considerable relief. It allowed
me to contemplate the possibility of making a change, yet another
change, that would be better; and it calmed me down enough so that
I could try to focus on the present and near future, to try to integrate
the different ways of life in city and town.

There is nothing bad, and everything good, about having one's
own house with a porch and a yard. I am grateful for this newfound
privacy, seclusion, and peace. I love to come into the airy, pale-yellow
living room—spacious, quiet, and serene—and to read a book, or to
drink tea. I miss the variety of the city, and its cultural life, but not
the noise, pace, and visual clutter, and I will never forget the effect
one selfish, uncooperative person can have on a community.

Once the worst pain of a parting is over, and when one has found
good things about a new place, it is possible to go back to the old
place and to be less nostalgic, less self-doubting, and hardier. One has
made the decision and survived the move and early stages. Once I allowed myself to admit that I might someday move back, I could visit
Cambridge and Boston without feeling so desperate. In the process, I
was reminded of how crowded and noisy they had become, and how
I preferred the openness of my new place. Yes, I still feel isolated and
out of the cultural loop, but there are many consolations for what a
Cambridge friend (who feels rebuffed) refers to as my exile. Living
in a private house, with the sun orbiting around your home over the
course of a day, is a great pleasure.

I have made places for myself in my rooms, kept cleaning, unpacking, and arranging, and noticed new aspects of the play of light as the seasons change. It is amazing how important the beauty of one tree can be for a human admirer who sees it every day, with leaves and without, boughs saturated with rain and sculpted in snow. I love finding ephemeral art in the house: the shimmering reflection of a stained glass window on a wall, the silhouette of a carved balustrade—like shadow puppetry—in a high-ceilinged hall. I am trying to be open to my new place, and to not regret what I have lost. I am trying to see what is here.

I still go into the city most days in much the way one continues to see a former husband, or an old lover. Both places, city and town, are becoming part of my life. I bought a subscription series to concerts in the nearby town of Wakefield, and renewed two subscriptions in Cambridge. I go to the Stone Zoo in Stoneham and the Franklin Park Zoo in Boston. Some Sundays I buy the *Boston Globe* in Melrose and get the north weekly regional supplement (with news of the towns north of Boston); other Sundays I pick up the paper in Cambridge and get the city weekly (with news of Boston's neighborhoods, plus Cambridge and Somerville) bundled in. I subscribe to the *Melrose Free Press*. I have made my peace with the local annoying supermarket by concentrating on root vegetables. I am going to start baking my own bread.

When I'm commuting, I try to avoid rush hour, and I use back roads wherever possible. While I feel guilty about using Route 93 less and residential neighborhoods more, I was in danger of becoming enraged and explosive, a social menace in the making. Driving smoothly on familiar roads, thirty minutes each way, is just enough time to listen to a jazz set on the radio, or part of a news program. By shunning big, anonymous, fast-moving roads, especially the Route 128 beltway, which makes me feel I'm in the dentist's chair, I learn the connections among neighborhoods and feel less disjointed.

Driving the Main Streets and Broadways of the towns north of

Boston is a lesson in how each town was settled and the move of immigrant communities that is still going on. Along the way, I check out these communities and shop for bean sprouts, take-out dumplings, arancini, and homemade tortillas. Now I know that there's an Italian produce market in Malden, a natural foods grocery in Medford, and a lakeside nineteenth-century Jewish cemetery in Wakefield. Stoneham has a performing arts theater. Revere Beach, a honky-tonk scene with a long white beach, is fifteen minutes away.

I try to drive ecologically. I take Sophia, my five-year-old Honda Civic hatchback, for an oil change every four months. I drive in the highest gear and try to maintain a constant speed. Sophia gets thirty-five to forty miles to a gallon and has no air conditioner.

I am trying to see if I can be at home, and productive, in both places—transurban, a citizen of city and town. I would like to continue to be in my own home *and* to maintain connections to Boston and Cambridge. An alert and attuned individual should be able to have ties with multiple communities, to pledge to do so and to figure out how. I want to live in a world where we are less defined by where we live and more defined by our interests, involvements, and contributions. I am trying to learn how to traffic not only between city and town, but also between community and privacy, involvement and stillness, doing and being.

Soon I will have my first winter in Melrose. I will not be able to walk over snowdrifts and past artsy snow sculpture (mimicking classical modes) en route to movies in Harvard Square. But I can walk in the local public golf course and watch children sledding down hills in their bright parkas and flying scarves, and feed red and tawny cardinals black sunflower seeds in my yard, and curl up in the warm lamplight of the Melrose Public Library. I can try to be alert to the town. Just yesterday, a bright, crisp October day, I stopped at the local chain supermarket I am trying to like to pick up a gallon of milk. At a particular place in the parking lot, which I had thought unremarkable, I entered a zone of homey aromas, an intermingling

of just-baked pizza, warm bagels, and Irish soda bread, emanating
from three local establishments. I lingered between the neat yel-
low lines of parking spaces before reentering my car, parked behind
Melrose Elks Lodge ("Benevolent and Protective").

If, in three or four years, I move back to Cambridge or Boston—
by then leaving a well-established garden with stands of Japanese iris
and hardy cyclamen beneath a weeping cherry—I hope to care less
that friends will compare me to a woman who remarries her former
husband. If I stay in my adopted town, won over by quiet and serenity, relationships with trees, and having planted clumps of exotic iris
not for every taste (in a range of copper, cocoa, and rust), it will have
been an arranged marriage that worked. Either way, I'll be glad to
be in love again.

———————————————

LYNDA MORGENROTH is a Boston-area freelance writer and essayist. She has
written widely on art, architecture, urban culture, and social issues, in part as
a longtime contributor to the *Boston Globe,* and is the author of an urban field
guide, *Boston Neighborhoods: A Food Lover's Walking, Eating and Shopping Guide
to Ethnic Enclaves in and around Boston.*

BETWEEN CITY
AND SUBURB:
AUTOMANIA

AMERICANS HAVE A DEEP-SEATED AFFECTION FOR
their cars (I confess to this) and consider driving a basic
right. Most automobile owners are probably not aware
that they pay only a small fraction of the true cost of
driving. In *The Elephant in the Bedroom,* authors Stanley
Hart and Alan Spivak point out that government subsidies for highways and parking make up between 8 to
10 percent of our gross national product, an astonishing
figure that doesn't include the cost of automobile pollution. The question for those of us who drive every day
is: What would a public transit system have to provide
to induce us to take the bus or light rail and leave the car
at home?

SELECTIONS FROM
ROADKILL BILL

KEN AVIDOR

Cartoonist and writer Ken Avidor has no doubt about the effect of auto-mobiles and highways on our environment—and on the psyches of those who rely on them. His Roadkill Bill *cartoons allow us to laugh, if somewhat shamefacedly, at ourselves and at the society that we have built in homage to cars and highways. His characters clearly enunciate the values promoted by automania.*

STARRING . . .

ROADKILL BILL

 He's a frequently squashed rodent—of precisely what species we may never be told—a cute and lovable victim of consumer excess and the American way of life. So if you're scouring the aisles of Toys "Я" Us in search of Roadkill Bill action figures, you've completely missed the point.

SUNNY THE SUNFLOWER

 Known as "the flower with the power to explain just about everything," Sunny is a peaceful and bleeding-hearted yet fearless forb; a tireless advocate of herbalism, permaculture, and green economics; a follower of Gandhi and Schumacher; founder of "Sunny's Anti-Corporation Diet."

ANGER MAN

 He's the overweight, wasteful suburban consumer seeking status, happiness, and convenience in the ownership of more and more things. He is reactionary, defensive, and selfish, lashing out at those he perceives as threats to his privileged, destructive, unsustainable lifestyle.

MEL THE MALFORMED FROG

 He's essentially a friendly Frankenstein created in the pursuit of progress. But he's nonetheless a proactive victim. Any resemblence between Mel's mouth and the Nike swoosh logo is of course purely coincidental.

KEN AVIDOR IS a writer, illustrator, sculptor, and cartoonist. His weekly comic strip *Roadkill Bill* has appeared in *Pulse of the Twin Cities* since 1999. His artwork and writings have also appeared in *Car Busters Magazine* and *Funny Times.* The first collection of *Roadkill Bill* comics was published in 2001 and is still available from Car Busters Press. Avidor is currently working on a graphic novel called *Gondwanaland.*

WHAT MAKES A CITY LIVABLE?

THE AUTHORS OF THESE SEVEN ESSAYS SUGGEST
some of the attractions that raise a city's livability quo-
tient. These include city centers and neighborhoods
where pedestrians, not cars, have the right-of-way for
strolling and shopping; renovated neighborhoods and
revitalized waterfronts; well-designed urban infrastructure; and mixed-use neighborhoods that encourage
street traffic during the day and in the evening. Features
that promote our interaction, whether for business or
for leisure, contribute to an enlivened urban life.

▶ THE CHARLES RIVER. PHOTOGRAPH BY BOB DINATALE.

CAMBRIDGE WALKING

SARA ST. ANTOINE

The author recounts her transformation from native Michigander immersed in a car culture to someone who chooses not to own a car at all. For her, walking in Cambridge provides myriad benefits, from ease and exercise to a stronger sense of kinship with the people in her neighborhood. She credits the historical layout of Cambridge as well as the current city government with making Cambridge a place where walking is a viable and ever-rewarding mode of transportation.

In the spring of 2001, the city of Cambridge hid one hundred gold shoes in parks, along sidewalks, and in other places where pedestrians might find them. It was a bit like a collaboration between Willy Wonka and the Easter Bunny. If you found a gold shoe, you won a gift certificate for a pair of walking shoes, and your name entered a drawing for a thousand-dollar shopping spree in Harvard Square. Within days, gold-shoe fever infected many Cambridge residents, myself included. While a sign outside the public library kept track of the number of remaining hidden shoes, we displayed a new level of attentiveness as we walked the city streets. We eyed tree branches and bike racks and the dark, grungy spaces under bus stop benches with hopeful curiosity. When an out-of-town friend came to visit, I told her about the gold shoe hunt and saw, in moments, a marked change in her behavior. She grew distracted. Her eyes shifted in every direction and she even veered across the sidewalk to peer over a low concrete wall—casually, as if it were something she did every day. Apparently we never outgrow our enthusiasm for a good treasure hunt.

The purpose of the gold shoe hunt was not, of course, strictly entertainment. The city hoped to call attention to walking, rewarding those who already logged substantial hours on foot and hoping to entice nonpedestrians out of their cars and onto the sidewalks. There might have been some interest in promoting the cardiovascular benefits of pedestrian travel, but for the most part, the city encourages walking for the community's quality of life; the fewer people driving, the cleaner, safer, quieter, and more pleasant both residential and commercial areas will be.

These are all goals I support wholeheartedly, though sometimes I think giving rewards to Cambridge pedestrians is akin to creating incentives for Phoenix retirees to play golf or Las Vegas tourists to play slot machines. According to the U.S. Census, fully 24 percent of Cambridge residents walk to work, compared to a national average of only 3 percent. Another 25 percent use public transportation, compared to 5 percent nationally. And 12 percent of Cambridge households have no car.

My husband and I have lived without a car in Cambridge for six years, and in that time, we've come to know a sizable cross section of its community of walkers. There's the elderly man who walks the length of Broadway every day to pick up groceries at the market, dressed always in a sport coat and moving with a more awkward gait each year. There's the gangly, dark-haired woman who seemed to walk her dog so incessantly that I thought she was off in the head until I realized that her dog changed from spaniel to samoyed to mutt: she is, it appears, a professional dog walker. In the early morning and evening hours, the sidewalks fill with commuters striding purposefully to their offices or public transportation stops. In the hours between, the teenagers in their low-slung jeans dominate the sidewalk, walking three across and moving so slowly one can sense the aimless languor of adolescence in their every step. There are nannies and young mothers with their strollers, a woman with a leashed cat, and an American Indian man who sports a red bandanna in his long black and gray hair. But perhaps my favorite pedestrian to watch is the celebrity poet who lives on our block. She doesn't so much walk as meander, literally unable to maintain a straight course. I watch her weave from one edge of the sidewalk to another, in a pace nearly as slow as the teenagers', and can only think that her mind is so occupied with imagery and language that it hasn't the capacity to govern the movement of her feet.

Choosing not to own a car is not something I ever anticipated as a young person growing up in Michigan, the land of automobiles. Everywhere I turned, someone was affiliated with the automotive industry. My father has worked many hours as an arbitrator for the United Auto Workers, my cousin's husband is a Ford executive, and my brother was once managing editor of *Car and Driver* magazine. When I was in high school, Michigan encouraged automobile driving with such fervor that sixteen-year-olds with the requisite driver's education class credits could get their license without a driving test (which goes a long way toward explaining why, to this day, I cannot parallel park). My hometown had plenty of walkable areas, but two-car families were still the norm in the seventies and eighties, and families with teenagers often had three or four.

Over the years, though, I grew increasingly fond of the carless lifestyle. I lived in big cities with excellent public transportation systems and smallish communities where walking took care of most my needs. Though I briefly owned a car when I had to, I found over the years that living without a car gave me more freedom than having one, contrary to what car advertisers would have you believe.

In this time, I also became more attuned to the problems associated with cars. Yes, they fuel the economy of my home state, and they indirectly financed my college education, but they're also noisy and polluting, and they've helped destroy places I love. When I return home to Ann Arbor for a visit, I spend most of my time in the city center, which retains its essential charm despite the inevitable loss of its earlier hippie character. But there is more traffic everywhere, and if I venture at all past the center of town, the changes are dramatic: oversized houses, cookie-cutter condominium complexes, chain-store strip malls, and corporate headquarters occupying the places where I once visited friends at their horse farms or took hay rides through a farmer's field. The older parts of town have a tidy efficiency about them, like a nineteenth-century grandmother sitting on a slender wooden chair. The new areas sprawl—the term is perfectly apt—like a couch potato who stretches out and usurps the space designed for two or three. The *Ann Arbor News* reported several years ago that in recent decades, Michigan's urbanized land has been increasing at a rate six times greater than its population growth. Fewer people are living in bigger houses on more land, and using more resources to get there. And this happened in large part because we started building communities around automobiles instead of around humans. Watching this happen to places in Michigan that I've always cherished has fed my resolve not to build my life around a motorized vehicle (even if that does, ironically, translate into some sort of state blasphemy).

In Cambridge, it isn't hard to live without a car. The city was laid out for people and horses, so it's compact and human scaled, with many businesses and institutions located just a short walk from our home. Like many urban residents, I can reach basic necessities like a dry cleaner, Laundromat, bank machine, and corner grocer in a few minutes. Still greater rewards lie just five or ten minutes away. Just the other day, friends who used to live in the neighborhood were reminiscing about the evenings when they'd walk up to a nearby intersection and purchase wine and cheese on one corner, a loaf of fresh-baked bread on another, and homemade ravioli and tomato sauce on a third; one small walk, one large meal. We're lucky, too, to have a major natural foods grocery store just a ten-minute walk from our house. When the parent company built a new, bigger store about a mile and a half away, it looked like they'd close our little neighborhood branch. But customers responded with an outpouring of letters, many of them suggesting that a corporation with such a supposedly strong environmental ethic ought to honor the needs of pedestrians. Miraculously, the company decided to keep our neighborhood store in operation.

I'm sure one can find a strong sense of community in places built around cars, but I've always found it more readily in places where pedestrians proliferate. An inevitable intimacy develops when you routinely encounter the same store owners. Our corner florist is said to be the best person to talk to if you want to know any neighborhood gossip—who's selling their house, who bought it, what it went for. The family-owned pharmacy down the street has a steady flow of elderly and not-so-elderly walk-in customers who chat while they wait for their prescriptions to be filled. The weather, the Red Sox, the best brand of laxatives—all are fair topics of conversation in this pharmaceutical bonding ritual. It's probably not surprising that these pharmacists know the name of my cat; he is, after all, the member of the family who requires the most medication. Even so I was amazed one day when I raced in for a last-minute prescription and one of the pharmacists held up a stapled paper bag and said, "Pickup for Spenser Kitty?" then added, "It's all ready to go. We hear you're late for your train."

Walking creates an unspoken social network that extends beyond neighborhood store owners. The other day, my husband and I were returning from the store when we passed by a woman with a strong New Jersey accent smoking with friends on her stoop. We've walked by her countless times and almost feel as though we know her now. In fact, there are dozens of people who fall into this category; we don't know their names, but we've seen them so often that we feel a strange kinship. They've become characters in our lives whom we talk about and wonder about, even if we've never said more to them than a simple hello. "We should have a party," my husband mused, "and invite them all to come." It was an intriguing idea, and we spent the rest of the walk making a list of who we'd include: the New Jersey woman and her friends, the biracial gay couple who spend hours tending their corner garden, the thirtysomething twins we never see apart, the feisty old lady next door who weeds her flower bed in high heels, and our fellow walkers, too—the dog walker, the celebrity poet, a few of the teens. It was an eclectic group, to be sure; we've made connections to people who might not necessarily form a circle of friends. But in a way, that's reassuring. It means that diversity is part of our neighborhood, and that our sidewalk society can transcend those differences.

To walk in Cambridge is often not a social experience at all, of course, but a sweet stretch of solitude and introspection. I weave through the neighborhood streets instinctively choosing the path that offers the greatest rewards that day: maximum leaf cover on a hot summer afternoon, fewest hills on the days when I'm weary, best front-yard crocuses on those first tentative days of spring. Unconsciously or consciously, I've charted this information onto my mental map of Cambridge, and I both draw upon it and update it as I walk. Even as my mind works over other matters—what to have for dinner, perhaps, or how to sort out a work-related dilemma—I find myself noting the human and natural goings-on around me: which tree's leaves are turning, who has a "welcome home, baby" sign in their window, which cat has gone missing. Oddly, the combined activities of walking, observing, and internal musing often elicit my best thinking, as if considering new corners and perspectives outside has opened up new ones inside, too.

When I walk, my pace is inarguably slower than it would be if I were driving, but it's also steady. There is none of the frustrating stop and go that drivers experience constantly in busy neighborhood streets. At heart, we all want freedom of movement, and like most people I can take great pleasure in cruising down an open road in a car, listening to music and watching the scenery pass by. But one doesn't find many open roads in the city (or anywhere else these days, for that matter). The prevalence of road rage around these parts is the clearest indication I know that car driving isn't giving people the sense of freedom they expect. But walking is different. You may have to pause, but you're never stuck. You move almost seamlessly through the city, with few blood-pressure-raising surprises.

Most days my route is defined by basic needs: I'll take a break from work midafternoon and run errands on foot—dropping off a package at the post office, picking up a video, getting cash, and then buying a load of groceries on the way back home. Afterward, I'm done with the day's errands and my day's exercise, and I feel restored by the dose of sunshine. But the experience of walking varies considerably, depending on the purpose, the weather, and the season. On fall weekend afternoons, my husband and I will make our way down to the Charles River for a long walk by the water and the geese, surrounded by the frenetic activity of runners and bikers and in-line skaters. On summer nights, we'll walk home from Harvard Square enveloped in darkness, our fellow pedestrians moving in and out of the streetlamp glow like performers entering and exiting the spotlight. On the rarest of winter weekends, we'll wake up early to a city hushed with snowfall. Knowing it won't last long, we'll pull on boots and trek to our favorite bakery for a brief excursion into this silent, snow-draped world.

Walking has its disadvantages, of course. Some days, a heavy backpack of groceries strains my shoulder muscles and by the time I return home—bread squished, a container of olives drooling onto my backpack—I'm crabby and tired. Other days, the rain or heat or cold makes me yearn for the climate-controlled bubble of an automobile. And, too, Cambridge is a twenty-first-century city where most people travel by car. Given the narrowness of the streets and the growing size of the average automobile, it takes very little for the streets to feel overrun with traffic. We pedestrians can start to feel outnumbered.

Because of this congestion, I'm always grateful for the efforts the city government makes to look out for its walking residents. Not only are there several full-time city employees devoted to addressing pedestrian concerns, but a volunteer citizen group meets monthly to give input on pedestrian issues. The group organizes walking events and educational projects, reviews every major development project, and debates such issues as crosswalk safety and jaywalking. No pedestrian-related issue is too small for this dedicated bunch; vigorous internal debates rage over whether our sidewalks ought to be made with bricks (the aesthetic choice) or concrete (apparently a safer surface in wet or icy weather). Throughout Cambridge, the work of the city and its pedestrian committee shows up in ways one could easily enjoy without noticing. In some areas, for example, planners have reconfigured streets and erected traffic islands to make it easier for pedestrians to cross lanes of heavy traffic. Elsewhere, they've extended curbs to discourage cars from cutting sharp corners and installed experimental walk signs with digital clocks to let pedestrians know just how many seconds remain before cars will once again be rushing across their path.

While walking works in Cambridge for most needs, my husband and I do turn to other modes of transportation for longer trips. We make ample use of the city's bus, subway, and commuter rail systems. We frequently call cabs for early-morning trips to the airport or on late nights coming back from downtown Boston. We rent cars for weekend trips into the New England countryside. And when none of those options works easily, we now have Zipcar. An innovative transportation company, Zipcar owns a fleet of new cars and parks them throughout the city for registered members to use when they need them. The company pays for the cars, the insurance, the upkeep, the parking, and the gas. We members pay an hourly fee plus mileage. The idea is that many people need a car only for the occasional errand, and so it's easier and more cost-effective to share cars than to have your own. At the same time, because you have to pay for each use, you'll keep your driving to a minimum and reduce the overall number of cars on the road. We've been Zipcar members for a year now, and the process has worked without a hitch. When it's terribly cold outside, or public transportation just won't do, it's nice to know there's a hybrid Honda Civic parked just around that corner that we can borrow for a few hours. But the best part about Zipcar is that it keeps us from making driving our central mode of transportation, allowing us to preserve the almost-car-free lifestyle we like best.

One can never know what the future will hold, but for now I will happily be a Zipcar renter, a cab hailer, a public transportation taker, and, above all else, a pedestrian. Walking lends a rich simplicity to my days, a small measure of ease in a fast-paced world. I know there are many places in the country where walking isn't practical or easy, or where I couldn't accomplish one-tenth of what I can do on foot in Cambridge. So although my peripatetic habit may be doing something good for the community, I tend to think of it the other way around. Walking is a gift, yes, but one the city of Cambridge has given to me. And that's something I value more than any gold shoe.

SARA ST. ANTOINE grew up in Ann Arbor, Michigan. She attended Williams College and the Yale School of Forestry and Environmental Studies and now lives in Cambridge, Massachusetts, with her husband (who also enjoys walking) and her cat (who would, if someone would just let him out). She writes educational materials for World Wildlife Fund and edits the *Stories from Where We Live* series for Milkweed Editions.

CITY PLACES, SACRED SPACES

TERRELL F. DIXON

Writer and educator Terrell Dixon compares his experiences with nature in Houston to his experiences in the Arctic National Wildlife Refuge as he breaks down the traditional American dichotomy between nature and the city. He urges that we adapt Henry David Thoreau's notion of "sauntering" to our contemporary urban lives. Once we recognize that the urban nature walk is not an oxymoron, we are free to see the sacred in our urban landscapes, and thus to acknowledge and cherish the nature of American cities.

It began as an ordinary bedtime stroll around the block with my dog, Rocky. In my Montrose neighborhood, near downtown Houston, walking the dog is often a social event. We residents sometimes stumble over the name of our human neighbors, but we can call out the canines—Dooley, Taylor, Bella, Louise—with ease, and our evening walks with them set the stage for casual chats about housing prices, the ongoing battle against town-house blight, politics, the weather. This walk, however, was too late at night for such meetings, and it led me to what has become a very different kind of walk—a contemporary, urban version of what Henry David Thoreau, in his essay "Walking," called "sauntering." He understood sauntering, as we still do today, as walking in a way that is free from a specific destination, setting forth on foot to see where the walk itself takes us. Thoreau also saw another layer of meaning in the word. He argued that the word *sauntering* derived from the custom, in the Middle Ages, of walking "à la Saint Terre," to the Holy Land. "Sauntering" thus became a way to connect with the sacred in the landscape. His thoughts have helped to shape my attempts to come to terms with life as an environmentalist living in the heart of the nation's fourth-largest city. It is true that Thoreau's mid-nineteenth-century America was a time, unlike ours, when those who loved the natural world could easily disregard the city; it was an easy walk from the village of Concord to the rural landscapes that he loved. Yet his use of sauntering to emphasize a basic connection between traveling a landscape on foot and recognizing its spirituality, between the act of walking and seeing the sacred in the landscapes around us, can still have meaning for the over 80 percent of Americans who now live in cities. It remains a powerful notion, one that can help us improve the nature of urban life.

What happened that night occurred at the edge of an open lot just around the block from my house. As I stood by while Rocky nosed around the weeds and tree trunks, I slowly became aware of an unfamiliar sound. An intriguing bird call began to quietly stand out from the eight-lane hum of Highway 59 traffic just three blocks away. It was a quavering, softly resonant series of descending notes, repeated in a way that, to my untrained ears, sounded neither familiar nor territorial, but simply—there is no other word for it—mysterious. I kept listening, and I rooted myself in that spot for so long that the dog stretched out on the ground for a nap. But for all of my peering into the tangle of trees in that wooded lot, I could not see the source of the call. The sound stayed with me. I was drawn back to that small piece of neighborhood open space over and over again, to listen and, also, to look.

The bird that night was—as my bird-watching friends explained with a mixture of long-suffering patience and mild disdain that often marks their explanations to me—an Eastern screech owl. To them, it was a very ordinary bird. I, however, keep no lists, and since I like to watch and listen to everyday birds as much as if not more than to catch a brief glimpse of a rare one, my enthusiasm remained intact. My fascination with the bird and its place grew.

My lack of knowledge did not mean that this was my first memorable owl encounter. The first was with two great horned owls in far west Texas. My wife and I had just left Big Bend National Park in the crisp clear coldness of an early January morning. Each trip to that part of the world brings a sense of seeing things anew, but this visit came on the heels of vision-restoring surgery and each vista and each rock face appeared with a startling clarity, detail, and power. The owls, perched in a small tree fifteen feet from the edge of the road, loomed out of the early-morning gray as we sped by. They stayed in place while we slowly turned around and parked just across the road from them. We kept quiet and were able to watch them scan the landscape for prey, and to watch also as one of them eased off the branch and glided into the field for a rodent meal. Although they surely knew of our presence and although they rotated their flat faces our way occasionally, the size of those owls and the stillness of their regal bearing exuded a self-confident majesty and evoked a world where they ruled with an easy, unquestioned authority. Those large owls on that small tree, just outside the national park boundary, out in a huge expanse of high plains desert, were the heart of our wilderness experience. They elicited a respect for the power of nature that lingered during the long drive home, and after.

Years ago, in a different part of Houston from where I now live, an owl took residence in a failing oak tree in my front yard. This was fine, except for one odd characteristic of this owl: the way he responded to the sheen of moonlight on my silver hair. Friends assumed it was an aesthetic issue, though I preferred to think of it as a territorial one. Most of the time, I could work with the flowers and shrubs and enjoy the small front yard as I wished; I could walk anywhere, even in the dark. On clear nights when the moon was half full or more, it was unsafe for me to venture within twenty feet of the tree. Out he would come, in an awful silent rush, propelling himself straight at my head. Sometimes he pulled up short and veered away at the last possible second, other times he nipped, just barely, the offending silver strands. Each time he terrified me. All of this was vastly more entertaining to my friends and neighbors than to me. I learned much later that this, too, was an Eastern screech owl. At the time, I was relieved when it was time to sell the house (to a young brown-haired family) and cede the front yard space to him.

My personal history with owls was thus both memorable and mixed, although there was a consistent element of awe in each of the encounters. The screech owl in Montrose was different, and though my personal history left me with no doubts about its ability to be ferocious if necessary, my experiences with this owl fed into my daily life. We shared a neighborhood, and I was curious about it. I learned, not surprisingly considering this individual bird's choice of home, that the Eastern screech owl has a high tolerance for human activity. It does well in cities and suburbs, and its name stems from the grating, piercing screech it utters when it is agitated or afraid. The mellow, descending song that so captivated me is a way to signal the owl's presence in a nesting territory, and it works also as a way for owls of both genders to signal their mates. It is often used when other owls or humans approach. This call occurs most frequently at a crucial time in the life of the species: the period of fledgling dispersal when the young are out of the nest but still in the area. The role of the owl in human culture turned out to be richer than I knew. In addition to the well-known associations of owls with wisdom and with death throughout the literature of the Western world, there are also other cultural traditions whose views of the owl fit well with that first call that drew me into the owl's world of urban nature. Some

Native American stories view the call as a lament for an earlier time, a golden age when men and animals lived in perfect unity.

After this encounter, when I walked the neighborhood I expected more than the physical exercise for Rocky and for me. Over time, I learned that the medium-sized open lot sustained a good deal of natural activity. Butterflies came to that area: cloudless sulphurs could show up at any time; black swallowtails and monarchs were fairly frequent in the spring. The red flash of a cardinal's wing could light up the whole back of the woodlot. Huge numbers of very small American toads suddenly appeared in the puddle that formed where the tree roots break up the sidewalk. Then they seemed to disappear until those summer months when their chorus took over the evening air. One spring, an early-morning opossum looked back at me for just a moment before plunging off the back fence and back into the small wild of the open lot. Another morning, sitting on my back porch and looking over a garden that backs up to the open lot, I watched a red-tailed hawk, high in a tree, rip apart the squirrel pinned in its talons.

I also came to look at other parts of the neighborhood in a new way. I went often to this first lot, but I also started sauntering through the neighborhood, walking with no particular goal other than to discover the nature of the neighborhood. There was, once I could at last choose to see it, a richly textured natural fabric, one that flourished below, between, around, and on top of the built world that traditionally commands the attention of human urban dwellers. Where once I saw Arts and Crafts homes, interesting human neighbors and their canine companions, I now saw also increasingly diverse parts of the natural world. That first screech owl moved on, but I learned to listen for and find other screech owls in other parts of the neighborhood. One spring, neighbors pointed out a yellow-crowned night heron nesting in a corner tree a few blocks away. In the light of a full moon, the heron's crown stood out in splendid silhouette. The green mass of beautiful live oaks that line the neighborhood streets slowly began to emerge as individual trees, some with infinitely complex and gnarled above-ground root systems that tug at the eyes like sculpture. I learned that one magnificent tree, a live oak whose branches arch all the way across an esplanade and two wide lanes of city street, appeared on a city list of champion trees.

I am not a naturalist. Despite my enthusiasm, my knowledge of neighborhood nature remains rudimentary at best. Nonetheless, since that first encounter with a screech owl I have begun to walk my way toward a new understanding of my neighborhood and of urban nature. I have also begun to rethink how we can know and preserve nature in the city.

Most of us think of the nature walk, if we think of it at all, as an activity from an earlier, less thoroughly urban age, something that took place in a period when cities were relatively small and the country was never far from the village or the town. The very name "nature walk" can feel like a relic from some earlier time when amateur naturalists walked the county countryside, cataloged the local flora and fauna, and, after thirty years, issued *A Natural History of Suchandsuch Shire* or *County.* And yet, among those who care about the environment, a consensus is building that our environmental concerns must extend to the city, that among our most pressing environmental concerns is finding new ways to inhabit and shape our cities. My experience suggests that the neighborhood nature walk can help with this.

In our city lives, we tend to restrict where we talk and think about nature to certain types of places. We have the option of driving to the nearest arboretum and walking along a proscribed pathway where we can read the plant and tree identification signs. Arboretums are good things, of course, and walking them can lead to other ways of knowing urban nature outside their boundaries, but our schedules can often fail to match up with arboretum hours, and the learning that goes on there sometimes seems more like a lesson than a saunter. Most city parks also require subway, bus, or automobile transportation, and they too tend to favor directive signage on planned walkways, codified instruction, and structured landscapes. I am not criticizing urban parks. I do not want to suggest that our city parks and arboretums are fatally flawed; they are not. They offer urbanites open space, green expanses, and chances to know the local flora and fauna. They are both wonderful and essential. They help maintain and increase the presence of nature in the city, and every American city needs more of them. I am simply saying that parks by themselves are not enough. We need to complement what they offer with urban nature walks.

In our neighborhoods, the nature walk becomes more than a relic, an out-of-town exercise, an occasional country indulgence, or even a guided—no matter how intelligent and well-meaning—urban nature excursion. It takes us into the neighborhoods where we live, as opposed to going occasionally into preserves set apart from the rest of city life. In it, we let our feet and eyes take us where they may; we engage in exploration, sauntering in our contemporary sense of that word; we amble without a set goal or predetermined destination, intent only on seeing nature in the neighborhood. When we do this, we begin to view our urban areas anew—to see trees as well as trucks, to note birds as well as the built environment. At the root of such strolls, there is daily delight and renewable joy, sufficient reasons in themselves to take them. But they also offer more. They possess the power to change how we conceive of our cities and their relationship to the nature that underlies, supports, and envelops them. The persistent, engaging sound of that Eastern screech owl in the neighborhood open lot opened my eyes and began the process of teaching me, a die-hard environmentalist living deep in the heart of Houston, to see urban nature and the city in a new way. The implications of this are clear. When urban nature becomes something more than an amusing oxymoron, when it emerges instead as an expected part of everyday life, we are already well on our way to making more places for nature in our neighborhoods and our cities. Once we begin to really notice nature in our neighborhoods, it is but a short step to protecting what we have and requiring more of it.

▶ ▶ ▶

Even after I realized that my walks were teaching me the nature of my neighborhood, it took a bit longer for me to recognize that as I walked something else was happening. For Thoreau, the notion of sauntering meant more than setting out on a nature walk without a predetermined plan. It also was a way to discover the holy in the landscape. He believed that by sauntering we learn the spiritual worth of a landscape, its place in the beliefs that sustain us. For him, of course, such walks always went away from the city and into the countryside.

For me, a Euro-American of Scottish and Scots-Irish ancestry, raised reading the poetry of the English Romantics and believing in Henry David Thoreau, John Muir, and the innate holiness of remote mountain hiking, the spiritual dimension of sauntering fit easily with my love of wilderness. When I hiked in "the big wild," the remote grandeur of Big Bend National Park or the Arctic National Wildlife Refuge, it was natural for me to see their landscapes as sacred. My personal history and the dictates of American environmental culture came together to exalt the act of walking in grand and remote places. But even after I came to take pleasure in my urban nature walks, I did not come easily to the realization that our city spaces could also be sacred places.

The change began, oddly enough, when I was far from home, traveling in a place that is in many ways the opposite of the urbanized, overdeveloped Texas Gulf Coast. Sprawling Houston, a perennial contender for the title of the country's most polluted airshed, is easily and often seen as an environmentalist's nightmare. The Arctic National Wildlife Refuge, on the other hand, is a sacred place for American environmentalists. We revere it as the most pristine wilderness among all of our American places.

Nonetheless, I learned something crucial about my Montrose neighborhood on the Aichilik River delta, near the Beaufort Lagoon and the Arctic Ocean. It happened late in the sixth day of a float trip down the Aichilik River, the river that marks the boundary of the contested 1002 study area of the Arctic Refuge. During the day's travel, we had gloried in seeing some of the abundant life that fills summer on the Arctic delta. There were a few caribou, their outlines visible against the far horizon, but the huge numbers that constitute the famed Porcupine herd had already left. It hardly mattered. Musk ox and their young watched us from a bluff above the Aichilik; pairs of arctic foxes hunted and played on both sides of the river; a snowy owl, resplendent and startling in its pure whiteness, surveyed the area from the top of a tussock; tundra swans flew overhead; and semi-palmated plovers fluttered from place to nearby place on the tundra, faking broken wings to lead us away from their young.

Later on, after the boats were pulled ashore and our tents put up, I sat down to record the day in my trip journal. In the soft blend of dusk and dawn that marks 2:00 A.M. in the Arctic summer, I responded to the majesty of the Romanzof Mountains of the Brooks Range and the rich vitality of animal life in the Arctic. I ended that day's journal entry, however, with my thoughts turning back toward urban nature, thinking about the neighborhood opossum and screech owls, and the small piece of neighborhood open space where they lived.

I had to laugh at the unexpected appearance of that particular memory amid the remote splendor of the Arctic, but re-reading my journal after the trip, this unbidden juxtaposition of open lot and Arctic Refuge began to make sense. For me, it comes together in the following way. In Euro-American culture, we have traditionally tended to locate spiritual meaning in two types of landscapes. Scenic national park wilderness areas are the most obvious kind of sacred place. Places like the Grand Canyon and Big Bend, for example, feature nature on the grand scale, and they provide a scenic grandeur that generates a sense of awe and wonder. These icons of nature's beauty have a sacred status reinforced over time and reiterated by landscape paintings and calendar photographs, by nature writing and by televised travel and nature shows. At this point in our cultural history, their sacred status is both long-standing and incontrovertible. Even though our very love for these places is bringing crowds and pollution, most Americans who care about the environment still share an almost automatic reverence for them.

Pastoral places can constitute a second type of sacred landscape. While wonder is also part of our response to these places, it is more muted and stems not so much from a sense of grandeur as from our apprehension of order. We respond, it seems to me, to what we feel to be the order and harmony, the pleasure of humankind working in harmony with the processes of the natural world, that permeate our walks in a pastoral landscape. Since the rural pastoral landscapes so widespread in Thoreau's time are essentially unprotected and rapidly diminishing, our appreciation of sacred pastoral places is often intermingled with a sense of impending loss.

It became clear to me as I wrote about the appearance of the Montrose open lot in the pages of my Aichilik journal that there is a third type of American landscape that also can have sacred status: urban nature. Like its wilderness and pastoral counterparts, it elicits wonder. But in the sacred urban site, wonder often stems not from the perceptions of nature's grandeur or even its harmony, but from what we recognize as an unobtrusive strength, a power most often expressed in the persistence and the resilience of the natural world. In my case, the charismatic beauty of the snowy owls on the tundra led my thoughts back to the Eastern screech owl families: how their small wings enabled them to fly in tightly wooded space, how they used the darkness to persist and flourish in the city.

Wonder at the persistence of urban nature differs from the awe we feel in the face of grander scenic spectacles, but it does share a common source, one that cuts across all types of landscape and brings together the grand, the rural, and the urban. The common source ties together each place where we humans apprehend the spiritual value of the landscape. Each of these otherwise very different types of sacred places fosters awareness of a life force that is greater than our human selves, one that contains us and all that we create. As I have come to see our world, all landscapes—wilderness, rural, urban—have innate sacred potential. Spirituality becomes manifest once we take time to attend to the land and thus are able to observe the great cycles of the natural world—the changes from day to night, the shifts from season to season, the process of courtship and procreation, the passages of birth and death—enacted within that place. Mountain ranges are thrust up and then worn down over millennia; musk oxen stand, shielding their young, on an arctic bluff; wheat is planted, tended, and harvested; urban owls mate, their offspring fledge and disperse, and the owls call out to approaching humans. The sacredness of a place emerges when we come to *see* that place and *know* the life it sustains. This can occur in the Montrose or in the Romanzof Mountains. It finally requires neither grandeur nor harmony, but it does require that we pause to know the landscape, to acknowledge the ongoing processes of individual lives other than our own and how these lives express the great cycles of the natural world. When we do that, landscape takes on a sacred quality.

I am aware that this view runs deeply counter to some traditional concepts of sacred landscapes. Some religious traditions see the sacredness of a landscape as dependent on designation by a divine authority. Also, for some environmentalists, to link an unknown, somewhat scruffy lot in my Montrose neighborhood with some of the most cherished and celebrated landscapes in America may at first seem like sacrilege. The same historical and cultural forces that hindered my recognition of the sacred in urban nature push all of us to dismiss and degrade urban nature. Traditionally in American thought, we have striven to separate what we value in nature from the city. The artificiality of this separation, which stems from the British Romantic poets and was amplified by the transcendentalism of our most important nature writers, is only now being recognized and rejected. Though we are beginning to change, an important strand in our environmental culture still situates the sacred only in spectacular or pastoral landscapes and chooses either to ignore urban nature or to treat it with condescension.

There are practical as well as philosophical reasons to outgrow this division. When we try to make sacredness into an exclusive attribute of remote wilderness and rural places, we secularize and trivialize the landscapes where most Americans spend most of our days. We become more and more profoundly *dis*placed. This accelerates our ongoing degradation of urban nature. Perversely, trashing the landscape with malls and freeways comes to seem more natural than sauntering.

▶ ▶ ▶

This essay should not conclude without a disclaimer, something to the effect that the magic of my Montrose sauntering is hard to replicate. The Montrose is an early-twentieth-century version of a suburb, on the edge of downtown, and thus has different properties than the new suburbs that are fifteen miles of ten-lane freeway from the city center. Or, if I chose a more direct disclaimer, I might utter the kind of injunction that once accompanied the early extreme sports television shows: Do not try this at home. To be more precise and more forceful, I could say something like this: If you live in the kind of far-flung suburb characteristic of contemporary America, the suburbs that ring Houston and other cities and that bear names like Greatwood Pines, and Silver Lake, and Ranch Meadows, *be absolutely sure that you do not try this at home.*

New suburbs like these do make a nature pitch, offering the opportunity to buy into what one recent advertisement described as a "a tranquil nature community surrounded by the beauty of nature":

> We at Wildwood Homes believe that families need to see
> the sky, the trees, the geese flying overhead, and an expanse
> of land on which to live.

In reality, suburban developments usually ignore the ecological cost of continued suburban sprawl. The ads tell us that nature is not in the city, that nature is in the suburbs we develop. This kind of development, of course, perversely becomes a kind of self-fulfilling prophecy: the suburbs destroy the biodiversity of natural areas around a city that would otherwise feed and support nature in the city. And the nature that the developers provide is mostly a de-natured nature, places where woodlands have been destroyed in favor of a few new trees planted in straight rows, where wetlands have been drained and replaced by artificial lakes.

The Montrose neighborhood in Houston, like newer suburbs, has a name intended to evoke the beauty of nature. The original developer named it after Montrose, Scotland, which he considered to be one of the world's most beautiful places, and it was developed in the early part of the twentieth century, when the City Beautiful movement influenced notions of what developments ought to be. It has sidewalks and huge live oak trees spreading over wide streets, an occasional tree-lined esplanade (one of those, appropriately enough, is the middle of Audubon Street), and, still, miraculously, some lots that are de facto natural spaces, as yet unaffected by town-house blight. It is not to be mistaken for paradise—highways and busy thoroughfares encroach and are likely to be more troublesome. As the old neighborhood has been gentrified, housing prices have risen, and this may increasingly limit access to housing to the wealthy. And yet my section of the neighborhood still invites us to walk, and when we walk, we can choose to saunter and to see the natural world, to discover and cherish city spaces that can be sacred places.

As we work to design our cities anew, it is unlikely that we will employ the old model that shaped Montrose. There are too many of us, and our cities are too large to make that feasible in our plans for the future. But as we build toward greater urban population density and its expected benefits, we also need to allow space for nature. A meaningful twenty-first-century environmentalism must cherish not only the grandeur of our national parks and the beauty of our rural places but also nature in our cities. Our concept of urban nature must mean more than a formal park at a stop on a light rail line. We need to be sure that each neighborhood leaves us room to saunter.

TERRELL DIXON teaches "Literature and the Environment" at the University of Houston, Central Campus. His essays and articles on urban nature have been published widely, and he is the editor of *City Wilds: Essays and Stories about Urban Nature*. This essay is part of a book in progress about urban nature in Houston.

▶ "FARMER'S MARKET ON NICOLLET MALL." PAINTING
BY DARCY FERRILL.

FOOD FOR THE CITY, FROM THE CITY

KRISTIN BRENNAN

As community outreach coordinator Kristin Brennan says, the words
urban *and* agriculture *do not usually go together, yet in cities throughout
the world, residents are growing vegetables and fruit in their backyards
and in community gardens. In the Dudley neighborhood in Roxbury and
Dorchester, Massachusetts, more than 150 gardens dot the city landscape
and the Food Project, a nonprofit organization, brings young people from
the urban and surrounding suburban areas to participate in growing food
for community residents and for shelters throughout Boston.*

It was a city neighborhood known for its fires. A place in which
a three-story home burned every night for a decade, the smell of
smoke wafting to nearby houses and keeping residents awake with
fear that their house might be the next one to be firebombed. An area
used as the city's trash can for all sorts of illegal and toxic dumping.
Residents shunned by the government and the banks with blatant
refusals to provide loans for home or business improvement. An environment filled with such a stench of decay—from the burnings and
from the trash—that people held their noses as they walked down
the street. A community simply stunned by its own circumstances,
totally shut out of the process that could change them—all the while

knowing that there *had* to be another way. The scars of the Dudley Street neighborhood in Roxbury and Dorchester, Massachusetts, were dramatically represented in its polluted vacant lots, trash transfer stations, bankrupt businesses, and crumbling buildings and homes.

Today, though, Dudley Town Common is alive with purple-T-shirted teenagers eagerly unloading themselves and their freight from a pair of cargo vans. Their knees are dirty and their fingers smell like basil. The backs of their necks are darkened and their hands are rough and callused. The adrenaline still surges from a morning of pulling red peppers and eggplants gently from the plants, lifting skinny carrots from the soft soil bed, snapping collard green leaves from the hearty stems and gathering the huge leaves into bunches of ten with sturdy rubber bands around the bases. The vegetables come out of the truck, stacked neatly in bright orange crates heavy with the weight of beets, corn, and potatoes. The young farmers pass the crates to one another, forming a line to empty the truck of the vegetables. Onto long tables, arranged in bushel baskets and steel tin buckets, the newly harvested produce is guided into various categories—greens, roots, brassicas, fruits, summer vegetables. Signs are raised, price boards are tied to the sides of tents, and a cash box is opened for business. Soon the tables are surrounded by a crowd of people and the scene sounds like a marketplace of old: prices and products, requests and thank yous, shouted in a jumble of Cape Verdean and Haitian Creole, Spanish, Portuguese, and English. Two months ago, these teenagers had no gardening experience. Now they have pulled weeds, spread compost, set up drip irrigation systems, and harvested vegetables.

Sylvia arrives in her old gray Chrysler. Spotting her, two of the young people leave the market activity to assist with her old card table, two small buckets of tomatoes, a crate of collard greens, and a huge bunch of callaloo. The young people comment on how lovely Sylvia's tomatoes look or inquire, "What do you do with callaloo again?" They talk about the past week's weather and how the rain, sunshine, and temperature affected the crops. Sylvia offers insights and observations backed up by thirty-five years of gardening experience—how to anticipate blossom end-rot on tomatoes, how to combat cucumber beetles without using chemicals. Maybe she'll add a tidbit about how her homeland of Jamaica produced heartier greens or sweeter tomatoes. While they chat, they set up Sylvia's market stand together, close to the other tables so that scales and grocery bags can be shared. The lingering customers suddenly sight the callaloo. Sylvia welcomes her regular clientele. On the opposite side of her stand, plenty of room remains for the possible arrival of Honorio with his corn and shell beans or Bob with his peaches and apples.

This farmers' market is in the center of an urban neighborhood, on the Dudley Town Common, easily seen and easily accessible to walkers, bus riders, and motorists. It is run by a twelve-year-old nonprofit, the Food Project, an organization that brings urban and suburban young people together to grow organic vegetables and fruits in the city and suburbs of Boston. Two acres of farms in the city produce most of the fresh food brought by the young people to the Dudley Market; some vegetables—corn, winter squashes, cucumbers—come from the suburban farm. The food couldn't be more local: the urban farmland is only five blocks from the market site. The farmland once held twenty-two houses, and, when they were burned to the ground, it became a two acre stretch of rubble and trash. When the Food Project, with young people and volunteers from the community, came to clear it, with the dream of an urban farm, a couple of young people said, "We shouldn't do a garden here. It's a dump. It will just be ruined." Slowly, as the trash was cleared, the land began to breathe, preparing itself to give life to over 10,000 pounds of vegetables each season.

Dudley Street winds through one of the poorest sections of Boston, stretching for about two miles through the eastern section of Roxbury into northern Dorchester, dotted with sub shops, community centers, old Victorian homes, a community garden, an elementary school, and several apartment complexes. The Dudley Town Common, a park halfway down, holds the neighborhood's timepiece, a large clock poised on several pillars, proudly displaying the hour, consistently ten minutes fast. Three buses stop regularly at the park, headed downtown, or deeper into Roxbury, or east toward Dorchester. People gather on the benches, placed among maple and oak trees, to watch and wait for public transportation. On market days, they wander over to the color and scent of fresh vegetables and gather their produce for the week.

The real treasures of this urban place that make the market possible are nestled between and behind the three-story homes that line the neighborhood's one-way streets: tall rows of corn with bean plants circling up the stalks and squash plants on the ground, holding in its moisture. No space is wasted. Along the shady sides of the houses, lettuces, collard greens, spinach, and callaloo grow abundantly. On pergolas covering driveways, grapevines wind in and around trellises, drooping heavy with bunches of grapes by the end of the summer, and creating canopies of shade. In the yards where you might expect to see an oak or a maple tree are apple, pear, and peach trees, branches sagging with the fruit of the season. Often these gardens are hidden in backyards and you can only sneak a glance at the tops of the corn stalks or the apple trees. But on other streets, where vacant lots have been abandoned by their owners, local gardeners have created small urban farms. In the spring, they are carefully tilled, composted, and planted. In the summer, they fill out to create lush and dense green space. In the fall, the plants are heavy with the bounty of the harvest, colorful and delicious. In the winter, browned cornstalks stand tall when snow covers the garden floor. The tour of the Dudley neighborhood gardens is not a brief one; 165 gardens lie within a mile of the market.

This land was covered in orchards in the 1700s. The narrow side streets were rows of apple and pear trees, pruned judiciously, flowering, fruiting, harvested, and brought to the market just around the bend in the growing city of Boston. The Roxbury Russet and the Bartlett pear, two lasting heirloom varieties, originated in the soil of the Dudley neighborhood. As Boston expanded, orchards were slowly replaced by urban growth, real estate, businesses, schools. The farmland became part of the city, and only a few small Victory gardens dotted the landscape. After decades of explosive economic growth and the emergence of a thriving urban community in the 1950s and 1960s, the Dudley neighborhood experienced serious disinvestment in the 1970s, when many families moved to the suburbs. As the value of the land declined, many landlords intentionally burned their properties, finding they could profit more from insurance than from their tenants. The Roxbury fires left thirteen hundred vacant lots. Huge stretches of cleared land, eerily reminiscent of the orchards that preceded them, were covered with rubble from the fires.

Reclamation of the land and the neighborhood, largely through grassroots efforts of its residents, gained momentum in the late 1980s. Residents connecting and reconnecting to the history and value of their urban place began to imagine and create something new. Over time, vacant lots were transformed into affordable housing, community centers, health clinics, and local businesses. Even more strikingly, some of the land was returned to farmland. Orchards were returning, but in a new form. With the influence of neighborhood residents from Cape Verde, Jamaica, Puerto Rico, and the American South, many of whom had grown up on farms in their homelands, urban agriculture became a salient feature of land redevelopment. Essentially, food—producing and making it available in the community—was considered a priority for a livable urban environment.

Gardening as an essential part of urban life came naturally to many residents. Honorio Correia had been growing vegetables and fruits in his backyard for all of his nearly seventy-two years. In the city of Mosteiros, on the island of Fogo, the largest of the Cape Verde Islands off the west coast of Africa, Honorio's father owned nearly two acres of land. The Correias' urban farm was bordered by other homes with large gardens—an urban area where corn grew high next to beans, collard greens, and squash, and pigs, chickens, cattle, and goats roamed the yards. The food needed by the households, except for rice and some grains, was provided by the land that bordered the home. The farm was only a five-minute walk from the city school, a ten-minute walk to the local store, a fifteen-minute walk from Mosteiros's downtown. When Honorio compares his birthplace to his present home in Roxbury, he says, "Pretty much the same." Honorio's first apartment in the Dudley Street neighborhood looked out onto small patches of grass, wide enough for only one or two tomato plants. As Honorio's assets have grown, so has his garden: adjacent to his current home on Brook Avenue is a small urban farm, overflowing with corn, squash, beans, collard greens, and peaches.

Making food central to a city neighborhood's life means more than putting seeds in the soil and waiting for nature to complete the process. The land in the Dudley Street neighborhood was not as healthy and as fertile as it was when orchards covered it. Various urban uses introduced dangerous chemicals and pollutants into the soil. Some lots and backyards required deep cleaning before being safe for growing food. With the help of the staff and young people from the Food Project, Honorio's small urban farm was remediated, its lead levels reduced by hundreds of parts per million. Likewise, the Food Project has worked with gardeners to build awareness of possible soil hazards through soil testing, informational visits, and demonstration workshops. The challenging aspects of urban agriculture are as instrumental in bringing the community together as the beautiful, delicious vegetables that arrive at the market. The Dudley Street neighborhood gardeners gather not just to sell the food, but also to ensure that it is grown safely.

Agriculture in the city enlivens urban communities. When the young people associated with the Food Project spend a summer interacting with the land, the residents, and the gardens in Roxbury and Dorchester, they know it's different from other places they've been. Gardens bring people outside. Emma, a fifteen-year-old Food Project participant, says, "My moment of beauty was just walking down the streets near the Roxbury lots. People were sitting on their porches, greeting each other. I just saw a community. I don't have that where I live . . . everyone stays in their own houses." Danielle, the Food Project's urban farmer, bumps into her fellow farmers as she travels from one lot to another. Language barriers may prevent deep exchanges, but the camaraderie is apparent, and the important vocabulary is well known—rain, or *chuva,* is either plentiful or not. When volunteers come to work on the Food Project's two acres, they cannot believe how many people are using the land in the city. But the residents are not caring for quaint yards; the land is closer to wildness, with no straight lines or rows, but dense green places with overlapping and climbing plants.

When the Food Project began working the urban land in the Dudley neighborhood, it was not new to farming in general. In 1991 the organization began with twenty teenagers on two acres in Lincoln, Massachusetts, with a vision to bring young people from different backgrounds to grow vegetables for the homeless. Over twelve years, the program has expanded to include twenty-one acres in Lincoln and two in Roxbury and Dorchester. More than 400 young people have spent at least one summer of their lives weeding, tilling, and harvesting while learning about themselves, service, food systems, and the community. Many of them have stayed on for more summers and for programs that last through the academic year. Real and interesting work has kept teenagers coming back, creating an expanding base of strong leaders who work in partnership with the staff to cultivate the farms, to organize in the communities, to run workshops, to write newspaper articles, to connect with young people all over the country involved in agriculture, community, and the environment, and to advocate for local agriculture and food systems. Most strikingly, the Food Project has ensured that the Dudley neighborhood is infused with energetic and passionate young people engaged in community agriculture.

For the people of Dudley, farming has created a livable community. Formerly abandoned land has been reclaimed and turned into beautiful, productive spaces. Air, water, and soil are filtered and renewed by plant life. City dwellers are actively engaged with the land. Families are more self-sufficient and have control of their food choices. People are eating fresh vegetables, not trucked from the West Coast, but harvested in their own backyards or their neighbors' backyards. Varieties of vegetables and herbs from Cape Verde, the West Indies, Latin America, and beyond are being grown and preserved in crevices of backyards and side lots. Farming in the city brings residents closer to the source of their sustenance, it allows them to participate in and benefit from a local food economy, and it creates a community that knows food deeply. It is not a new phenomenon. The exchange of food has been joining people for centuries. Societies that have engaged in vibrant trading of crops at marketplaces inevitably delve into the broader fruits of cultural exchange—the sharing of languages, culture, religion, literature, and worldviews. Throughout history, while fruits and vegetables were being thrown from ships to wheelbarrows to be carted to homes around the world, agreements were formed, wars waged, ideas exchanged, friendships made, minds stretched, and perspectives changed forever. Right now, in Roxbury and Dorchester, where vegetables are grown in backyards and on abandoned lots, cared for and harvested by residents and young people, transported to kitchens in baskets or to the market in a pickup truck, set up on bright stands and tables, food is consumed in all of its wonder right down the street from where the soil gave it life.

Here, in this city neighborhood, food takes center stage. Here, food is grown in every nook and cranny. Here, large gardens with organic vegetables border fast food shops and, in homes, fresh collard greens are served on the side of burgers or ready-made pasta. Here, in this sunny spot in Roxbury, among people from around the world, Sylvia sells her callaloo, collard greens, and tomatoes, which were harvested that morning off the garden soil that her husband tilled for the first time thirty-five years ago. Here, the Food Project gathers teenagers from around the city and suburbs to engage in care of the land and in food production; from these experiences, they deepen their understanding of themselves, their communities, and the relationship between the two. Here, young people put their fingers deep into soil that has known neglect and pollution, care and fertility, and they pull out sweet carrots, forgetting about pizza and chips if only for an hour or two as they crunch into the day's harvest. In this place, food is certainly the end goal—beautiful, delicious, and bountiful vegetables that fill the markets, the shelters, the residents' tables with color and flavor. Yet it is the process of planting, growing, and harvesting in this city spot that creates the occasion—the time, the place, the activity— for people to deeply engage in urban life through the most basic of human practices, sharing food. And because of this phenomenon, this city place is not just livable—it is *alive*.

KRISTIN BRENNAN lives in Roxbury, Massachusetts, where she coordinates the outreach program of the Food Project, working with young people and local gardeners to promote awareness of urban soil health and organic methods for reducing chemical use on city gardens.

▶ "SKYLINE." ACRYLIC ON CANVAS BY REBECCA SILUS.

MIXED USE IN THE CITY

MARY FRANÇOIS ROCKCASTLE

Mary François Rockcastle, writer and educator, explores her history with cities and her attitudes toward urban living as she reflects upon her family's move from an old house in a Minneapolis neighborhood to a studio/ loft on the northwestern edge of downtown. A native of Plainfield, New Jersey, Rockcastle grew up in the shadow of New York City and spent meaningful time there. Questions about the livability of New York City contributed to her move to Minneapolis in 1975. Now, nearly thirty years later, she examines the elements that make downtown living pleasurable and looks ahead to changes she hopes will be made as a new urban neighborhood blossoms along the river in downtown Minneapolis.

"City of wharves and stores—city of tall facades of marble and iron! Proud and passionate city—mettlesome, mad, extravagant city!"

—*from Walt Whitman, "City of Ships"*

I open the sliding glass door and walk onto the roof of the building we soon will call home. It is located on the corner of Washington Avenue and Eighth Street, on the northwestern edge of downtown Minneapolis. In the course of its long history, the building has housed such disparate functions as the manufacturing of farm implements and clothing, the storage of Packard automobiles and theater props, and the sale of architectural antiques. To my right are the homes and churches of north Minneapolis, the Government Center clock tower to the left, the dome of the Basilica of St. Mary straight ahead, the river behind me. *What will it be like to live here?* Will I miss the green trees and lawns, the privacy and quiet of the Lowry Hill neighborhood where my husband and I and our two daughters have resided for eighteen years? All around me gleam shifting planes of concrete, brick, steel, and glass.

I have always felt at home in the city. I love its intricacy and sensuality—the sounds and smells, the visual feast of so many sizes and shapes and types of people and buildings. The city feeds my imagination, my curiosity about people, my pull to the exotic, my love for art and culture. I am inspired by the fact that all around me human energy is at work—thinking, making, imagining the future.

I was born and raised in Plainfield, a small city in north central New Jersey, twenty-four miles southwest of Manhattan. My parents, both New Yorkers, wanted their children to know and appreciate the city as well.

▶ ▶ ▶

My father grew up in a brownstone apartment on Bainbridge Street, in the Bedford-Stuyvesant neighborhood of Brooklyn. He played stickball in the streets and alleys, took the elevated train to Coney Island on summer afternoons, hung out with his buddies on stoops and fire escapes. My mother's family was wealthy in comparison, for they owned a house in Queens and a *car.* Their favorite summer pastime was to spend the day at Jones Beach. While my grandmother sat dreamily under the beach umbrella, my mother and grandfather rode the waves, coming up only for air or lunch or games in the sand.

The city became as familiar to my brothers and sister and me as the homes of our grandparents. We knew the vicissitudes of traffic; the dark whoosh as we entered the Holland Tunnel; the steel trusses on the Goethals Bridge; the glimmering masts, the ferries, the nasal honk of barges below. We knew where the Statue of Liberty stood in the harbor, where the Empire State Building rose against the skyline.

My mother made it an annual ritual to take each of us into the city for our birthdays. We traveled by bus to the Port Authority and from there walked up Forty-second Street to Fifth Avenue, where we visited the public library; stopped at Schrafts for lunch and hot fudge sundaes; strolled uptown to Rockefeller Square, Saks department store, St. Patrick's Cathedral, and Central Park. Sometimes we visited the Metropolitan Museum of Art or the Museum of Natural History. Sometimes we saw a play or a movie. I remember seeing *Camelot* with Robert Goulet and Julie Andrews, *The Great White Hope* with James Earl Jones, *Cat on a Hot Tin Roof* with Elizabeth Ashley and Keir Dullea. Sometimes we took the subway downtown to Greenwich Village and SoHo.

▶ ▶ ▶

The year I graduated from high school, I got a job as a production assistant in the textbook department of the Institute for Certified Public Accountants, located on the corner of Fifty-third and Fifth Avenue. I worked there every summer for the next four years. By the end of that time, I had friends who lived in the city whose apartments I could use whenever I wanted to stay overnight. I was drawn like a moth to the dazzling light of New York City culture: to the theater, the ballet, opera, and film. I kept track of readings at the West Side YMCA and frequented the Village Vanguard and jazz clubs on upper Broadway. I haunted the sale racks at my favorite shops, spent lunch hours rooting through bookstores, saved my pennies for dinners at Chez Jacques, a French restaurant that served the best coq au vin in midtown Manhattan.

▶ ▶ ▶

Eventually, though, I grew tired of New York. Was I worn down by its frenetic pace and clutter, or was it just a time in my life when I needed to make a change, to emancipate myself from the close corners and comfort of home? Suddenly the dark side of the city was in ascendance: the daily rush to catch the subway or train; people *always in the way*; my own and other people's rudeness; litter; people sleeping on newspapers in doorways; the oppressive heat.

As I journeyed by train each day between New Jersey and New York, I gazed sadly at the marshes and tidal flats of Arthur Kill, that narrow band of water between New Jersey and Staten Island. This wetland oasis—home to gulls, waterfowl, herons, egrets, and ibises— is surrounded by landfills, railroad yards, petrochemical plants, and port facilities. I could only imagine the level of contaminants in that water, which could turn from bilious green to sparkling blue, depending on the angle of sunlight. By this time, I'd graduated from college and was trying to decide on a future for myself. Should I stay in New York and try to get a teaching job or a job in publishing? Or should I look for another city, a little smaller and slower, where I might be happier?

▶ ▶ ▶

During my junior year in college I spent seven months in Oxford, England, and discovered how deeply *place* could shape and affect one's moods and outlook. I experienced, almost as a shock, the pleasure and power of landscape. The sinuous River Cherwell that snaked through the city, the blond, pebbled paths of University Parks, the gardens at Christ Church, the buildings that shimmered like marzipan from the thirteenth-century tower of the University Church of St. Mary. I stood on Boar's Hill just outside the city and gazed with pleasure at the spires, feeling a fellowship with Thomas Hardy's Jude, who had climbed a tree to catch *his* first glimpse of the city. Was this why the seashore resided so deeply in my mother's bones, why she turned contemplative and serene whenever we neared the ocean? It was as if all the complications and worries in her life disappeared as soon as she heard the whisper of waves or the screech of seagulls. Was it simply nostalgia for the happy days of her child-hood? I don't think so. I believe the happiness she experienced merged with something primal and particular in the place itself, something that traveled deep into her interior and mirrored what was there. Certain places can have that effect on us, can be another kind of soul mate.

▶ ▶ ▶

What does it mean, then, to be a *livable city?* It depends, in part, on the individual, doesn't it? On character and lifestyle and past ex-periences. And on economic class and where one can afford to live. In 1974 I decided to go to graduate school in a city (a college town would never do) *not* on the East Coast. Minneapolis was lauded as a clean, enlightened, liberal city—one with a thriving downtown; an excellent educational system; great cultural facilities; beautiful parks, lakes, and rivers; and strong public amenities.

So I came. For twenty-seven years I've lived in Minneapolis, and for over a dozen I've worked in St. Paul. The Twin Cities are not as exciting as New York, and less diverse, but they're more livable for the person I am now. I cross and recross the Mississippi River five days a week. Each day, on the trip home, my heart speeds up at the sight of the Minneapolis skyline. I feel energized by the present and connected to the past. The Twin Cities are worth appreciating—for their cleanliness and civility, their order, their liberal political history, their geographical beauty, their lakes and rivers. East Coast transplants complain about the blandness here; they bemoan the phenomenon called "Minnesota nice." Sometimes I miss the frankness and assertiveness of those old conversations, long for the verbal pyrotechnics of my own extended family, complete with dramatic facial tics and rapid hand movements. But for the long term I feel saner, more healthy, more *listened to* living here.

My husband, Garth, has always wanted to live downtown. An architect educated in urban design, he is passionate about the city. When our first child was born, we bought a house a few blocks from Walker Art Center and the Guthrie Theater, with a view of the downtown skyline from our attic window. The house was a real fixer-upper, good for a young, restless architect. Our two daughters grew up happily here. They thrived in the Minneapolis public schools, spent transformative time in the Boundary Waters of northern Minnesota. Our oldest is now in graduate school in landscape architecture in Philadelphia, having been inspired in college during a course called "Green Cities." Our youngest, a senior in high school, also is looking East for college.

Before she leaves, though, she'll have the experience of living in a studio/loft downtown. I thought we would have to wait until she graduated, convinced she'd never want to leave the family home, but she's eager to move in. She *loves* the idea of living downtown. She's followed the design process with her dad, including the reuse of an old elevator shaft running through the middle of our unit, and a small greenhouse room at the top.

▶ ▶ ▶

What *is* a livable city? Is it the city you're born into, the city you come to know and love? Is it the city you discover, the one you *choose* to live in, having reflected on your own nature and the nature of cities and the pleasure to be derived from living in a particular place?

Is it the city you help to *create* by investing and living in a downtown neighborhood?

I can't help but ponder these questions as I crisscross the roof. Our building is two blocks west of the river, in the thick of the warehouse district. History reverberates here. *Memory fragments,* my husband calls them: warehouse names etched in faded brick, remnants of cobblestone streets, traces of an old railroad half-buried in asphalt. The block is quiet; not much street life is visible. The businesses here are trade rather than retail. There's one coffee shop, one bar, a few restaurants.

The riverfront is the place to be, it seems, evidenced by the explosion of new and renovated housing. There's some higher-density housing in the area, buildings designed to reflect in scale and materials the history of the neighborhood. The closer you get to the river, however, housing is in town-house subdivisions. No allowance is made there for nonresidential buildings: no shops, restaurants, or offices.

I'm greedy. I want the diversity and richness of cities I've loved in *this* downtown. I want delicatessens, candy stores, churches and synagogues, restaurants, shoe repair shops, newsstands, drugstores, hair salons, fruit and vegetable stands, workout studios, bookstores. I want other cultural facilities, like the Guthrie Theater and Open Book, the center for literature, to relocate along this edge of downtown. I want to see people out and about at all hours.

My husband designed our building with storefront-like entrances and stoops on the ground floor, hoping to attract residents who wish to merge their business and home lives. This approach lends itself to a more lively street culture, that animated life on the street that makes downtown living so pleasurable. We hope that other buildings in the area are renovated into studio/lofts, apartments, and businesses; that a real urban neighborhood blossoms here, complete with shops, offices, restaurants, cafés, bars, and cultural and entertainment facilities. In such a place we can sit at our window and look out on the busy, vibrant life of the street. We feel *safe* because people are living and working here and paying attention to what goes on outside as well as in. Public spaces are integrated into the neighborhood for people to gather and children to play. There's a mix of old and new, and of different architectural styles. There's density without overcrowding, and a range of residential opportunities and prices to attract different economic classes.

I close my eyes and imagine the neighborhood in a few years. Streets buzzing with commerce, culture, and entertainment. Outdoor cafés crowded with men and women reading the Sunday paper. People passing on the street whose faces have become familiar after I've seen them day after day. Lights glowing like tiny hearths in windows all over the city. Past and present and future converging as memories merge with everyday life in the midst of movement and energy, hopes and dreams being realized and reborn.

MARY FRANÇOIS ROCKCASTLE is the author of the novel *Rainy Lake*. She is the director of graduate liberal studies at Hamline University and the founding editor of *Water-Stone,* a national literary review. Her awards include a Bush Foundation Fellowship and a Loft-McKnight Award of Distinction.

THE EMPTY HARBOR
AND THE DILEMMA
OF WATERFRONT
DEVELOPMENT

PHILLIP LOPATE

Essayist Phillip Lopate looks at the New York City waterfront as a once-thriving harbor that has lost its function—as has occurred in many other cities whose port activities have been moved, thanks to containerization, upriver or elsewhere. The ancient connection between city and port is being severed. What are the consequences for metropolitan areas? In the case of New York, blithely optimistic projections of reconstituting the waterfront for leisure/public space/high-end residential or office use have encountered decades of delay and unacknowledged resistance, while those segments that have been built are for the most part mediocre and unimaginative. The author considers some of the reasons why this is so and offers recommendations for transforming the waterfront, given the reality of the now-empty harbor.

The advent of containerized shipping, with its demands for acres and acres of backspace to load, unload, store, and truck the containers, has meant that, over the past forty years, in city after city around the world, port functions have had to be moved further inland or upstream, to rural or suburban areas where there was more available cheap land. This severing of the age-old connection between city and port is having profound effects, which we may not fully grasp for a considerable while. At the moment, all we know is that one metropolis after another is faced with an empty harbor and a good deal of underutilized waterfront property.

In my own native New York City, the waterfront has become the great contested space. Newspapers regularly carry announcements of some plan for a stadium, recycling plant, soundstage, wetland, park, marina, ferry, electrical generator, or museum that is then fought over by the local community board, developers, and municipal and state governments. Over the past few decades, New York, like Washington Irving's Rip van Winkle, always seems to be reawakening from long slumber to discover it possesses . . . a shoreline! "The new urban frontier" is what a 1980s Parks Council report called the city's waterfront, inviting, it would seem, the brash gold-rush behavior often associated with American frontiers.

Why is it, then, that developing the waterfront continues to have a forced, reluctant quality, as if New Yorkers were trying to talk themselves into a root canal? Are there unconscious resistances that may need to be examined?

There is, first of all, this particular city's historic habit of turning inland. It has often been remarked that, unlike most great cities on water, which tease and flirt with their liquid edges in a thousand subtle, sensuous ways, New York has failed to maximize its aqueous setting. This underutilization of the waterfront is mentioned as a curious negligence, as if it just happened to have slipped the locals' minds. Actually, the main reason this shoreline resource remained so long "untapped" is that it already had been allocated for maritime and industrial uses. These functions may not have provided the best urban design, public space, or environmental protection, but they were a huge economic motor driving the region's economy. So the present, fabulous opportunity, we must bear in mind, stems from a vacuum left by the port's demise.

Shabby and makeshift as much of the old working port may have been, its vitality issued from the way that purpose had dictated its construction. As more boats came in, as more docks were needed, they got built; warehouses were erected to hold the goods loaded off the ships; customs offices, shipping agents, chandlers and rope makers, retailers of barrels and packing cases, brothels and seamen's churches, taverns and boardinghouses and union halls all sprung up around the docks. Nothing can replace the beautiful, urgent logic of felt need. When it is met in an ad hoc, accreted manner, urbanists speak glowingly of "organic" city growth. I put *organic* in quotation marks because I don't believe any large human endeavor such as constructing a metropolis can ever be spontaneous or unplanned: the term *organic* tends to cloak a good deal of maneuvering by powerful special interests, such as the shipping lobby. So let us say, then, *additive* or *incremental* instead of *organic,* to connote the lot-by-lot assemblage of a classic New York streetscape.

Now that the old port is gone and the river's edge sits dormant, waterfront recycling makes a certain sense ("We got all this valuable riverview property close to the center of town, we got a populace starved for public access to water, we might as well do something about it"). But that reasoning still has a slightly abstract air, lacking as it does the keen urgency that commandeered the old port's growth. And that lack produces an ache—call it the ache of the arbitrary: we wish we could feel driven to redevelop the waterfront because our very life depended on it. Instead, we are faced with more tepid drives: the profit motive of real estate developers (but they can make money elsewhere) and the altruistic motive of community advocates for parks and a cleaner, greener environment. Yes, each of these interest groups may be passionately committed to its agenda, but there is not the same imperative to act promptly as in the past.

Some of the resistance is historical: Broadway and Central Park together had helped establish Midtown as the city's fashionable center, while its waterfront districts were associated with bad smells and low rents. All recent efforts to draw maximally upscale residential development to the water's edge have had to overcome that centering organization and the hierarchical superiority of the center to the periphery. In other words, however desirable a river view may be, for the wealthiest clientele it can never replace proximity to Bergdorf's.

The sense of urgency is further vitiated by the incredibly long time that waterfront development projects seem to require from inception to completion. Manhattan is now entering its fifth decade of waterfront "rebirth" (the original plans for Battery Park City were drawn up in 1962). While New Yorkers might self-pityingly assume it takes forever to get anything built or repaired in the city because local contractors are uniquely corrupt, the truth is that it is a slow process everywhere on the planet. Analyzing why it takes so long to redevelop the waterfront, planner David Gordon wrote: "In the four cities I studied, under ordinary circumstances, it took five to ten years just to achieve the political and technical consensus needed to start a major waterfront technical project. This phase was considered complete when the plan was approved. The most important factor affecting approval times was the complexity of the political environment." (In other words, how many layers of government had to agree to the plan was more important than how much acreage the final project might cover.)

Then there were problems of "land assembly, site clearance, environmental remediation, and new infrastructure." Anything involving underwater inspection or construction also led to prodigious expense. The typical waterfront project is brought in years behind schedule and hundreds of millions over budget partly because the companies and officials involved issue overly optimistic projections, knowing that otherwise they might lose political support for funding. We who are living through the great leap forward of waterfront revitalization should cultivate patience, a long-range perspective, and possibly reincarnation skills, because we may not see the changes in our lifetime.

In New York, there is a further clash between the waterfront zone—a separate corridor with redevelopment issues unto itself—and the neighborhoods it traverses. Traditionally, the working waterfront has had a separate visual character, a more rough-hewn quality than the inland areas. The riverside highways that have come to rim the island compound the problem of getting to the Manhattan waterfront. These perimeter highways ignore the grid, or, rather, intentionally oppose a powerful counter to them, a moat between the everyday city and the water. They have also introduced disjunctions in scale, which can never be more than awkwardly reconciled, between highways meant for thousands of speeding cars and the buildings abutting them. In theological terms, the West Side Highway and the Franklin D. Roosevelt Drive constitute the original sin of Manhattan planning. We may repent, we may patch, but we can never regain our wholeness. These massive highways will not go away anytime soon, short of putting a lid over them, which, desirable as that may be, would be very costly.

▶ ▶ ▶

In New York, the waterfront has undergone a three-stage revaluation, from a working port to an abandoned, seedy no-man's-land to a highly desirable zone of parks plus upscale retail/residential, each new metamorphosis only incompletely shedding the earlier associations. We may think of Manhattan's shoreline as a golden opportunity, a tabula rasa for leisure and luxury development, but the ghosts of stevedores, street urchins, and shanghaied sailors still haunt the milieu. Physically, no area of New York City has changed as dramatically as the Manhattan shoreline, thanks to natural processes, landfill, dredging, and other interventions. Only by considering the waterfront's past can we account for New York's current, perplexing relationship to its future.

We can expect the waterfront to remain for decades an unresolved zone in which polished sections and decrepit shards of the old industrial port coexist in an unsettling or perversely pleasing disharmony. What used to be said of New York—"it would be a great city if they ever finished it"—can now be said of its waterfront. It is the nature of dynamic cities to remain incomplete, in flux, to be torn down and rebuilt; that is one aspect of their ability to grow. And perhaps it is for the best that waterfront development takes so long to transpire, because it keeps open at least the possibility of a more incremental, mixed-use, historically sensitive approach to the river's edge. Still, a part of me wishes they would wave a magic wand and let me see, once and for all, this brave new waterfront we are promised. I want to be blissfully disappointed all in one gulp.

What to do with the New York waterfront? The art of waterfront design is not a secret: there already exists a body of highly evolved thinking that represents the collective wisdom of architects, landscape designers, and city planners on that subject. And yet, the empty harbor presents a most recalcitrant challenge.

The hardest thing for cities now is to replace their vibrant old ports with lively, casual urban texture. Different as they are, the three most important recent projects that have begun to transform the Manhattan waterfront—Battery Park City (a new town), the South Street Seaport (adaptive reuse of an old historic quarter), and the Hudson River Park (a "green necklace" of public access)— all have in common a certain antiseptic, deadened quality, as though the theoretical air of the original prospectus renderings clung to them even after they were translated into physical realities. All three have made wonderful additions to the open public space of New York. Yet all three resist integration into the nitty-gritty, everyday city, partly from failure for the skin graft to take, partly from explicit intent. The original marketing of Battery Park City as a residential zone depended in part on its being perceived as separated from the city, safely insulated from the "undesirable aspects" of urban life. "This combination of a unique location and an air of isolation was exactly what determined the commercial success of the project," wrote Han Meyer in his useful book *City and Port*. Meyer further noted that South Street Seaport, with its comfortably suburban retail, "has become an enclave, which may be a successful tourist attraction" but "remains an isolated phenomenon in the context of contemporary New York and a rewarding target for sarcasm and irony."

Why is urban design today so at odds with the spontaneous uses people make of the city in their casual daily routines? To untangle that question would require an analysis of how developers seek assurances that a project will attract one social class and not another, which leads to a suburbanized, vanilla aesthetic; how the discipline of city planning has become tentative, guilt-ridden, uncertain of its mission; how new construction technologies foster a monotonous gigantism that impedes the flow of street life. While acknowledging that "the city of daily life is simply difficult to incorporate into the built work, given the means and concepts that architects typically use," planner John Kaliski nevertheless insists that "as urban environments continue to evolve, designers must find new ways of incorporating the elements that remain elusive: ephemerality, cacophony, multiplicity, and simultaneity." New York's writers, visual artists, and choreographers have long celebrated these very elements. One thinks of Frank O'Hara positioning himself in Times Square and reporting on overlapping sensations; or the street photography of Weegee, Helen Levitt, and Gary Winogrand; or the city paintings of Reginald Marsh and Yvonne Jacquette; or the "sidewalk" dances of Merce Cunningham and Jerome Robbins; or the movies of Martin Scorsese and Sidney Lumet. Is there some way of incorporating the city's everyday, syncopated spirit into a design for the new waterfront? Or is the discipline itself so programmed to work against the

city's flux, by pinning space down into single-use, static forms, that it
would be hopeless to try?

▶ ▶ ▶

Any redesign on the waterfront must start from the premise of public
access. A venerable legal principle, dating from the Roman era, as-
sures the citizenry the right to public waterfront access. This noble
principle sometimes has been honored more in the breach than in the
observance, but recent lawsuits by citizens' groups have helped to re-
establish the precedent. Because it took such a battle just to ensure that
right, and because New Yorkers have so often been faced with threats
of massive luxury housing taking over the river's edge in boom times,
there is an understandable fear of allowing any private use to con-
taminate the shore. I think this is a mistake. By all means, the public
should be able to get to the water's edge, to walk along the riverfront
and enjoy sea breezes. But that does not mean that the entire waterfront needs to be protected by a prophylactic green belt. That would be
a very monotonous and antiurban strategy. Why would it be so terrible
to have a Ferris wheel or a Chinese restaurant or some other spark of
urban life by the waterfront? We ought to remember that people do
not relocate to New York to commune with nature: the pleasures of
living in a big city derive partly from surrounding oneself with the
street's retail enticements. Why this horror against allowing commerce
to invade the new waterfront? There seems to be some fundamental
misconception that confuses public access with open public space,
untouched by the private sector. Many of the great "people magnets"
in the world—think of the Piazza Navona in Rome, or the Piazza San
Marco in Venice—are a mixture of public and private.

If the only way to ensure public access to the waterfront is to keep
the whole area around it commercial-free public space (a dubious
proposition at best), then why not put architecturally prominent public buildings at the periphery, as other great cities have done? The

waterfront could house schools, libraries, courthouses, post offices, police stations, firehouses—could be a destination point for ordinary citizens in the course of their daily routines, not just when they are in a leisure-seeking, park mood.

Parks are splendid; and surely quiet, contemplative places have a crucial role in the daily life of cities. But they can also be an over-done solution, from lack of imagination if nothing else. In trying to secure public waterfront access, many communities have regarded demanding that all vacant areas be turned into parkland as the safest strategy. James Howard Kunstler put the matter well in his book *The City in Mind* when he spoke of Boston's decision to turn over to green space the land liberated from burying the Fitzgerald Expressway ("the Big Dig"):

> In the context of contemporary cultural confusion, "green space" or "open space" essentially means build nothing. It is a rhetorical device for putting city land in cold storage in *the only currently acceptable form,* that is, covered by grass and shrubs, aka *nature.* This happens because we have lost confidence in our ability to produce buildings worthy of our spirits and aspirations. . . . Citizens are now thoroughly conditioned to expect the worst. A large fraction of the public has actually taken this attitude a neurotic step further and decided categorically that urbanism is a menace to the human spirit and therefore that the only acceptable use of vacant city land is for installation of the putative antidote to the city: nature. . . .
> . . . To make matters worse, "green space" and "open space" in this context are always presented as abstractions—and if you ask for an abstraction, that is exactly what you will get. You'll get a . . . berm! But a berm is not a park. A bark mulch bed has no civic meaning. This is "nature" in cartoon form.

Another reason for this omnipresent park solution to the waterfront problem is a rarely discussed collision of values between environmentalism and urbanism. Over the past twenty-five years, much of the energy and organizational acumen fueling waterfront revitalization has come from environmentalist groups. They were the first to have understood that nothing salubrious could happen to the waterfront until the Hudson River began to be cleaned up; they lobbied for it, made it happen, and deserve all the credit for the happy results. They continue to be understandably suspicious of any large-scale development on the waterfront, knowing how it might tax the existing infrastructure and lead to more pollution. As marine biologist Mike Ludwig, a champion of Hudson River Park, told me, "You ask yourself, How can I hold onto the gains in water quality and minimize further degradation of the environment? If you make it a park, you have at least precluded the most damaging possibilities, such as a hundred thousand people flushing the toilet at the same time in the same building, as happened with the World Trade Center."

Most urbanists have an environmentalist side: it's part of the liberal package, and if you love your city enough, you don't want to see it destroyed or degraded by pollution. Many environmentalists, however, are not similarly predisposed toward the urban: their idea of heaven is not New York City but the wilderness. Now, it would seem to me that the hope of the world is for urbanists and environmentalists to join hands, realizing that their common enemy is suburban sprawl, which removes thousands of natural acres every week and drains the fiscal and civic energies of big cities. Given that the most energy-conserving environment in America is probably a Manhattan street, a truly progressive environmental activist might lobby for *greater* density in cities, as well as against office parks or shopping malls in the hinterlands. But I do not see ELF radicals spray-painting graffiti in support of infill; congestion goes against their whole moral sensibility. And congestion at the waterfront now seems doubly objectionable—even though the historical pattern of many older cities, such as London, has been to grow outward from the docks, with highest densities achieved closest to the river's edge.

What I would like to see in some of the waterfront is a compromise: low-rise density that will not overtax the sewage treatment plants, but will begin to invite the activity of a human hive, or casbah. Is that too much to ask?

In order to gain perspective on what is happening to New York, I have looked to inspirations abroad, only to discover that the dilemma of waterfront development is global. Everywhere, in London, Glasgow, Buenos Aires, and Honolulu, cities are faced with converting their abandoned industrial waterfronts to other uses. A Washington-based organization called the Waterfront Center, run by Ann Breen and Dick Rigby, puts out handsome, glossy coffee-table books such as *The New Waterfront,* celebrating what it calls "a worldwide urban success story." Examples range from Boston and Singapore to Cape Town, Kobe, and Whangarei. "We like to think that the popular success of many new waterfronts is a tangible sign of the vitality of cities," they write, "even in a world increasingly dominated by suburbs. That the inherent magic of water will draw people together at certain places or for special events is proof that the growing sense of isolation in our cities does not have to be."

Aquapolis, a magazine published, appropriately, in Venice, analyzes in a more critical spirit the issues faced by cities on water. "The post 1960s global transformation of maritime technology has required ever larger land and water areas to discharge the port function, and the port function has been forced to migrate towards deeper water and more extensive land sites," writes geographer Brian Hoyle in the pages of *Aquapolis.* "In urban terms the result is a vacuum, an abandoned doorstep, a problematic planning zone often in or very close to the traditional heart of a port city, a zone of dereliction and decay where once all was bustle, interchange and activity."

While some comfort may be taken from the knowledge that re-inventing the waterfront is a worldwide problem, and that no society has dealt with it in an entirely satisfactory manner, the ubiquity of mediocre solutions is still saddening. In city after city, the same ideas for recycling the old waterfront are put forward: (1) an aquarium; (2) a festival marketplace; (3) a convention center; (4) a museum; (5) a sports stadium; (6) a residential enclave, or town within town, à la Battery Park City. "You will see a surprising similarity in projects constructed in every part of and in every climate of the globe," observed planner Richard Bender in *Aquapolis:*

> This is because projects more often express the processes of organization, finance and management that create them rather than the lives and conditions of the communities where we find them. Too often, this development creates a kind of citadel, walled off from, raised above, or turning its back on the adjacent community. Too often, these new projects form their own ecologies, overpowering the connection between the natural systems on the land behind and those of the water's edge.

In waterfront development—even though enlightened planners persistently counsel that it would be better to work incrementally and in a modest, hybrid manner—the economics of such projects lead again and again to the monolithic. Developers who have the start-up capital and teams of lawyers tenacious enough to work through years of regulatory approval tend to want the highest return on their investment, by squeezing the maximum number of million-dollar co-op apartments or high-rent offices out of their property. If the developer is the regional government, it will usually want some massive cultural or theme park project it can exploit as a logo.

The postindustrial city has been driven to reposition itself as a center of culture and leisure in order to attract the technology firms and tourism it needs for its economy. Remnants of the historic port will be razed or else so "restored" and "preserved" for tourists as to lose all connection with authenticity (see South Street Seaport). Even small interventions in the waterfront's fabric require a momentum that carries the developer into much larger schemes than originally foreseen, and the waterfront becomes a dumping ground for gigantic, hollow spectacle. "The most striking aspect of many recent urban projects," concludes Bender, "is the increasing scale of their parts and, at the same time, the decreasing richness of the 'mix' of activities and uses they contain."

▶ ▶ ▶

In promotional materials and slide-show lectures for waterfront projects, there is always a sentence thrown in about "the magic of water," accompanied by assertions that "people have a remarkable tendency to be drawn to the water." No real estate or recreational development can go forth without appeal to the spiritual properties of H_2O. That water is life-giving and life-sustaining, no one would dispute. I merely wonder why, if this substance is so universally mesmerizing, its magnetic qualities need to be reiterated so often in planning statements. We do not, for instance, feel obligated to make claims in a stock prospectus that money has great attractions, or, in a handbill for phone sex, that erotic pleasure has a strong, almost undeniable appeal. Could it be that we have our doubts—that the case is not so clear-cut?

The mystical longing to get to the edge; the impossibility of doing so. Prevented by highways, railroad yards, fences, gradient problems, environmental laws against reaching the water, there is yet another issue that is never discussed, namely, you get there finally and there is—nothing, an emptiness, the river flowing interminably by, now nearly devoid of ships or other human presence. Granted, there is something soothing in itself about watching moving water, for twenty minutes at the maximum, and there is something beautiful about the sunlight or clouds rippling on water, about the natural landscape intruding on the cityscape, good for shall we say another fifteen minutes, but this play of water and light that is supposed to be unquenchably rewarding soon becomes a sterile delight for the urbanite raised on spectacle and shopping. The empty harbor becomes, paradoxically, the zone revealing to us our own shallow impatience, alienation from nature, unattainable sexual desires, professional pettiness, the substance of our nattering inner monologue. We *say* all we want is access to the water; we *mean* access to inner peace, to meaning, to purity, to a mature acceptance of our place on earth, and other such improbables. The water's edge is the infinitely beckoning, infinitely receding mirage of our consumerist society: the place that will finally tell us we have arrived.

▶ ▶ ▶

And yet, it should be possible, shouldn't it, to have a relationship to the water that is more day-to-day, functional, less contrived-aesthetic or compensatory-spiritual? Those who use the river regularly understand the language of its tidal changes, its placid moods and rages, where it is shoring up dangerously, when it is rising. Ferryboat captains, professional and amateur fishermen, divers, Coast Guardsmen, harbor police, canoeists, swimmers, and marine biologists have specific, quirky things to say about the waters surrounding a city. Such was the technical lore possessed by the *New Yorker* essayist Joseph Mitchell's harbor monologuists, and he listened to them all, patiently and with fascination, as I to my regret cannot. But I can see that if the waterfront is to come alive again, it must regain a sense of purpose, and not just become a theatrical backdrop.

In short, we need a true water policy. So far, almost all the planning attention for New York's waterfront has gone into land-use policy, with very little thought, beyond lip service, about what should take place on or with the water. Intrepid kayakers, canoeists, swimmers, sailboat enthusiasts, and anglers have made forays into the Hudson River (the East River is more treacherous), to establish that it can be done, but there is still very little supporting infrastructure for them along the shore: places to tie up small craft, sandy beaches, electrical outlets for motor-powered boats, fishing piers. South Cove in Battery Park is lovely, but its timbers are for show. No boat can dock there, as we learned after the attack on the World Trade Center.

September 11 taught us how unbalanced our waterfront policy had become. Carter Craft, director of Manhattan Waterfront Alliance, analyzed the problem as follows:

> The fight to create waterfront access was won by the aesthetes. Decades of decay and encroaching blight had to be beaten back. Flowers replacing corrugated steel. Grassy lawns where working piers once stood. Come September 11 this limited design palette was a recipe for disaster. "We didn't have anywhere north of Battery Park where a tugboat could pull up," said Andrew McGovern of the Sandy Hook Pilots. "The bulkheads in Battery Park City weren't strong enough, and even if they were, there is nothing to tie up to. The first couple of days of the disaster we were bringing everything by water—food, firemen, body bags, acetylene—all of it was brought over to Manhattan from a pier in Jersey City, a condemned pier." The region finally realized that the water is more than just a quiet vista.

Since all those "unsightly" waste transfer stations on the Manhattan waterfront had been eliminated, interim transfer stations had to be installed along the Hudson and the East Rivers to receive equipment and to discharge waste materials excavated from ground zero. The World Trade Center attack, which destroyed several subway stations, also caused ferry service to be reactivated between Brooklyn and Lower Manhattan, showing how much more could be done with water transportation in the city. An expanded ferry service, such as existed at the turn of the twentieth century ("Those wonderful long ferry rides!" wrote Lewis Mumford. "Alas for a later generation that cannot guess how they opened the city up, or how the change of pace and place, from swift to slow, from water to land, had a specially stimulating effect upon the mind"), could, in the future, not only link Manhattan with the other boroughs, New Jersey, and Westchester, but also circumnavigate the island perimeter, connecting various waterfront amenities. The New York Olympics 2012 Committee has a water-based vision of ferrying athletes to the main sports arenas and facilities, most of which happen to be on the water, thereby guaranteeing the athletes won't get stuck in traffic on the Long Island Expressway; afterward, the city could inherit a fine ferry network and conceivably integrate it into its own mass transit system. Most major New York hospitals are also located on or near the water, and water ambulances could transport patients for emergency surgery.

Finally, the waterways could be used again for shipping goods into the city. Granted, Manhattan will never have enough backup space for containerized shipping; but once the shipments have been broken down in Newark, why can't they be placed on barges and brought up the Hudson or the East River and distributed from there? We could again have working docks all along the waterfront. Where is it written that trucks alone must deliver goods to the metropolis? For that matter, we could reconnect a rail freight system to the waterfront, maybe by rehabilitating the High-Line and building a rail freight tunnel out of Red Hook in Brooklyn. We could even restore pieces of the port on the Brooklyn shore, which has more backup space than Manhattan and a deeper channel than New Jersey. Of the four modes of moving goods—water, rail, truck, and air—the first two systems have been largely dismantled in the past century to benefit the two newer ones. This was a big mistake, since boats and trains are less polluting than cars and planes, and, in the long run, more economical.

Parenthetically, an increase in the river craft using the New York harbor would also make the waterfront more stimulating for passive contemplation, since gazing at the water is immeasurably improved by the sight of a vessel moving steadily through it.

▶ ▶ ▶

I am tempted to end with a few more concrete suggestions about what I think should be done. Perhaps I am too much under the influence of those critics who say, "Mr. So-and-So has failed to recommend solutions for the problems he calls to our attention, and therefore risks leaving the reader in a state of despair." I would not for anything leave you in despair. On the other hand, I am not a professional architect, landscape designer, or city planner, and would hate to have to bluff the part.

As it happens, recently I came across a report titled "A Better Edge" that the architect James Sanders prepared for the Parks Council in 1990. Reading through it, I was heartened to see many of the viewpoints I have stumbled on, through my own halting reasoning processes, corroborated by the report's author, even as I was edified to see how much further Sanders's thinking went, with fresh proposals and imaginative refinements I could never have figured out by myself. The summary I now offer is a blend of my ideas and those (the majority) I have purloined from him.

Now that everyone recognizes that "waterfront access" is a good thing, this concept needs to be made workable. Especially in a city such as New York, where there are major physical impediments to reaching the rivers (highways, power plants, superblocks, railyards, housing projects, brownfields, factories, sanitation department parking lots, private development enclaves), as well as psychological ones (the tradition of nonpublic access), it becomes necessary to reach further inland and develop a clear and inviting procession, from several blocks away, that will lead would-be waterfront enjoyers toward their goal. Thought will have to be given to drawing pedestrians from

streets and avenues near inland subway and bus stations, with a wide
choice of routes down to the water. Strategies may involve extending the street grid further to the river's edge, redesigning the main
approach street to the water as a tree-lined, handsome thoroughfare,
displaying signage or pennants to alert pedestrians to follow the
water-bound route, improving sight lines to the water, and erecting
some culmination—a gateway, column, flagpole, or mast—that can
be seen from a distance, lit with strings of lights at night, to welcome
people to the waterfront.

To help the public across the physical barriers encountered at the
edge, it will be necessary to "breach the wall" wherever possible with
creative solutions. For instance, the underside and column supports
of an elevated highway structure can be reconfigured as arches or
vaults, using inviting materials at key entrance points. A farmers' market can nest under the elevated structure, receiving protection from
rain and snow year-round. Where the highway is not elevated but at
grade, pedestrian bridges and overpasses should be erected; but they
must be designed much more appealingly and imaginatively than in
the past, to overcome the public's resistance and fear of using them.

Once the public reaches the water, there should be wide paths to
accommodate pedestrian circulation. A continuous promenade is
desirable, with shade trees, benches, well-designed lampposts and
high-quality paving materials; but it must have the variety, incident,
and urbanity of a popular boulevard for it to be truly pleasurable.
There can be cantilevered lookouts, pushing out over the bulkheads,
to relieve the circulation of walkers, joggers, and bicyclists at densest
points. There should certainly be some central civic public area—a
square with a fountain, artwork, café, or bookstall—built into the
promenade every so often. Where it is impossible for the city to
acquire land from private owners to make a continuous promenade,
public plazas can still occur where the street ends at the waterfront.

There is no end to pleasurable activities that can draw people
to the waterfront. Fishing piers, with basins and tables for cleaning

fish, a bait shop, and handrails notched with rests for fishing poles, represent one possibility. You can reintroduce pleasure piers, those semienclosed public recreation structures popular in days gone by, and offer court games such as handball and racquetball, shuffleboard, miniature golf, concerts, dances, public lectures, classes, carousels, carnival rides. Offshore, you can have floating swimming pools, with clean, chlorinated water and changing rooms—and even a floating beach, using a barge vessel filled with sand. Water theaters with live performances or floating movie screens can bring a dramatic flair to the riverfront; view towers can offer panoramic vistas; water clubs and restaurants can be equipped with retractable glazed doors, open in the summer months, shut in the winter.

Ultimately, however, the edge must become something more vital and necessary than a place just for pleasure strolling, looking out, and imbibing: it must draw people as a site of routine, day-to-day activity.

For this to happen, the water itself must be restored as a circulation system, and the waterfront as a place of transfer. That means a combined, integrated system of ferries that cross the rivers and bays, connecting opposite shores; water jitneys that travel along a shoreline and connect with the ferries; and water taxis that take individual customers or small groups to destinations on demand. Such a network will bring people to the waterfront and mitigate the isolationist tendencies of waterfront projects.

In addition to this boat transportation system, there can be excursion boats and pleasure craft, including motorboats, kayaks, and canoes. All these boats will need new docks. While ferries require substantial docking facilities, those for water jitneys and water taxis can be slighter. Pleasure craft need many small-boat launches up and down the waterfront, not necessarily more full-sized marinas for stationary yachts. There can also be seasonal mooring docks, floating and movable, designed for small boats to tie up, and canoe and kayak launches. Boathouses, lighthouses, windmills, and watershops, selling oysters from barges, could add color to the waterfront edge.

In general, to achieve a better balance in waterfront planning, the emphasis should shift from very large projects, which have garnered most of the attention up to now (because they commanded the resources for outlasting the approval process), to small-scale and moderate-scale projects. The city should help small entrepreneurs to operate on the waterfront, realizing that often it is the smaller projects (such as the River Café, BargeMusic, the Fireboat House Environmental Center on East Ninety-second Street) that have ignited a vital spark at the river's edge. In line with that thinking, structures built on the waterfront should, whenever possible, employ a light, transparent architecture so that they do not themselves become new barriers.

Where the public enters at a higher elevation than sea level, such as the bluff at Highbridge Park, a cascading edge can be effected, through flights of stairs or ramps that curve intriguingly and are frequently interrupted by landings equipped with seats for overlooks. At the seawall, there can be steps leading down to the water, with rising tides covering the bottom steps and retreating tides uncovering them. "Stepdowns," or platforms reached by ramps or steps, can be carved into the bulkhead or project out from it. The bulkhead itself may be decorated, so that different sections acquire a neighborhood identity.

Not everything need be bustling and crowd-attracting. Sites of intimacy or discovery, little gardens and coves almost hidden away, make for a restorative change of tone and a waterfront that rewards recurrent exploration.

A softer edge can be achieved, in places, by nurturing wetlands and grassy lawns sloping down to the water. Fragile wetlands environments can be protected from the public by wooden boardwalks. Lagoons could be introduced, with artificial lakes and paddleboats rented by the hour, and smaller basins notched out of the shore, designed for toy and model boats. One could take a playful attitude toward the shoreline: just as Frederick Law Olmsted and Calvert

Vaux artificially composed seemingly wild, Edenic landscapes in Central Park and Prospect Park, so the edge of the island might be sculpted to give it more varied, dramatic, and "naturalistic" coast.

Lest all this sound like an impossible fantasy, please consider that many of these strategies existed as part of the everyday reality of nineteenth- and early-twentieth-century cities. They are drawn from New York's own traditions and practices—largely forgotten, I realize, but by no means impossible to put into practice once again. The quickening of the urban pulse at the waterfront will go a long way toward achieving the goal of making truly livable cities.

PHILLIP LOPATE is perhaps best known for championing the personal essay, as a practitioner of the form (his collections include *Bachelorhood, Against Joie de Vivre,* and *Portrait of My Body*), and as the editor of the anthology *Art of the Personal Essay.* He has also written novels *(Confessions of Summer, The Rug Merchant)* and poetry collections *(The Daily Round).* He teaches at Hofstra University and in the Bennington M.F.A. program. His latest work is a forthcoming book-length meditation on the New York harbor, past and present, called *Waterfront,* of which this essay is an excerpt.

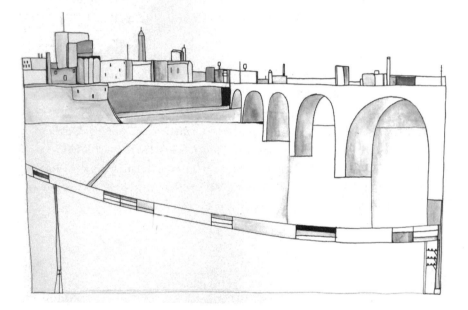

▶ "STONE ARCH BRIDGE." INK AND WATERCOLOR BY
REBECCA SILUS.

REINVENTING A VIBRANT RIVERFRONT

JUDITH A. MARTIN

Over thirty years, the downtown Minneapolis riverfront has evolved away from its industrial heritage. Geographer Judith A. Martin recounts the ways in which citizens, public officials, and federal, state, county, and city agencies have played a role in the process. Today's central riverfront, filled with public space and thousands of upscale housing units, presents a new form of downtown space: leisure, workspace, and residential uses all intermixing in public and private spaces on both banks of the Mississippi, adjacent to the downtown core.

A new high-amenity, service-economy downtown emerged nationally and internationally in recent decades as cities moved away from their industrial and multicommercial core beginnings. The Mississippi River has played a prime role in transforming downtown Minneapolis.

While many have written lyrically of the majesties of this river in this place—the Mississippi River surely has the power to conjure historical association and contemporary imagination—the riverfront has not always been a magical place for Minneapolis. As elsewhere, heavy industry reigned here for decades, and few people actually used the riverfront. The complexities of the river's divergent uses and history are still readily apparent. Industrial structures, big and small, old and new; downtown Minneapolis with many construction cranes; St. Anthony Falls with its lock and dam—all play roles in the evolving riverfront story. The lyrical Mississippi necessarily contained prosaic elements: the politics, economic realities, and planning ideals that imbued discussions of the central riverfront through Minneapolis; the individuals or groups with a vested interest in what happened here. This area's eventual transformation from an industrial backwater to highly desirable residential and recreational location is a complex story. With other cities, it may represent a new configuration of the downtown itself.

The Minneapolis riverfront shares a common American urban succession story ranging from occupation to industrial decline in 100 years, and on to service-economy reuse in recent years, after decades of abandonment. As elsewhere, this is a story of ever-changing mixes of private investment and public/planning initiatives. But the Minneapolis central riverfront, old and new, also presents a unique path from settlement to decline and reuse. Its history encompasses the city's railroad and flour-milling concentration, a 1917 City Beautiful plan, and finally a mix of initiatives from citizens, the city, and the county. The central riverfront's transformation required financial support from these, plus the Metropolitan Council, the state, and the federal government, in addition to bold speculative investments. Two elements stand out in this story: the durability of the vision of the 1917 Plan of Minneapolis and the sustained appeal of the river itself.

The surprise on the Minneapolis riverfront today is that major portions of the 1917 plan were actually implemented. Achieving this took seventy or eighty years; only modest changes occurred between 1940 and 1980. During some of these years, a painting of an idealized riverfront hung in the public library, the lone reminder of an early vision. Still, today's riverfront is much closer to that 1917 painting than to its 1917 economic and physical reality. Most of the flour mills are now closed, and the railroads and factories are long gone. The Mississippi here remains a working river, a commercial corridor, and a natural resource. Both banks have become up-market residential zones, office settings, and a city-metro park—the livable city indeed. The Mississippi River and its banks have reemerged as potent economic forces for Minneapolis, functionally distinct from their historic origins. One lesson from this story is that sometimes planning goals may be painfully slow to be realized, but a better product may also emerge.

INDUSTRY AND POWER

The Mississippi River and its surrounding banks served as *the* economic core of the Twin Cities region from the 1870s to the 1930s and remained important economically into the 1950s. Celebrated from the first in poems and panoramic paintings, the early years were in reality the years of Mark Twain's steamboats, the levees, the sawmills, and the river serving as an open sewer. In Minneapolis, after the first generation of settlement in the 1850s, the riverfront was a heavily industrial world of flour milling and trains. The great fortunes of the city were made here, memorialized still in blazing neon signs: "Pillsbury's Best" and "Gold Medal Flour." New technology was created here, revolutionizing flour production and turning St. Anthony Falls' water power into electricity. By the end of the nineteenth century, and well into the twentieth, Minneapolis milled more wheat than anyplace else in the world; the downtown riverfront was massively reconfigured to serve industry. But this industrial powerhouse diminished by the 1930s. If most city residents ever thought about the Mississippi River after World War II, it was likely as a "problem" landscape: filthy, polluted, smelly water; large industrial buildings, often empty; and people without apparent employment.

The agents of change in this era of industrialization were private investors who saw potential fortunes to be made in the sheer volume of water rushing over St. Anthony Falls. Businessmen built the mills, the railroads, and even the massive Stone Arch Bridge. City involvement in this era was limited to selling leases and providing infrastructure—streets and most bridges. The vision for the riverfront in the late nineteenth century was commercial success and what would today be termed "exploitation." This was a landscape laid out as the center of the regional economy and of the future. Until the early twentieth century, this vision succeeded brilliantly.

CIVIC INTERVENTION

The riverfront has been a development and planning focus for the city of Minneapolis for many decades. As the city's birthplace, then the long-neglected and unloved backside of downtown, it shifted from a prominent position in the city's nineteenth-century self-identity to an afterthought through most of the twentieth century. Once known as "the Mill City," Minneapolis proudly proclaimed itself the "City of Lakes" in the early twentieth century. Minneapolis citizens ignored the great river as the industries that built the city shifted production elsewhere, and the river became more and more polluted.

The riverfront revival is commonly dated from the late 1960s and early 1970s, when industrial decline was readily apparent and federal money was available to effect landscape change in blighted urban areas. But it clearly has roots in one earlier document: the 1917 Plan of Minneapolis, sponsored by the Minneapolis Civic Commission. Here, among plentiful City Beautiful ideas about grand civic design, planner Edward Bennett and his colleagues provided a utopian vision of what the riverfront could be. The actual 1917 riverfront was an unmistakable railroad landscape, dirty and sometimes dangerous, serving flour mills and their ancillary provisioners. It had been thus since the 1860s. The authors of the *Plan of Minneapolis* hailed this landscape as holding potential for people, for recreation, and for the sublime enjoyment of nature, particularly the Falls of St. Anthony.

One of the few full-color plates in the plan displays a grand vision of a green landscape with stately amenities, and with significant construction above the railroads, in the manner of New York's Park Avenue. In an era when parks, such as New York's Central Park, were thought to provide green relief for relentless industrial urbanism, the 1917 plan set forth a vision of a green-edged Mississippi River. The "greatest of all great possibilities" label for the downtown riverfront must have struck a World War I audience as laughable at best, but, more likely, as implausible and impossible. The 1917 plan was not simply a set of pretty drawings, though these abounded. It proposed concrete suggestions for achieving its lofty goals, including special assessments and bonding, and it also mentioned the city's condemnation powers. The model was the implementation of the Burnham Plan for Chicago (1909).

Some fitful attempts to transform the nearby landscape occurred early in the twentieth century, but the riverfront itself long remained untouched. Around World War I, a federal building and the Gateway Park Pavilion, both Beaux Arts civic spaces, replaced older structures a few blocks from the river (see map on p. 125). In the mid-1930s, Minneapolis constructed its new downtown post office on Gateway Park, in an early downtown riverfront cleanup effort. Here, the city attracted federal financial resources to effect a landscape change. This pattern would later be repeated in the nearby Gateway clearance of the early 1960s, leveraging federal urban renewal money for a twenty-two-block clearance effort. Several decades of improvement efforts clearly spawned some ideas about future reuse, but there were setbacks to these visions, too: the 1956 opening of the Lower St. Anthony Falls Lock and Dam and the early 1960s Upper Lock and Dam seemed to highlight the riverfront's ongoing industrial future.

Agents of change in the early twentieth-century City Beautiful era were as financially motivated as their counterparts in an earlier era, though their means differed. The Commercial Club represented a fusion of public and private interests, applying a national improvement vision to Minneapolis. This group appeared to embrace a "civic" solution while also anticipating private financial returns, consistent with the temper of that time. It is doubtful that mill investors and their allies would have promoted a green river edge to the city if they saw a secure industrial future there. An era of riverfront industrial decline was setting in, and Minneapolis commercial interests looked beyond the historic flour-milling origins of their capital. Moving beyond heavy industry to a big idea for the future was cost-free for them; they owned the land and could wait for a future time of civic improvement. In fact, through the next five decades, there was little change in the riverfront. A small number of government initiatives, such as the post office, did not constitute a substantial transformation. That had to await future "big" ideas.

CIVIC INTERVENTION: FIFTY–FIVE YEARS LATER

Transformation of the riverfront from industrial backwater to hot real estate market owes much to projects occurring in other U.S. cities, starting with the late-1960s renovation of a run-down chocolate factory into San Francisco's Ghirardelli Square. Over the next fifteen years, James Rouse successfully developed three waterfront festival markets: Quincy Market in Boston (1976), Harbor Place in Baltimore (1980), and South Street Seaport in New York (1983).[1] These projects refocused the attention of American cities, including Minneapolis, back toward their long-deserted waterfronts. They also underscored the enormous recreational potential of what had become emphatically *derelict* spaces in most cities. Rediscovered decades after being abandoned, the Mississippi riverfront, too, still seemed to have the power to amaze and entice those who ventured near.

For 1960s urban adventure-seekers, could there have been a more simultaneously inviting and intimidating place to explore than a riverbank that had been left to hoboes and their campfires? Few seriously imagined the changes about to occur over the next three decades. By 2000, the central riverfront was the city's hottest new residential neighborhood, with a completed riverfront parkway on the downtown side, an archaeological excavation (Mill Ruins Park) near the Falls of St. Anthony, festivals and fireworks galore, the prospect of a relocated Guthrie Theater, and several thousand housing units. The transformation from a 1960s hobo landscape to today's offices, hotels, and expensive ($300,000 to $1 million and up) town houses and lofts relied on plans, on significant public investment, and on major private initiatives.

Recent progenitors of riverfront change in Minneapolis came stunningly close together in time. Three stand out: (1) the creation of a National Historic Register District (1971), encompassing all of the central riverfront, several blocks deep, from just above the I-35W bridge to Plymouth Avenue; (2) *Mississippi/Minneapolis,* a 1972

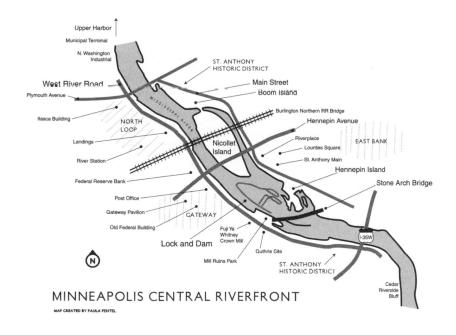

MINNEAPOLIS CENTRAL RIVERFRONT

MAP CREATED BY PAULA PENTEL

publication containing a major vision that was adopted as a plan for reshaping the existing riverfront away from its long-term uses; and (3) a Walker Art Center exhibit titled *Mississippi River* (1976) that helped to publicize the churning ideas of the time. The same period saw the passage of the federal Clean Water Act and state passage of tax increment financing, an important riverfront development tool. These were the necessary precursors to physical change, though alone, none could foment the transformation that many espoused. Their coming close together signaled that rethinking the riverfront's historic uses was timely, given the changing economic environment of the river and of the city. All clearly articulated the early-1970s intent of riverfront planning. The four primary goals were:

▶ To remove barriers to redevelopment, including incompatible heavy industrial uses and railroads.

▶ To convert the riverfront from practical utility to public amenity by linking the central merchant to the established system of lakes, creeks, and parkways that formed the continuous Grand Rounds of the city park system.

▶ To preserve and interpret the area's history.

▶ To develop a mixed-use community with vibrant residential neighborhoods.[2]

These goals highlight the new policy of transition from long-term industrial uses to something quite different. Having the city proclaim that railroads were now incompatible uses to development and that the riverfront was to become an "amenity" adjunct to the city's vaunted park system represented a clear step away from the past. Policy was the necessary first step in a decades-long implementation process.

In many ways these goals may be viewed as a complex puzzle, one that shifted over time as pieces came into view or disappeared.

Completing the puzzle required the long-term commitment of many actors, working together over long periods of time, sometimes without any certainty of funding for projects. Often large obstructions— gravel manufacturers, contaminated waste deposits—loomed. Timing was critical, as was the political will of elected officials at many levels to keep the goal of riverfront transformation alive.

Change agents in recent decades became more numerous, involving a complex of public and private interests. Government at many levels was key, especially the city of Minneapolis, including elected officials, the planning department, and the redevelopment agencies (Housing and Redevelopment Agency, then Minneapolis Community Development Agency). The city had a financial interest in the riverfront at different times; more importantly, it played a coordinating role throughout decades of riverfront planning. First came the early 1970s' Riverfront Development Coordination Board, a joint-powers organization to coordinate efforts of the park board, city planning, public works, and the HRA. This was supplemented in 1982 by a still-functioning riverfront TAC (a staff technical advisory group representing everyone at the city, metro, or state level with an interest in the riverfront, plus the National Park Service). The independently elected park board has played a significant role in trading, acquiring, and protecting parcels of land, working toward creation of a 200-acre linear park. The park board's long-term guiding goal was to link the riverfront to the city's well-regarded park system. Another city agency, the Heritage Preservation Commission, has enforced adopted preservation guidelines as new development has come forward.

Hennepin County also played a role: acquiring the historic Stone Arch Bridge for biking, walking, and potential light rail access, reconstructing the Hennepin Avenue Bridge in a historical style, and moving a span of an upriver historic bridge to Nicollet Island, creating better access.

The state also played an important role, with multiple representatives working on behalf of the central riverfront. Most important,

perhaps, were Minneapolis's state legislators—John Sarna, Carl
Kroening, Jim Rice, Phyllis Kahn—who tenaciously found riverfront funding again and again. The Minnesota Historical Society
and the State Historic Preservation Office were steady partners,
especially through the state-chartered (1988) St. Anthony Falls
Heritage Board. This organization is responsible for interpreting riverfront history and has developed self-guided tours and an
extensive system of historical markers. Minnesota's Department
of Transportation bought the Stone Arch Bridge from Hennepin
County to ensure its preservation for public use.

The regional Metropolitan Council provided park and open space
funding as the riverfront became part of a regional park system.

The federal government also played a role, designating the riverfront a National Register Historic District in 1971, designating a
seventy-two mile stretch of the river through the Twin Cities the
"Mississippi National River and Recreational Area" in 1988 and as-
sisting in the extension of the National Great River Road (West River
Road in Minneapolis). The Army Corps of Engineers operates the
St. Anthony Falls Lock and Dam, and has been an active riverfront
participant. All told, over $200 million in public money has been ex-
pended to acquire, clean up, and rebuild parts of the central riverfront,
with more still to come, to ensure public access.

As in the nineteenth century, private investors have been crucial
in the evolution of the central riverfront, ranging from early individuals who saw potential in the dilapidated riverfront to larger developers of recent years. The earliest group included some pioneers:
architect Peter Hall, who rehabilitated the Pracna restaurant on the
east bank, and Reiko Weston, who built her pioneering Fuji-Ya restaurant on the west bank just above the falls. Both ventured onto the
riverfront at a time when few others would. The Zelle family owned
the Salisbury Mattress Factory building that became the late 1970s
festival market St. Anthony Main, and John Kerwin rescued the de-
caying Grove Street Flats on Nicollet Island. The first big developer

was the local Boisclair Corp (and Kajima, its Japanese partner), which built the mixed-use Riverplace project on the east bank in the early 1980s. Since 1997, major local housing developers (Brighton, Rottlund, Sherman and Associates, and Hunt-Gregory) have added thousands of housing units, in both old and new structures. Any who remember the eerie feeling of venturing to dinner at Fuji-Ya or First Street Station in the early 1970s, or wandering Nicollet Island with its warehouses, donkeys, and goats, recognize the enormous risks taken by the early riverfront investors. To date, the amount of private investment in the riverfront is well over a billion dollars.

No list of riverfront involvement can overlook the crucial role of citizens. As early as 1970, Southeast Minneapolis residents initiated the River Ramble, a walk along the railroad tracks and the bluff to underscore the potential that they saw there. Those residents' long-ago efforts have since been vindicated. Contemporary riverfront users owe a great debt to longtime residents, many with very modest means, who intervened early to help shape the river's future. Many especially worked to save historic assets. Residents mobilized to get most of the central riverfront designated a National Register Historic District, to save structures such as the nineteenth-century Nicollet Island houses, and the nineteenth-century North First Street commercial buildings. On the east bank, citizens worked hard in the late 1970s to limit heights on the Riverplace project and to ensure the maintenance of historic structures on and near Main Street. Further citizen involvement has been steadily present throughout recent redevelopment.

THE BIG PLANNING IDEA

> Minneapolis is on the doorstep to providing the kind of complete environment that has been lacking in American cities for several decades. There is no other part of the city that can better serve to fulfill this long awaited renaissance than the river area.[3]

As the bedrock document underlying central riverfront transformation, *Mississippi/Minneapolis* deserves special attention. It became the plan and also contained many enforceable design guidelines. This visionary document was divided into three major sections: a survey of uses, past, present, and future; the plan, with concepts, objectives, images, and a framework; and actions to be taken. The survey included a section identifying the riverfront's historical assets. It was also clear about these existing challenges:

▸ Industry and related activities presently account for almost 30 percent of Riverfront land—including manufacturing, warehousing, storage, railroads, and utilities. Railroads presently occupy approximately 10 percent of Riverfront land. . . . Much of this land is essentially unused, containing rusty rails or no rails at all.

▸ The general categories of land use along the river which are most detrimental to the overall economic picture are: vacant land; excess or underutilized railroad land; underutilized and poorly used land and facilities; unnecessary street rights of way. . . . A significant portion of these lands can and should be redeveloped.

▸ Water pollution severely limits recreational use and aesthetic enjoyment of the Mississippi in Minneapolis. Coliform counts prohibit body contact with the water; floating solids and Riverfront debris discourage pleasure boating; . . . fish kills, damage to waterfowl, odors, and obnoxious vegetation growth all discourage aesthetic appreciation. . . . The major cause of Riverfront litter is the lack of a Riverfront image.

▸ The Mississippi in Minneapolis has been misused. Polluted by upstream agricultural and sewage effluent, and within the city limits by urban runoff, electrical heat waste, and combined sewer discharge—unused as it flows through the city except for water supply, navigation, and as a carrier for effluent—its varied use potential and proper designation as a major resource for Twin Cities residents have been neglected.

▶ It seems almost inconceivable that a city of nearly half a million people in the center of a metropolitan area of four times that number, and straddling a twelve-mile segment of the greatest river in North America, has but three distinct places [the University's Showboat and two restaurants] on that river where any kind of entertainment or culture can be enjoyed.

The *Mississippi/Minneapolis* plan section was elegant in its simplicity, citing a need for a riverfront location as a criterion for inclusion in future plans. Activities without a need for river access, or whose continued presence was deemed detrimental, included industries such as warehousing, wholesaling, and outdoor storage functions, as well as excess railroad capacity. Recognizing that Burlington Northern's rail line would remain on the riverfront for some time (it still operates), the plan urged consolidation or elimination of many other lines. Activities deemed appropriate for a riverfront site included water-oriented recreation; open space; housing and commercial uses that create an amenity; educational uses; and industry that needs the river in order to function. The plan called out Nicollet Island, Main Street, and Hennepin Island as major attractions of the central riverfront, specifying a ban on private development that was inaccessible to the public. *Mississippi/Minneapolis* promoted a continuous riverfront greenway, eventually linking up to the existing West River Road. Paramount above all was the goal of making the riverfront accessible to pedestrians and cyclists. Specific case study areas along the length of the city's riverfront identified many opportunities for new housing, for cultural and educational facilities (such as an industrial museum and a new symphony hall), and for river-front viewing and access points. In addition, the plan noted that high-rise housing should be on the top of the bluff line, with terraced housing following the terrain of the bluff.

The action section of *Mississippi/Minneapolis* was quite detailed, although it claimed great flexibility. It established priorities for implementation, with Nicollet Island ("the key to the renaissance"), Main Street, and the east bank residential development identified as the first areas to be addressed. The next priority level was assigned to Hennepin Island (as open space), and to two areas further away from the central riverfront—the Cedar-Riverside bluff, and the upriver Municipal Terminal. Areas of lesser priority included the entire west bank (including the north loop), the North Washington industrial area, and the looming question of overall river access. The one non-negotiable element was the high level of interagency coordination deemed necessary for the plan to succeed.

The action plan identified clear time lines for development, many of them quite ambitious. Between 1972 and 1975 all of the following and more were to happen: Nicollet Island was to be developed as open space, which implied demolition of all residences and indus-trial structures (the former would prove contentious), and Hennepin Island was to be made accessible (which required staircases to be built down the bluff); Main Street was to be closed and restoration efforts begun; recreational open space on University Flats was to begin; River Road was to be extended to Industry Square; reclama-tion of the river edge of Boom Island was to begin; residential devel-opment was to begin in several areas; and necessary zoning changes to allow these uses were to be completed. Activities in 1976–80 were to include completing River Road into downtown, completing and con-tinuing housing in several areas, beginning the Boom Island marina, completing the river-edge walkway into downtown, and starting the development of a cultural center. The riverfront effort was to be completed between 1981 and 1990, including finishing all of the residential development as well as new industrial parks north of downtown, and removing the post office.

The action section included investment projections, though it acknowledged that actual costs were likely to vary substantially. But the expectation was set regarding the ratio of public funding to private. The plan projected a potential $400 million to $500 million investment, 85 to 90 percent of which would be private money. Public money would be concentrated on Nicollet and Boom Islands, and to a lesser extent on industrial efforts in the upper harbor. A critical question was posed: "What will the costs be if [the plan] is not carried out?" Implicit was the sense that riverfront transformation was crucial to the future health of the city at a time of declining population, and that time was of the essence. Financial discussions led naturally to a consideration of partnerships, supported by this bold statement: "The Minneapolis Riverfront is a citywide and regional asset and therefore its rejuvenation is a citywide and regional responsibility." Partners were expected to include city agencies and boards, Hennepin County, federal agencies (especially the Army Corps of Engineers), and several state agencies, as well as the state legislature. There was also a call for regular riverfront events and for ongoing conferences on the river to keep improvement efforts in the public eye.

IMPROVEMENT OVER TIME: THE RIVERFRONT TRANSFORMED

Implementation of *Mississippi/Minneapolis* was necessarily slow and incremental. St. Anthony Main, an east bank festival marketplace, opened in 1978, near the earlier Pracna restaurant. Visiting this complex to shop, dine, or attend events was *the* introduction to the riverfront for thousands of Twin Citians. An adjacent upscale high-rise residential building, Winslow House, also appeared in the late 1970s. And there were clear signs of more to come, as parkway land was acquired and passenger service to the two downtown railroad stations was diminishing. But the pace was necessarily slow, with impediments remaining. One example: the planning department's Mike Cronin spent the better part of ten years convincing railroads to remove tracks and share lines.

If the 1970s were largely a time for riverfront plans to gel, the 1980s were a time of action. This decade's dozen-plus technical reports and planning documents demarcate dramatically increased interest in the riverfront. These documents included goals and guidelines for historic preservation, regional park plans, environmental impact statements, and larger conceptual plans. Most were directed toward specific project areas or topics (the interpretive plan), and most attempted to establish clear standards for specific developments.

The breadth and variety of these plans represent scales that shifted from the entire riverfront down to a particular two- or three-block area. For the first time, there were regulations in place addressing shoreland environmental concerns and specificity about the relationship between size and shape of buildings relative to the riverbank, as well as restrictions on types of uses. Projects completed during the 1980s made Mississippi riverfront revival in Minneapolis seem real for the first time. Among them: the large, mixed-use projects; an upscale hotel created from a mill-turned-rendering-plant; impressive offices created from a burned-out mill; new residential units on Nicollet Island and in the Itasca, Riverwalk, and RiverWest Buildings; new office space; a new printing plant for the local newspaper; and opening of the first downtown stretch of West River Parkway and Boom Island Park.

In the 1990s the redevelopment pace steadily increased. A further set of plans, proposals, and actions appeared; the bulk of them continued to refine the planning concepts set forward in the 1970s and 1980s. To a large extent, this group of plans focused as much on public actions as on private development. Much of the latter, such as the 360-unit River Station development, came forward as a specific project proposed within the context of already existing guidelines and criteria. Improved public access to the riverfront was the strong focus of this group of plans. The other big change in this decade was a neighborhood review process that all developers had to address. Among the many 1990s projects were hundreds of housing units, some additional office and commercial space, a large number of cultural facilities, and massive park and parkway improvements. Development dramatically shifted to the north loop, the area abutting the river north of Hennepin Avenue, during the decade.

IMPACT OF PLANNING

To what extent have the goals set out nearly thirty years ago for the central riverfront been achieved? To recap, with commentary:

▸ Removing barriers to redevelopment, including incompatible uses and railroads: largely accomplished, as has most of the pollution cleanup. Rails are gone, utilities have been upgraded, roads have been built or rebuilt.

▸ Converting the riverfront from practical utility to public amenity by linking the river to the Grand Rounds of the park system: largely accomplished. The riverbanks are largely in public ownership. Parkways have been built and connected to the city's Grand Rounds. Bike trails and pedestrian paths exist. Programming has steadily increased and will continue to explode with Mill Ruins Park, the uncovered mill foundations made into riverfront park space.

▸ Preserving and interpreting the area's history: Many historic riverfront structures have been preserved, including the centerpiece Stone Arch Bridge. The Heritage Trail and tours are in place, and the Mill City Museum interpretive center will open in 2003 in the Washburn-Crosby Mill ruins.

▸ Developing a mixed-use community with vibrant residential neighborhoods: Thousands of new ownership and rental units have been built on both banks, at varying densities and price levels—most market rate or more expensive, though some are affordable units. Housing continues to appear in old mills and as new construction.

Early and more recent plans have been implemented to a high degree, but there were some deviations. Most significant perhaps was that commercial office space was neither imagined nor planned in the early documents. To the surprise of many, in the past decade or so, the riverfront has become a vibrant office market: architects, graphic arts firms, publishers, the city development agency, and the Federal Reserve Bank are among those who have offices there. Commercial office developers have renovated industrial buildings, built new ones, and refashioned former retail spaces. Hotels have been added into this mix, underscoring the mixed-use character of the larger riverfront.

The best way to align the various plans with actual riverfront transformation is to attach some development costs to the various projects that have been completed. The 1972 adoption of *Mississippi/Minneapolis* was followed by two decades of additional project plans, and current riverfront development activity has continued apace. The original rough expectation of 10 to 15 percent public dollars and 85 to 90 percent private investment held as a standard. Currently there is a 25–75 percent division between public and private investment on the larger Minneapolis riverfront. The total investment to date is a billion dollars and still growing.

A sampling of 1970s to 1990s riverfront projects by category demonstrates the public-private financial breakdown. Five commercial projects, with a total cost of $294.2 million, garnered $58.2 million from public sources and $235.9 million in private funding. Five residential projects, with a total cost of $111.9 million, drew $13.5 million from public sources and $98.4 million from private ones. Mill Ruins Park, entirely publicly financed, will cost over $11 million.[4]

Some of the major institutional players had to adopt new ways of working collaboratively, in particular the park board and the Minnesota Historical Society, both of which had long histories of dominating projects under their domain. City elected officials had to listen to and cooperate with elected officials from higher levels of government. In some agencies, the same person has been consistently at work on riverfront efforts for over twenty years (MCDA's Ann Calvert and Dick Victor, and Fred Neet from Minneapolis Planning), making them, in effect, the keepers of the plan. The sheer scale of the riverfront effort was so large and so ambitious that no single agency could dominate.

REMAINING OPPORTUNITIES AND CHALLENGES

While the central riverfront in Minneapolis today is worlds away from its industrial beginnings, challenges have not evaporated. Some are relatively straightforward, such as creating more and better pedestrian and bicycle connections to the riverfront. Reknitting the connection between downtown and the river that had been severed for over a hundred years is crucial. Progress on this front has been steady, starting with the removal of multiple railroads and rail lines and of the Washington Avenue viaduct. But two- and three-block stretches of impenetrable barriers—the post office, the new Federal Reserve Bank—remain. All new development must ensure public riverfront access.

Another challenge is helping newcomers to the riverfront to recognize both the past and the present, and ensuring that they are tolerant of this mixed reality. Although most of the railroads are gone, and most of the industries have vanished, the present riverfront still includes inevitable remaining industrial uses. One is the Burlington Northern Railroad line, crossing the river on Nicollet Island, which may add commuter rail at some point. To some degree the river remains a working river; barges and tugboats are a regular sight.

A third challenge is ensuring that Minneapolis and other cities never again turn their backs on the majestic body of water in their midst.

Perhaps the greatest challenge remaining is the plan to extend riverfront revitalization northward to the city limits over the next forty to fifty years.

▶ ▶ ▶

The central riverfront today is a transformed landscape compared to thirty years ago—or even a decade ago. The Mississippi River through Minneapolis continues to be part of a large watershed cleanup effort. The industrial working river is diminished, though still present. The new-economy workplace landscape continues to evolve. The presence and power of financial resources increasingly are felt, particularly in the thousands of new upscale riverfront residents. So is the riverfront's role as part of a growing parkway connection. Historical artifacts—the hulking mill and grain elevator structures, the emerging ruins of nineteenth-century mills and canals, the city's earliest remaining commercial structures—add to the inherent interest of this large space. *Mississippi/Minneapolis* imagined a mixed-use space; what has evolved is more complex than what was imagined. The central riverfront today may point toward what will be a signature of successful twenty-first-century downtowns: a mixed-use open space, partly residential, part playground, part new-economy workplace, which clearly conveys a distinct sense of place in a global market.

I conclude this historical overview of a complex planning process with a personal observation. A riverfront resident for over two decades, I have spent countless hours on the river, reading on a dock, boating through the locks, or just walking nearby. It is an amazing space to be in, simultaneously containing runners and bikers, parents with buggies, railcars filled with coal, boatloads of tourists, and barges full of wheat or scrap metal. Despite the railroad cars and barges, it is an amazingly quiet place—and it is still a place where I can feel miles away from civilization, even with downtown nearby. Down on Hennepin Island, or on Nicollet Island's eastern lower bank, it is possible to *imagine* the wilderness landscape that this riverfront was a century and a half ago. It is still a place to spy beavers and herons, and, at certain times of day, to experience stillness and quiet right in the middle of a city.

NOTES

1. Judith A. Martin, "If Baseball Can't Save Cities Anymore, What Can a Festival Market Do?" *Journal of Cultural Geography,* Fall/Winter 1984, pp. 33–46.
2. MCDA, *Riverfront Revival—Twenty-Five Years of Collaboration and Change along the Mississippi Riverfront in Minneapolis,* January 1997.
3. Minneapolis Planning Department, *Mississippi/Minneapolis,* authorized by the city council, 1972. Epigraph from p. 45; excerpts from pp. 11, 13, 23, 33–34, 42, 19.
4. MCDA, *Riverfront Revival—Collaboration and Change along the Mississippi Riverfront in Minneapolis,* May 2000.

REFERENCES

Lucile M. Kane, *The Falls of St. Anthony: The Waterfall That Built Minneapolis,* Minnesota Historical Society, 1987

St. Anthony Falls Rediscovered: The Architectural Heritage of Minneapolis's St. Anthony Falls Historical District, Minneapolis Riverfront Development Coordination Board, 1980

FEDERAL, STATE, AND REGIONAL REPORTS
Minnesota State Comprehensive Outdoor Recreational Plan, 1980
St. Anthony Falls Historic District Regulations, 1980
State legislation creating the St. Anthony Falls Heritage Board and the St. Anthony Falls Heritage Zone, 1988
National Main Street Program Office, 1992
Upper Mississippi River Trail Corridor, 1992
Mississippi National River and Recreation Area: Comprehensive Management Plan, 1994

CITY AND LOCAL REPORTS
Central Riverfront Urban Design Guidelines, 1981
Central Riverfront Regional Park, 1982
Heritage Landing Guidelines and Criteria, 1983
Marquette Block/Coke Site Guidelines and Criteria, 1983
Mills District Guidelines and Criteria, 1983
Mills District Plan, 1983
West River Parkway Environmental Impact Statement, 1983
Minnesota Technology Corridor Plan, 1985
The Upper River in Minneapolis: A Concept Plan, 1985
Mills District Streetscape Plan, 1986
Riverfront Recreation, Entertainment and Cultural Plan, 1987
Metro 2000, 1988
Mississippi Mile: Redevelopment Activities along Minneapolis' Central Riverfront, 1989
Minneapolis Mississippi River Corridor Critical Area Plan, 1989
Marquette Block/Coke Site Guidelines and Criteria, 1990
St. Anthony Falls Interpretive Plan, 1990
St. Anthony Falls Heritage Trail, 1991
Stone Arch Bridge Plan, 1994
Minneapolis Downtown 2010, 1996
Nicollet Island Plan, 1996
Historic Mills District Plan, 1998
Mill Ruins Park Plan, 1999
Update to Historic Mills District Plan, 2001

JUDITH MARTIN, University of Minnesota professor of geography and director of urban studies, has taught and written on diverse subjects such as urban planning, neighborhood development, historic preservation, urban renewal, comparative urban design, and metropolitan governance. She is actively involved in the formation of urban public policy, serving on the Minneapolis Planning Commission for twelve years and as a Fellow of the Lincoln Institute on Land Policy for five years. She is the editor of the Metropolitan Portraits book series, published by the University of Pennsylvania Press.

▶ "EASTMAN FLATS." ACRYLIC ON CANVAS BY
REBECCA SILUS.

THE BACKSIDE
OF CIVILITY

EMILY HIESTAND

Traveling to a state-of-the-art water treatment plant, through the largest engineering project in American history, and over a reclaimed swath of urban land, the author, a public works hound, proposes that well-designed municipal infrastructure is the corpus of a livable city.

Growing up in the 1950s South, I received a strong dose of the idea that anything with an engine, anything that shot flames, anything that involved lug wrenches or voltage need not especially concern a young lady. Ditto the flying-saucer-shaped vat that was the town water tower; the gray electrical transformers with coils inside a chain-link pen behind the dry cleaner; and, of course, the ultra-secret atomic plants into which our fathers in Oak Ridge, Tennessee, disappeared each weekday to split, or fuse, or manage the atom. So it was a surprise, even to me, that I grew up be a public works hound, the kind of person who likes to poke around bridges and waterworks, power plants, rail yards, and shipping terminals—the hefty infrastructure operations that are the bones and muscles, the sinew and spine (not to mention the gastrointestinal tract) of every industrialized community on earth.

I like the word *infrastructure* too—a robust double trochee with a hint of syncopation. *Infra,* from Latin, means "underneath" or "lower down than." As *infra dig* means "beneath one's dignity," *infrastructure* means "beneath the structure." It is a word that colludes with Western culture's old and poignant hope to, by golly, figure out what's really going on in the material world. The way I am using the word here, to mean the public works and subservices of an industrial economy, evolved from more specialized meanings. When *infrastructure* first migrated into English from French, circa 1920, it was used chiefly to describe military installations such as naval bases and cavalry barracks and the like. In American English, the word was quickly applied to the tunnels and culverts of railroad lines, and once it was linked with the railroad, *infrastructure* was free to travel. Soon it could be found signifying the subparts or underlying system of just about anything, even something as ephemeral as sound, as the metrical frame of jazz.

As a partisan of civic infrastructure, I have noticed that if the example in question is ancient and lying in ruin, if it is, say, a Roman aqueduct or the cistern at Mycenae, it is considered fascinating and highly visitable. But with only a few exceptions (the Parisian sewer system, for one) current-day infrastructure is rarely featured in portraits of our cities. Do we overlook these monuments to human ingenuity and nature's forces on purpose, because they are the unglamorous shadow city on which the fashionable city rests? Well, sure. And yet, as the poet Amy Clampitt asks, "What's landfill but the backside of civility?"

Over many years, ongoing field trips to the backside of civility have taken me to such places as a wind-power generating station on a North Sea island, a catfish farming equipment manufactory in the Mississippi Delta, and a Vermont dairy that purifies its whey runoff using sequenced beds of aquatic plants. In Grenoble, France, my husband, Peter, and I toured a wafer fab, one of the billion-dollar facilities that make the silicon chips that make the information society go. In a Tokyo train yard, we were smitten by a midnight-blue train, the elegant Nozomi, Japan's fastest train, which is named for the speed of mind and desire: the word *Nozomi* translates into English as "wish."

Fond as I am of such faraway travels, some of the most memorable infrastructure expeditions I have taken have been to facilities in my own home ground in metropolitan Boston. Close to home it is easy to make clear connections: from a substation to a living-room lamp; from a city filtration chamber to one's own bathtub; even from the present to the past. The day Peter and I paddled our canoe upriver from Boston's Inner Harbor, locked through the Amelia Earhart Dam, and headed northwest along the local Mystic River, we were following the annual spawning route taken for millennia by the alewife, the tiny fish used by Native Americans to fertilize their cornfields.

Often, an hour talking with an operator at a toll bridge or fish processing plant offers information about a city that you will not discover in its cafés, shops, and museums. Every ordinary power plant and waterworks can be revelatory on matters such as water rights, sound energy policy, economic equity, and population size—these essentials for creating peace and global security. By their very nature, facilities that deliver such basic needs as energy, warmth, water, food, fuel, mobility, and connectivity embody our reigning proposals, for better or worse, for conducting life on earth. When it is well designed, municipal infrastructure is the very corpus of a livable city.

Consider the new plant located on Deer Island, on the northern shore of Boston Harbor. Completed in 2000 after eleven years of construction, it is visible from several miles out at sea, thanks to a cluster of plump ovoid structures that loom, 140 feet tall, and rather perkily for such giants, on the tip of the Deer Island Peninsula. The eggs, as they are commonly called (and there are a dozen) cut a dashing, futuristic figure against the blue-green Atlantic: Rem Koolhaas meets the Jetsons meets Fabergé. I zoomed recently to the top of one egg in an industrial-strength elevator along with six visiting Sri Lankan engineers. As our small group stepped out onto a catwalk, the plant manager, Jeff McAuley, said of the massive structure below us, "This could blow up anytime."

He was kidding; we were perfectly safe, I think, but McAuley was getting our attention about the methane gas being generated deep inside the structure. Sometimes mistaken by passing mariners for a luxurious marina condominium complex, the twelve eggs are habitable only by microorganisms. "They are like your stomach," one of the Sri Lankan engineers explained, adding in a polite fluster, "Not like your own personal stomach, Madame, but the stomach of the human body." Technically known as anaerobic digesters, these big Berthas are the most dramatic feature of a state-of-the-art waste-water plant that treats and dispatches the effluents of the whole of metropolitan Boston—forty-three communities, two million people— handling the task so well that for infrastructure cognoscenti and policy makers from all over the globe, the Deer Island plant is all the rage—a must-see.

As we walked together through the Deer Island facility, the visit-ing Sri Lankan engineers were almost bubbly with excitement. Me too. The sleek gauges, dials, and computer monitors in the operation room of the treatment plant rival the deck of the starship *Enterprise*. Cavernous rooms below us are full of monster pumps and a maze of rather beautiful color-coded pipes. Above us, in the dome of each egg, floats a lovely oculus, a functional cousin of that calm, all-seeing eye in the Pantheon of Rome. The shop talk between McAuley and the visiting engineers is about such things as cryogenic oxygen chambers, centrifugal thickeners, and the diffuser heads on the nine-and-a-half-mile-long outfall tunnel—the gear and techniques of a multistage process that cleanses the city's wastewater of pathogens and converts its sludge into rich organic pellets that can be sold as landscaping fertilizer.

What sends me even more than the marvelous plant itself is the transformation the facility has worked on Boston's harbor. For many decades before the new plant came on line, our harbor was becoming

an ever more cloudy and diseased estuary, its flora and fauna dying
from the cumulative effects of heavy metals and toxins, and the mini-
mally treated sewage that was released twice daily on the ebb tides.
It is not too much to say that the treatment plant on Deer Island has
rescued Boston Harbor, restoring it to a realm clean enough to please
bluefish, striped bass, and sensitive marine mammals. People too.
Sometimes now, when Peter and I pilot our small red boat through
the outer harbor, our hearts rise as we see the slick, dark head of a
whiskered seal popping up from the sea.

"Why, why do we feel / (we all feel) this sweet / sensation of joy?"
asked Elizabeth Bishop about such unexpected animal sightings.
In these waters, the sensation arises in part because a seal is a sign
of life being restored. Boston exists because of the sea and its gifts,
especially cod—still called "the sacred cod" in some quarters—and
the reviving harbor is now turning the city's face toward the sea
again, reminding Bostonians that we are a coastal people. Peter
and I are typical: as the harbor grew cleaner, we were lured to learn
coastwise navigation, to keep an eye on tides, winds, and phases of
the moon, and to call each other when stripers and blues are running. Plying the harbor and Massachusetts Bay in a small boat, we
have been introduced to the powers of the sea, to sudden squalls and
enveloping fogs, and gradually, a few each year, to the thirty-four
islands that dot the harbor, among them Spectacle, Moon, Grape,
Graves, Button, and Bumpkin. Greatly admired for the adventure
and repose they offer so near an urban hive, the islands are places
of tide pools and salt marshes, wild roses, rabbits, ancestral burial
grounds and native history, nesting sites, swimming coves, and ruins
(of, for instance, resort hotels and the nineteenth-century Asylum
for Indigent Boys). Together the islands make up what might be
called a sapphire necklace, a watery companion to the linked green
parks that landscape architect Frederick Law Olmsted designed as
Boston's Emerald Necklace. On the most remote islands, the only
sounds are wind and waves. On the larger islands that are served

by ferries, new citizens from water-loving cultures like Haiti, Cape
Verde, and Brazil have shown the way; on any sunny summer
weekend, Georges Island is a fiesta of picnics, grills and spicy smells,
salsa music and soccer games, people snoozing under pines, reading,
wading.

All these pleasures and understandings, these ways of being, and
being in place, have come to our city courtesy of a wastewater and
sewage treatment facility—the plant where I am now creeping along a
catwalk that is tucked under the dome of one of the anaerobic digesters. Out the catwalk windows, the skyline of the Hub of the Universe
shimmers in the distance, while directly below lies the Rube Goldberg
complex, of pipes, Corten steel stacks, and clarifying ponds—all of it
surrounded by the Atlantic and coursed by fresh sea breezes.

Along with good shop talk and insights about dwelling, journeys
to infrastructure inevitably give the visitor deep respect for the souls
who build and tend these bastions. At Deer Island, I ate a sandwich
lunch on the seawall with a young mason named Kevin who is con-
tinuing a long family tradition of building local infrastructure. "My
dad built I-93," he told me, proudly, "and my granddad built the
Boston & Maine Railroad." I loved the way this young man gave his
forebears *total* credit for the massive interstate and rail transportation
projects, as if the two of them were his own personal Paul Bunyans.

BIG DIG

My admiration for the burly pinions of modern civilization coexists
with rather profound reservations about some of the logic and mo-
tives that drive our industrial world. Boston's central artery and
tunnel project is a good example. Roaming the construction site over
the past five years, I have often been agog. The largest, most complex
engineering project in American history, the "Big Dig" is one jaw-
dropping engineering feat and ingenious improvisation after another,

many required because the new construction is located directly in the midst of the old transportation corridor—which continues in full operation. Likened to performing open-heart surgery on a marathoner during a race, the project is the sort of enterprise for which we might wish we had reserved the word *awesome* (once the boss word of the Romantic sublime, now hanging out with *dude*).

And yet this impressive enterprise is a many-billion-dollar *highway* project. Alas, a highway project at a time when we might better be reviving the nation's near-death railroads, laying in bicycle corridors, creating the smart intermodal transportation links already found throughout Europe and Japan. Big Dig moguls passed on many opportunities to upgrade Boston's existing public transit, most egregiously failing to close the mile-long gap between the north and south rail lines that enter the city. In fairness, the project has delivered a good road, a poetic cable-stayed bridge, and some splendid communications and utility systems upgrades. But only fierce pressure from citizens held project directors to delivering a few, minor transit felicities to the urban core. Many American citizens now grasp that infrastructure projects that continue to bind our culture to oil dependency and spendthrift consumption contribute directly to global inequities and to compromised foreign policies that make us less, not more, safe in the world. I don't know the answers, but I think one of the questions must be: How do we put the promise of *techne,* the marvelous ingenuity in such evidence at the Big Dig, in the service of more sustainable, more pleasing ways of life?

PROMISED LANDSCAPE

When Boston's hulking Central Artery descends, at last, into its new tunnel, and the I beams and girders of the old elevated highway are carted off, one great plum of the Big Dig project will stand revealed: twenty-five acres of newly open land, civic territory promised for a people's park. Following the trace of the old highway, the park will arc from Kneeland Street in Boston's Chinatown district to the North End neighborhood of bocce courts and saints' days. Along the way, the park swings within a block or so of the harbor so close that breezes over the terrain are often laced with salt. Bordering the parkland are such neighbors as the New England Aquarium, Quincy Market, the Custom House Tower, South Station, and the stately Flour and Grain Exchange building. The park will also pass by a little luncheonette named Jake's and the cool, briny world of the James Hook Lobster Company.

In a mature city like Boston, new civic space of this significance is a great rarity. "A chance like this comes along once, maybe twice, a century," reflects Hubie Jones, one of Boston's most distinguished community builders and coleader of the international City-to-City Program. "And we must get it right," Jones says with feeling, "because this new park will affect the lives of Bostonians for generations." The jury is still out on whether Bostonians will get it right. A creative and transparent political process for shepherding the park into reality has not yet fully emerged, and as I write, there are several unanswered questions, including such humdingers as: Who is the client for the new park? Who will fund it? Who will take care of it? Can planners tame the six lanes of traffic slated to race along the narrow ribbon of land? Hovering over these many questions is another that subsumes them all: What should the new park *be?*

It turns out that envisioning a major new civic realm is not only about spatial ingenuity, but also about values. What values do the people of Boston want to inscribe on a new and symbolic landscape? As catalyst for that question, the terrain is already serving the city as a canvas for imagination and desire, a kind of screen onto which urbanists, artists, and skateboarders, lovers of nature and lovers of cafés, pols and preservationists are all projecting images of transformation.

The terrain has long been understood as connective tissue—a landscape that can physically reseam zones of the city that have been separated, for fifty years, by the overwhelming mass and sonic wall of the elevated Central Artery. Many citizens have seen that the terrain can also be connective socially—a realm of convergence that could increase the city's measure of commonplace civilization, the everyday pleasures and customs that can touch and dignify every citizen. "Boston is still struggling to achieve social integration of all our citizens," Jones comments as we are talking one day on the telephone. "And this park," he continues, "is a chance to create some common ground. I have seen it happen in other cities," he says, "and I have felt that pulse—in Chicago, for example, citizens pour into their city on weekends to enjoy the great parks and piers, the museums. And *everyone* comes. But here in Boston we have a paradox. Visitors find our city very special—historic, and friendly, and famously walkable. But many residents, especially people of color, do not always feel welcome in their own city, outside their neighborhoods. Can one park solve all of Boston's social problems? Of course not. But the new parkland is a once-in-a-lifetime opportunity to use physical change to foster a culture of collaboration."

At several public forums (convened by the Boston Foundation and the *Boston Globe*), Bostonians offered many ideas about the virtues to inscribe on common ground. For starters, fun. Citizens of the old Puritan capital have called for much joie de vivre—for cafés, and sledding hills, a hip-hop recording pavilion, and movies projected on the tunnel vent stack walls. Bostonians want a welcoming landscape that offers that most cosmopolitan pleasure of mingling with the spectrum of humanity. Citizens also long for connection with green and elemental forces, calling for groves of trees, a weather observatory, and—this swoon of an idea—a marine fountain that ebbs and flows with the nearby tides. Bostonians have called for a park that uses energy and water wisely, a sustainable landscape that is *urbi et orbi*—for the city and for the world. They would also like peace and safety, which means a park animated day and night, which means neighbors living by the park, which means homes. Affordable, please.

Citizens would like learning—a pavilion of history, a window to the tunnel below, a speaker's corner. Also Mozart Mondays, and blues and gospel festivals. One man wants a moose, another a moat, and some smart young designers would like to preserve a remnant of the steel highway structure as a trellis or a stage.

I have been following our citywide debate about the parkway-to-be, captured by a conversation that reveals both the strengths and the wounds of our community, and also because the new park promises to be an ideal place for *flânerie,* the open-ended wandering that is considered a respectable activity in some parts of the globe. By which I mean Paris. Paris thinks enough of its strollers to have given them a name—*flâneur* or, for the female of the species, *flâneuse.* Writes Baudelaire: "For the perfect *flâneur,* it is an immense joy to set up house in the heart of the multitude, amid the ebb and flow. To be away from home, yet to feel oneself everywhere at home." Note "set up house"—the blurring of domestic and public energies, Baudelaire's idea of metropolitan ease, of home as diffuse, embedded in flux and motion.

One hot day, I meet the architectural critic Robert Campbell at South Station, planning to stroll the length of the proposed new parkway in his company. Campbell received the Pulitzer Prize for his writing about architecture and urban spaces, and has a special affinity for Boston, which is his home. Because of the ninety degrees awaiting us this day, we do not immediately set out, but linger awhile in the cool terminal, studying an official map of the parkland parcels, drinking iced coffees, listening to the poetry of American place names rumbling over Amtrak's public-address system. On the map, Campbell traces the lines of Boston's major downtown streets—among them Causeway, Hanover, State, Milk, India, Broad, High, Oliver, Pearl, Summer, Winter, and Congress—and I see how many of these streets radiate toward the harbor, a little like the fingers of a hand, a pattern set long ago, when Boston's wealth came from the sea, rolling from the harbor up those streets to customhouses and banks. Because these splaying streets will cross and punctuate the parkway, it will feel less like a single entity than like a series of linked but individual spaces— none, Campbell points out, as large as our new, immediately popular park at Post Office Square. "The new parkway," he says, "is not an emerald necklace—it's a charm bracelet."

Walking along the terrain, it is easy to see that, like the park itself, the crossing streets could also be connective tissue, the principal lines of movement between the city and its historic waterfront. Designers envision boulevards of delight, pedestrian streets with arboreal colonnades and long "view corridors" to the sea. Even now, there are moments along the way where, in a gap between buildings, there is a sudden glimpse of a white sail, a tugboat nosing a tanker, a dazzle on blue water. The air grows salty as a sea breeze glides up an alley. And at State and Purchase Streets, a block from the Old Custom House Tower (once gushed over by Walt Whitman as the finest building in the land), you can glimpse what the designers are calling for: here, you can stand between a line of old granite wharf buildings, under an arch of honey-locust leaves, and see east clear to the water's edge, where a dark wooden whale is breaching on the roof of a small ticket hut. Near India Wharf, I catch a fragment of Coast Guard cutter heading out to sea. As I am watching the cutter disappear, Campbell broaches a question at the very heart of *civitas:* What rituals of daily life, and what ceremonial occasions, draw contemporary city dwellers together to share their landscape? What customs, what manners and understandings connect us to one another and to a place? Which is to ask—what makes us citizens and not merely consumers who happen to pass each other en route to shops? Like Hubie Jones, Campbell holds out hope that Bostonians will seize the potential in a reclaimed swath of land, that the city might, as he puts it, "invent the new public realm."

EYES FIXED, HEART OPEN

On another day, on another walk, I turned from possible futures to the quiddity of present reality. For much of its length, the land that may become civic treasure still lies in deep shadow under the highway. Elsewhere, the land is the color of desert adobe, baked by sun, pulverized by cranes, edged by Jersey barriers, loaded with foothills of rebar, and everywhere booming with sound—a landscape that defies the very idea of trees and cafés and climbing roses. But who will be surprised to hear that even in this condition, maybe especially in this condition, the terrain and its immediate environ are full of allure?

Those construction sounds, for instance. A throaty drumming and a deep, earth-rattling *whaump;* percussive *thwaupts,* a metallic high-hat of a sound; and an eerie twittering like swallows on steroids—all tones and rhythms that belong to the random music of life that John Cage taught us to hear, a music he might have scored as "Metropolis in Metamorphosis." What else can be found along the route? Three of the largest petunia planters ever constructed in the history of humankind, which can be seen—right now—on the Federal Reserve plaza bordering the parkland. Two men in suits who lean against the epic planters, one saying to the other, quite cheerfully, "Well, those guys are SOBs." And a wooden wall with peepholes, hung with many children's drawings: a willow tree; some orange lounge chairs; a drawing with the word *Future,* and another with the word *Anxiety.*

Along the route there are countless small things that would attract Flaubert, the man who wrote, "Often apropos no matter what, a drop of water, a shell, a hair, you stopped and stayed motionless, eyes fixed, heart open." Among the things that fix my eyes: The limestone trace of a long-gone staircase on a red brick warehouse wall. A man in a shirt and tie watching intently as a sailboat, the *Illusion* out of Miami, slips its mooring. Models of ships in a gallery window mingling with reflections of Boston's financial towers— whaling schooners ghosting through bank buildings and insurance companies. And at the old Northern Avenue Bridge, a bait-shack-style building, where a man in high rubber boots is offloading shellfish from Cushing, Maine. Inside the James Hook Lobster Company, the air is cool and damp, and the scent of the sea clings to littlenecks, blue-black mussels, and tangles of Jonah crabs. A polite young man will show you around a dim room where 60,000 lobsters (more in winter) await shipping. Both hard shell and soft, says Chuck, who can explain how filtered saltwater flows over the creatures, how the water comes from the harbor via pumps, and flows back, cleaner than before, some of it streaming from beneath the building, sounding, we agree, like a waterfall.

For the length of the planned park, the no-nonsense sidewalks teem with souls who would surely prefer to walk in a park instead: travelers emerging from South Station, blinking, rolling black suitcases into town (memo to planners: hold the cobblestone); a weary man pushing a cart of sandwiches, salads, and ice toward some meeting; a woman running lickety split in a long peony-pink dress and bright white heels—a late bridesmaid? Two middle-aged men in African robes, carrying leather cases. A thin woman in a tube top, pushing an old man slumped in his wheelchair. And a couple from Dresden, history buffs, carrying old and new maps of Boston, searching, they explain, for the exact, original, eighteenth-century site of Griffin Wharf, that vanished wharf where, in December of 1773, our civic predecessors dumped many chests of tea into the inner harbor, setting in motion a long and ongoing experiment.

At noontime, I come upon three Big Dig workers who have settled near the sidewalk on a berm of grass under a couple of linden trees. They are pulling Gatorade from coolers and their blue jeans are dusted white. Seeing my map, one of them asks, friendly, "Are you lost?" I explain that I'm walking the route of the proposed park. "Oh right, that park we're supposed to get." And what would these men like to see on the dusty land that is their job site? They're unwrapping subs; hot peppers spice the air. "Jeez, I don't know," one of the men muses. "We've got this spot," he says, gesturing at the grass, the lindens. "Pretty women talk to us. What more do we need?" I love this answer. Not everyone knows when a lunch, a tree, some buddies, and a little urban frisson add up to Enough. Upon some reflection, though, the man and his companions agree there is one thing that would add to the great fullness of the present. "You know what would be nice," he begins, and his pals nod as he adds to the city's wish list for common ground: "A stocked fish pond, now that would be really nice—a nice place to fish right downtown."

▶ ▶ ▶

When we were very young and full-time disciples of Nancy Drew, my best friend Ellen Jane and I spent many hours in Drewsian detective work, hoping to solve mysteries of the adult world. Even aside from the special-case conundrums of the atom that ruled our town, there were many things for which Ellen Jane and I did not yet have language. For instance, what were those hundreds of tall, flared, lacy steel structures that strode in long lines for miles over the east Tennessee landscape? We saw them when our families went west to Watts Bar Lake or east to Cades Cove in the Smoky Mountains. One summer afternoon when we were seven or eight, EJ and I lay on the long grass in her backyard trying to find the right word for these things.

Giants, I suggested—because of the towering size of the structures, the way they seemed to walk over the Tennessee land in seven-league boots. *Ladies' slips,* said Ellen Jane, noticing the dressmaker's model shape of the things: the full chest, narrow waist, a flaring skirt of steel.

Giants or ladies' slips. At age eight those were our best guesses for the eight-story-tall electrical pylons of the Tennessee Valley Authority that were electrifying and changing the face of the upper South. And looking back, I have to say those were very good guesses. Between the two of us, Ellen Jane and I at once mythologized and domesticated the vast TVA system, and in doing so we got something exactly right. The physical infrastructure of industrial society is at once heroic and ordinary, gigantic and intimate—always a membrane between the great and the small, between the collective and personal, things as close as our own skin and as remote as the distant future.

EMILY HIESTAND is a writer and visual artist. She is the award-winning author of *Green the Witch Hazel Wood,* a collection of poetry; *The Very Rich Hours,* a collection of travel essays; and *Angela the Upside Down Girl,* true stories about identity and place. Hiestand's writing has appeared in the *Atlantic Monthly,* the *New Yorker, Georgia Review, Salon,* the *Nation, Best American Poetry,* the *New York Times,* and *Partisan Review,* among other publications.

PLANNING
FOR CHANGE

PLANS FOR MAGNIFICENCE AND ORDER IN CITIES
are as old as the oldest societies, but a book that takes
into consideration the comfort and health of a city's
inhabitants became a reality only in 1898 with the publication in Great Britain of *Tomorrow: A Peaceful Path
to Real Reform* by Sir Ebenezer Howard. Building on
earlier town planning efforts around London, Howard
proposed a Garden City for the working classes with
decent, well-built housing as well as light, air, and the
benefits of nature.

   In the past century, urban planning for livability
has grown exponentially, both in theory and in practice.
Those interested in its diverse and argument-laden
history will want to consult this book's reading list. The
five essays included here offer ideas and practices that
have proven successful in American cities and in other
countries, innovative blueprints for making our cities
more accessible, more open to citizen participation, and
more equitable in the opportunities they offer.

IF YOU BUILD IT, WILL
THEY CHANGE?

BILL MCKIBBEN

*The city of Curitiba, Brazil, provides the world with a model of how to
integrate sustainable transport considerations into development of businesses, roads, and local communities. Writer Bill McKibben notes that
Curitiba first outlined its master plan in 1965, with the main goals of
limiting central area growth and encouraging commercial and service-
sector growth along two structural north-south transport arteries, radiat-
ing out from the city center. The plan also aimed to provide economic
support for urban development through the establishment of industrial
zones and to encourage local community self-sufficiency by providing all
city districts with education, health care, recreation, and parks.*

Here's the event, now three decades past, that started Curitiba
in a new direction: the city's mayor, Jaime Lerner, decided
not to proceed with a plan to reduce congestion in the southern
Brazilian city by routing a new freeway through the historic center
of the town. Instead, he announced that the maze of streets at the
city center would be closed to cars altogether, creating a pedestrian
plaza. This was the early 1970s. Except maybe for the old quarter
of Munich, there was hardly a pedestrian mall anywhere on urban
planet earth. So it was a brave thing for the mayor of a provincial

Brazilian city to decide that he would defy the town's business leaders and install one—literally do it over a single weekend, marshaling every city employee down to schoolteachers for the task of ripping up concrete and putting in cobblestones. When shopkeepers arrived on Monday to open their stores, they were outraged to find all the parking gone. Outraged until about midday, when it became clear that throngs of people were strolling the streets, stopping in to shop. By late afternoon, merchants in surrounding streets were demanding that their streets be ripped up too. The next weekend, when the local automobile club descended on the downtown to "retake" the street for cars, they found no police, no barricades. Instead, the Department of Public Works had unrolled half a mile of newsprint down the plaza and set out pots of paint. Hundreds of children were crouched there, drawing pictures. The drivers turned around and went home.

Changing the face of a city is a matter of blueprints, of dollars, of cubic feet of concrete, of cranes and bulldozers. Changing the heart of a city is more difficult, and more important—there's no simple way to bulldoze attitudes, to pour old feelings into plywood forms and let them harden in better shapes. And so Curitiba is an interesting story. Not because it has succeeded entirely, but because it has tried. Made a conscious effort to transform not only the shape of the city, and then through that physical transformation to reshape its citizens. To *unalienate* people. Not through propaganda, not through intimidation. Through respect.

Consider first the slum dwellers, the inhabitants of that rickety ring of *barrios* and *favelas* that circle every Latin American city. Go to Rio and, if you dare, wander the endless shantytowns, worlds to themselves, existing beyond the effective rule of law, even the effective reach of, say, the post office. You can meet fifth-generation residents—five generations of living next to open sewers, amid piles of trash.

Curitiba had always been relatively prosperous, mostly free of such spectacles. But in the 1980s, as agribusiness forced more and more peasants off the fertile land of its home state of Parana, the edges of the city began to swell with poor folk. The shacks started going up, and in the course of a few months, the health department noted an alarming rise in rat-borne diseases like leptospirosis. What to do?

The traditional answers, elsewhere in the hemisphere, have been to ignore the slums or to bulldoze them. Lerner and his team decided instead to try to incorporate their residents into the city, no easy task. Their initial problem, and initial opportunity, was the trash choking the alleys. There was no way to get garbage trucks down those narrow corridors, so they came up with an alternative. Signs went up all over the area, telling residents that if they carried a sack of trash to the nearest paved road at, say, ten A.M. on Tuesday, they would receive a sack of food in return. It took almost no time to clean up the shantytowns; residents got calories they badly needed; food for the program came from the remaining farms around the city, stabilizing what was left of smaller-scale local agriculture. It was a problem solved, and the lines of people clutching their sacks of trash were a moving sight.

But the city didn't stop with that. Soon it was distributing bus tokens, too, and whenever a big concert—Julio Iglesias, say—came to the municipal concert hall, some percentage of the tickets were handed out along the garbage lines. "We have to have communication with the people of the slums," says Hitoshi Nakamura, one of Lerner's longtime assistants. "If we don't, if they start to feel like *favelados* (slum dwellers), then they will go against the city. Before they feel like *favelados* we must get there and implant these programs. If we give them attention, they don't feel abandoned. They feel like citizens."

In certain ways, though, the poor are easy—they have desperate needs that you can meet. The middle class, the well off, are in some ways harder. Their needs are less pressing, subtler; their choices are more varied. As in the United States, so around the world: increasingly, people with any options have left behind the public realm and found themselves private schools, private transportation, private enclaves with private guards posted at the private gate. Private *attitudes*. Luring them back into the life of the city requires at least as much creativity.

In Curitiba that meant things like the downtown shopping plaza. But it also meant, say, a system of public parks that now provides more green space per inhabitant than any city on earth.

The money for that green necklace came from an unlikely source. When the federal government offered money for flood control, most Brazilian cities followed the example of the developed countries and "channelized" their rivers in concrete pipes, made them disappear from the center city. Curitiba took the cash and bought land, a series of parks along each of the rivers as they came into town, parks that featured lakes at their centers. When the rivers rose in the stream, the lakes in the parks simply expanded; for a few weeks, the jogging track or the bike path might have to be rerouted. But the rest of the year you had a park, a place for municipal bike rental stands, for outdoor restaurants, for city-owned skateboard parks and go-kart ramps. For the municipal Creativity Center, a former glue factory that now hosted a ceramics studio and a darkroom. For the city's very own remote-control airplane range. Did it work? Well, property values around each of the parks soared, enough that the increased tax collections paid for the improvements and then some. Did it work? So well that the biggest problem was how to cut all the thousands of acres of lawn the city now owned. And the solution, typically Curitiban, was to find a displaced shepherd newly arrived in one of the *favelas* and give him a truck and a municipal sheep flock, which makes its way from one park to the next, trimming and fertilizing.

The car, of course, is the ultimate symbol of the private worlds we now inhabit—our own transportation to take us exactly where we want exactly when we want, no questions asked, no concessions to anyone else's schedule, anyone else's taste in radio stations. Our own sheet-metal universe. This religion has spread outward from America to anywhere else where people are sufficiently wealthy.

(And with some baroque variations. A few hundred miles north of Curitiba, in São Paulo, street crime makes even driving too dangerous for the very rich, and so a fleet of private helicopters buzzes the city at all hours.) Wrenching people from their cars may be the hardest of all public policy projects, one we've essentially abandoned in North America.

But Lerner had a different vision, of a city that moved primarily on public wheels. Bus wheels, because subways were far too expensive. He built a pretty good bus system, but the growth in car traffic kept up, and so he stopped to reevaluate. He took a lawn chair and set it up next to the bus stop by city hall, and for several days he simply watched to see what slowed buses down, made them maddeningly lurching creatures. It was the wait while people walked up the stairs, put in their coins, and made their way to the back of the bus, he decided. And so he sketched a new kind of bus stop, one that was built all over the city within a few years. It was a glass tube, elevated a few feet above the sidewalk. You walk up a stair, put your fare in the box, and wait for the bus to come. When it does, the doors open as they would on a subway; twenty people a second can climb on or off. When you've built a bus like that, you can make it long. Curitiba's double-hinged "speedybuses" can hold 400 people. They can't be expected to snake through traffic, though—instead, they move on dedicated bus lanes and special bus-only streets, carrying traffic as fast as the New York express subways. But at a hundredth the cost. On busy routes at rush hour a bus pulls in every sixty seconds. Unlike New Yorkers, grimly peering out through scratched Plexiglas windows as the bus makes its halting way up, say, the East Side of Manhattan, Curitibanos can connect almost anywhere, whizzing through their city. The bus *serves* you—you feel in control of the city, not a victim of the tie-ups and bottlenecks and every-day-repeated traffic jams that mark every American town I know.

Does it work? Everyone takes the bus. Even with low fares, it pays for itself without tax subsidies. The fare box even pays for capital costs, for new buses and stations. Does it work? People in Curitiba use a quarter less fossil fuel, on average, than other urban Brazilians. That's a big number. Not enough to stop global warming, but remember, that savings comes before you install any fancy new engines or invent hydrogen fuel cells or whatever. It comes just from changing behavior. Does it work? At first some people detested all the bus lanes. It made driving more difficult. But when Lerner left office because of term limits, his approval rating was 92 percent.

But does it *really* work? Have any of these changes really changed *people?* Or maybe *change* is the wrong word. Has it managed to bring out the part of their nature, the part of all our natures, that likes the public world, the world of parks and plazas and barrooms and theaters, that likes to rub shoulders with the rest of the city? Change like that is essential if we're ever to deal with the core environmental and social questions we face. And change like that is harder to gauge. You need to leave statistics behind, try to get deeper.

The last time I was in Curitiba, I made it a point to talk with several writers who had lived there most of their lives, who had peopled their novels and poems with Curitibanos. The city, they agreed, represented an interesting test case. Populated largely by the descendants of European immigrants, it has always been a pretty stiff place. The rest of Brazil walks with a sway, but Curitibanos always stayed pretty much to the straight and narrow. *"Carnaval* is never much of a success here," says novelist Cristovao Tezza. "It's sort of something forced on us." Valencio Xavier, another writer, says that "when someone invites you to visit him in his house, you know he wasn't born here."

Lerner's reforms didn't change that character completely. "In some ways we remain spectators of the town," says Tezza. "I went to a rock show in the old part of town. It was an amazing spectacle—lights, lasers, stroboscopes. But people were just standing and watching. They didn't know if it was okay to dance." Still, they agreed, much was different. "Before in Curitiba things had always happened within four walls," says Xavier. "Lerner obliged us to walk. He had these street fairs; he made parks. Before we were like oysters that crack open just a little bit to get the world passing by. Now we are opening up."

"Look," says Lerner. "I know it's the right of people to live where they want. If you want to live in a condominium of wealthy people, that's okay." And in fact there are gated communities in Curitiba, a few. But government doesn't have to let everything inevitably slide in that direction. "You can also offer an option for people who want to live more . . . gregariously," he says. It's not a word many American politicians would employ. But it's the word that best defines a city worth living in.

Life is far from perfect in Curitiba. Too many of its residents are still poor. Lerner has run into trouble with leftists since he became governor of the surrounding state—he hasn't helped the landless, they claim. The antiglobalization campaigners don't like the fact that the city's success rests in part on the large corporations that have flocked there, lured by the good civic services, the safe streets. Too many of the reforms have been top-down, not democratic. Some residents say the stories about Curitiba's success are in great measure hype. It's not paradise.

But if you want paradise, you'd better look on a different planet. Curitiba offers what Lerner calls a "point of reference" for a world where urban too often means despair—even in places far richer than southern Brazil. For me, here's the "point of reference" from which to judge Curitiba:

When the mayor had sketched out his new scheme for bus stops, and city planners were getting set to build them, the first question was what material to use. The natural answer was glass—it is beautiful, and easy to clean, and durable: the glass in the windows of your home may have been there a century, and it works just as well as it did the day it was installed. But the public works commissioner wasn't so sure. The obvious drawback to glass is that you can chuck a rock through it. Maybe they should go with Plexiglas, he said, just to be safe.

No, said Jaime Lerner. "We have respected the people of the city, and they will respect the city in return." Glass it was. And the last time I was there, the shelters remained just as they'd been the day they were built. Gleaming. Uncracked. And busy.

BILL MCKIBBEN is the author of *The End of Nature* and *Enough: Staying Human in an Engineered Age* as well as *Maybe One, The Age of Missing Information,* and *Hope, Human and Wild.* He is a scholar-in-residence at Middlebury College and a contributor to a wide variety of publications, including the *New York Review of Books, Outside,* and the *New York Times.*

THE REGION
THE TRUE CITY

MYRON ORFIELD

Urban savant Myron Orfield explains how the future of the city is inter-
twined with the suburbs that surround it and shows that most suburbs are
hurt by lack of cooperation with their central cities. The author believes
that all communities can do better by working together.

The notion that "the suburbs" are an affluent, monolithic voting bloc still shapes American domestic politics, but it is an out-dated and dangerous myth that can cost unsuspecting candidates their elections.

An analysis of metropolitan swing districts—legislative districts that regularly switch from one party to the other—provides an important new view of the suburban political landscape. About 80 percent of the swing districts in the twenty-five largest U.S. metropolitan regions are in the fiscally or socially stressed suburban communities. These places are the true pivot points of American politics.

Politicians can win these voters with a platform of regional cooperation built on tax equity, coordinated land-use planning, and metropolitan governance. To stressed suburbs, regionalism means what every politician promises, but almost no one can deliver: lower taxes and better services. For older at-risk suburbs, it means fiscal stability, community renewal, and less social stress. For rapidly growing bedroom communities, it means sufficient spending on schools, clean water, and infrastructure.

But these are not the only places that stand to gain from regional reform. Despite the touted revitalization of central cities during the 1990s, all are still struggling with areas of great need. Central cities clearly would benefit from better relations with their suburbs.

And for citizens of affluent suburban job centers, at the hub of fast-growing congestion and dwindling open space, regional policies that redirect some of the region's growth back into its older communities offer the most realistic way to preserve their community's original character and proximity to open space.

SUBURBAN TYPOLOGY AND GROWTH

Despite its promise, American metropolitan regions have not embraced cooperation. Instead, individual communities have engaged each other in an intense and unequal competition for tax base and social stability. In region after region, this futile race has created far more losers than winners.

In fact, just a small fraction of the population—only 7 percent of people in the twenty-five largest U.S. regions—lives in affluent suburban job centers that boast expensive housing, upscale retail, and plentiful jobs. A majority of metropolitan residents live in suburbs that are facing the challenges of fiscal or social stress.

One American in four in the twenty-five largest regions lives in bedroom-developing suburbs. These places, which receive 60 percent of metropolitan growth, are chock-full of young middle-class families and school-age children but thin on commercial tax base. The unusually high ratio of children strains tax bases and often leads to overcrowded classrooms and low per-pupil spending—often significantly less per pupil than in the central cities they surround. Communities such as these are struggling mightily to pay for the schools, roads, and sewer systems they need.

Another 40 percent of metropolitan residents live in at-risk suburbs trying to stretch local tax resources that are even more inadequate than those of bedroom communities. These suburbs face burgeoning social problems, such as growing poverty in their schools, crime, an expanding population of older citizens needing services, and insufficient infrastructure. They must tackle these challenges without the central-city amenities of central business districts, cultural institutions, and gentrifying neighborhoods. Some older at-risk suburbs have become even poorer and more racially segregated than the central cities, and almost all are more fragile economically.

Regional polarization has had devastating consequences for the minority poor, leaving many of them trapped in segregated neighborhoods with limited economic and educational opportunities. Now it has begun to diminish the quality of life and opportunities of working- and middle-class suburbanites. Unplanned, often explosive development in every region is covering the landscape with new homes without corresponding growth in schools, roads, and sewer systems. It is destroying valuable and sensitive open space, causing traffic congestion, and crowding underfunded schools. The huge increase in "no growth" and "slow growth" policies suggests that no group—not even the wealthiest suburbs—is fully satisfied with the status quo.

There are virtually infinite examples of how regional competition hurts our metropolitan areas. Here are just a few.

IN PURSUIT OF AFFLUENCE AND JOBS

Along Highway 101 on the outer edge of the Los Angeles metropolitan region, the cities of Oxnard, Ventura, and Camarillo are engaged in battle. The spoils of this particular war are shopping malls, auto dealerships, and big-box retailers.

As in municipalities across the country, the fiscal well-being of these communities is tied to the tax revenue they can raise to pay for roads, schools, sewer systems, police forces, and libraries. Oxnard, Ventura, and Camarillo have taken it upon themselves to attract tax-generating developments to their segment of the Ventura County highway—dubbed "Sales Tax Canyon" by California planner and journalist William Fulton—at virtually whatever the cost.

In the past decade these three cities have funneled millions of public dollars into land acquisition, tax breaks, road improvements, and even cash payments to attract developers of tax-producing retail facilities. They have filed lawsuits to prevent neighboring communities from doing the same.

The result of all this has been the movement of hundreds of low-wage jobs, and the infrastructure that comes with them, from one community to another. Although these efforts have certainly brought tax revenues to individual cities, the efforts to attract them have been at the expense of other public investments. And the costs go beyond dollars. The new stores have devoured open space, added to growing congestion in the area, and drawn dollars from existing shopping areas.

Due to some unique state laws, this fierce competition among California local governments is focused on sales tax. But the same kind of self-defeating tug-of-war is repeated in regions across the nation, where thousands of cities are pitted against each other in a zero-sum game for tax base—it might be in the form of expensive housing, office parks, or retail developments—with little or no common economic strategy.

THE PUSH AWAY FROM THE CENTER

Rapid growth on the urban edge is often the outgrowth of chaotic social change taking place in older suburban communities.

In the mid-1990s, black middle-class families began to move into the city of Matteson, an attractive white-collar Chicago suburb of broad lawns, open space, and good schools about twenty miles south of the Loop. The new black residents were, by standards like education and income, at least the equals of Matteson's whites. Many were better off. But as soon as black households became a significant percentage of the population, there was a sudden sell-off of homes by white residents. Asked why they were moving, the white sellers cited declining schools and growing crime.

Neither claim was backed by evidence: school test scores and crime rates remained unchanged. But even if the stated reasons for leaving were flawed, the result was the same. As the white middle class left, demand for Matteson's big houses declined. Because the black middle class was not large enough to maintain demand, prices fell. Soon Matteson was growing rapidly poorer.

The transformation in schools is a powerful prophecy, setting in motion a series of dramatic transformations in housing and retail markets and ultimately the very stability of the community. This scene is being replicated in suburban areas in all large metropolitan areas—Prince George's County outside Washington, D.C., DeKalb County outside Atlanta, the eastern inner suburbs of Cleveland, and the rapidly "Latinizing" suburbs south of Los Angeles. The black and Latino middle classes are following the American dream to the suburbs, and the white middle class is moving away from them.

PRESSURE ON THE FRINGE

Flight from places like Matteson ramps up the pressure on the surrounding suburbs. As households move out, they bring with them a high demand for good schools and free-flowing highways to take them to jobs throughout the region. Such infrastructure comes at a premium, yet for bedroom-developing suburbs, roads are just one of many needs.

The fiscal squeeze facing these fast-growing places is evident in the Osseo, Minnesota, school district. The 22,000-student district includes a number of fast-growing, middle-class suburbs northwest of Minneapolis.

Leaders of these cities played the game that most middle-class developing suburbs play. They welcomed rooftops—lots of them— in an effort to attract a major mall and other significant commercial and industrial development that would help them pay the costs of services such as schools, roads, and sewer systems. Like most places that attempt this gamble, they lost.

Cities in the Osseo district attracted strip malls, Perkins, and Olive Gardens. But they never developed a significant commercial base, and they never received more than a few high-valued homes. Instead, the area filled up with busy two-worker families, living in thousands of modest ramblers, town homes, and a few McMansions.

The high ratio of children in places like Osseo contributes to low per-pupil spending. That fiscal squeeze is visible in the overcrowded classrooms of Osseo's schools. It is also visible in extracurricular activities. Kids in the north suburban districts of the Twin Cities— including Ossco—play a lot of hockey. But it is kids in the southern suburbs, places with more than their share of the region's jobs and expensive houses, and better-funded school programs, who most often take home the state tournament trophy.

Places like Osseo are home to the vast majority of middle-class families with school-age children. Home to a quarter of the regional population, they are experiencing 60 percent of the population growth. Already burdened by the physical demands of growth— roads, sewers, and parks—voters in fast-growing suburbs often resist additional taxes to support the growing needs of their schools.

In 2001, Minnesota passed an education budget that left many of the state's school districts facing deficits. Despite the threat of big budget cuts, voters in a number of fast-growing middle-class suburban districts, including Osseo, rejected local referenda that would have filled in some of the gap. Osseo officials responded by laying off teachers, cutting programs, and threatening to enact a four-day school week.

STRUGGLING TO COVER BASIC SERVICES

Not only schools are at risk when local governments can't keep up with the costs of growth. Fiscal strain is threatening the natural environment in many fast-growing suburbs, which exemplify the downside of unplanned growth in communities with few tax dollars to spare.

At the developing northern edge of the Detroit metropolitan area is Macomb County, an affordable suburban haven of mostly modest houses for industrial workers. Well into the 1980s, the notion of planning in Macomb County was often branded a form of socialism. But by the late 1990s, the results of this live-and-let-live attitude were becoming evident.

Failing septic systems were profoundly polluting wells. Several cities were convicted of dumping raw sewage into the tributaries of Lake St. Clair, the source of drinking water for the Detroit metro area and a major recreational resource, when rain overwhelmed already overtaxed systems. Officials closed Macomb County beaches eighty-two times in the summer of 2000 and thirty-one times the following summer due to high levels of *E. coli* bacteria from untreated sewage.

But neither Macomb County nor its municipalities, with tax bases relying mostly on small homes, has enough money to handle the cost of cleanup, which could reach $4 billion. Many Macomb communities have lower per-capita tax resources than even their troubled neighbor, Detroit.

HELP FOR THE WHOLE REGION

The incentives for rapid growth on the urban edge and disinvestment in the core are built into our nation's public policies. Tax policies promote wasteful competition among local governments. Transportation and infrastructure investment patterns subsidize sprawling development. The fragmented political nature of most metropolitan areas—with dozens, and sometimes hundreds, of local governments— makes thoughtful, efficient land-use planning difficult.

The many challenges facing America's metropolitan areas can be attacked effectively only by increasing cooperation and planning among suburban communities. A cooperative approach can strengthen all communities and regions and open opportunities for economic advancement and social mobility for all citizens. An agenda for regional reform draws ideas from both major political parties. It shares the Republicans' distaste for wasted money, land, and human potential and a goal of less complex and more efficient government. From the Democrats it borrows a strong commitment to ending discrimination based on race and class, and an environmental agenda for preserving natural areas and cleaning up the air and water.

1. *Local tax reform.* At the roots of metropolitan tax reform is a more equitable fiscal relationship between cities. This kind of reform is not unprecedented—it has close cousins in state school-aid systems that exist in virtually every state in the country. Contrary to popular misconceptions, such an approach could lower taxes and improve services for most U.S. suburbs.

These programs have several benefits. First, they reduce the competition for tax base among local governments in a region. They also reduce tax-rate disparities. Without such policies, central cities and at-risk suburbs are usually forced to tax themselves at a much higher rate than their better-off neighbors to compensate for high costs and relatively meager tax bases. Meanwhile, the few affluent suburbs are able to rely on their significant tax bases to offer high-quality public services at relatively low tax rates.

2. *Smart growth.* Combating sprawl and creating more-livable communities is a growing issue in the nation. "Smart growth" is an efficient and environmentally friendly pattern of development that focuses growth near existing public facilities. Smart growth provides people choice in where they live and work and how they get around.

Already sixteen states have adopted comprehensive growth management acts, and the ranks are growing. Regional land-use planning efforts, like those required in Oregon's statewide program, help officials coordinate investments in roads, highways, sewers, and utilities. Concurrency requirements like those in Florida mandate that infrastructure be online by the time development takes place.

Moderate Democratic and Republican governors like Mitt Romney of Massachusetts, Jennifer Granholm of Michigan, and John Rowland of Connecticut are smart-growth leaders. They understand that individual communities can do little to deal with the underlying regional forces contributing to sprawling development. They understand that when one community declares a growth moratorium, it simply pushes sprawl further out to the edge of a metropolitan region.

Achieving smart growth requires suburban communities to co-operate in land-use planning. That's a challenge, but one that yields enormous benefits by protecting open space, building infrastructure more efficiently, and stabilizing older suburbs.

3. *Reinventing government.* Just as our framers formed a "more perfect union" between the states, so must we form a more perfect union among metropolitan communities to prepare for the future. Two centuries ago, our fragmented government found itself unable to deal with the challenges of growth and external threats. Today our existing regional governments are unable to deal effectively with growth or—it is becoming apparent—to handle challenges from within. With hundreds of local governments stealing expensive homes and

shopping malls from each other, there is little sense of how to fit all the pieces into a comprehensive whole.

Regional institutions already in place in most metropolitan areas can serve as a backbone for greater regional cooperation. Federal law requires that every major region in the country have a body to coordinate hundreds of millions of transportation dollars. In their current incarnations, these relatively unknown forums, metropolitan planning organizations, are appointed bodies of local officials. The challenge is to make these existing shadowy regional governments more effective on issues of growth and more accountable to the people they serve.

Political candidates who can pull these strands together into a regional platform will find eager listeners in the stressed suburbs.

––––––––––––––––

MYRON ORFIELD is the founder of the Metropolitan Area Research Corporation and president of Ameregis, a research and geographic information systems firm in Minneapolis. A former Minnesota state senator, he is an adjunct professor at the University of Minnesota Law School and the author of *American Metropolitics: The New Suburban Reality*.

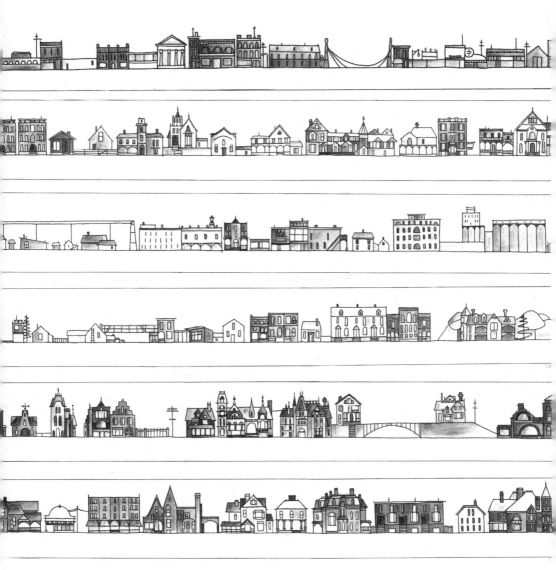

▶ "SOME PLACES I MIGHT HAVE LIVED." INK
AND WATERCOLOR BY REBECCA SILUS (HERE
AND OVERLEAF).

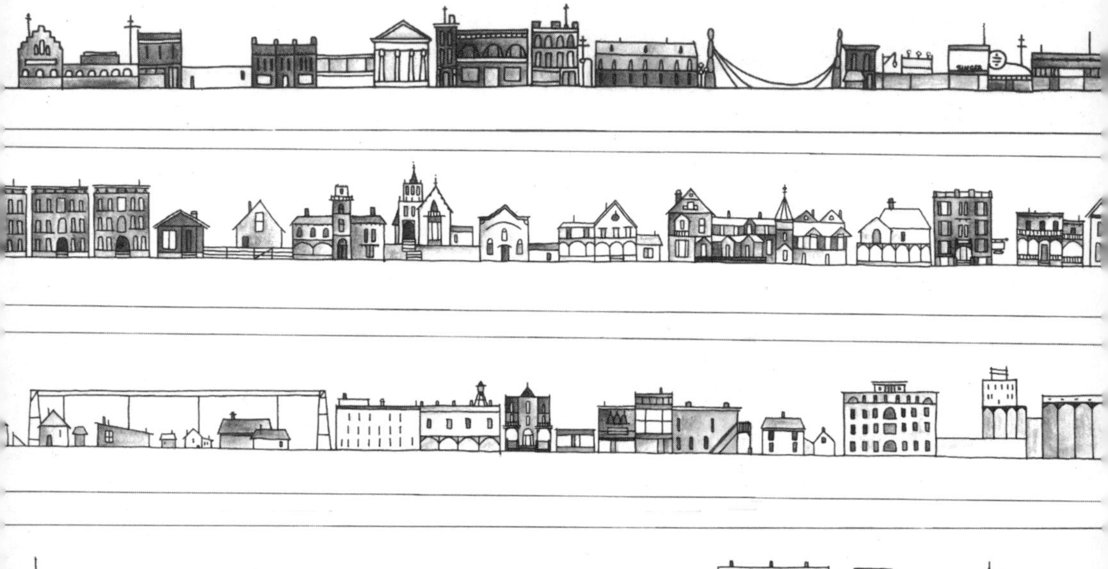
SINGER

OPPORTUNITY-BASED HOUSING

john a. powell

The distribution of opportunity in cities and regions is often, as john a. powell explains, effected through the location of housing. He elucidates the ways in which we have inscribed racial inequity into the urban land-scape by locating housing for people with low incomes and people of color in opportunity-denying space. He asserts that in addressing issues of social justice and equity, we must deliberately locate housing close to what pow-ell calls opportunity sites, especially for low-income communities of color.

L ivable cities and metropolitan areas provide opportunities for
those who live in them. Unfortunately, these opportunities are
not equally distributed, nor equally accessible. While this is historically true, recent demographic shifts, declines in private housing stock,
and changes at the federal level have made it almost impossible to
gain access to affordable housing. This crisis not only limits the ability
of low-income households and households of color to find a place to
live, it also limits their access to high-quality education, employment,
health care, and other opportunities.

This isolation is not simply the result of differing income levels
among whites and people of color, but is the product of a host of dis-
criminatory and subordinating practices and policies.[1] In this more

complicated pattern, and with the nonwhite population growing, entire metropolitan regions are divided by both race and income. Indeed, the operative divide is no longer city versus suburb; it is one of access to opportunity versus isolation from opportunity.

Housing is an important element within a web of other opportunity structures that affect the life outcomes of metropolitan residents. While providing shelter is a vital function, housing is much more than shelter. By its location and mix, it can enhance or impede access to other opportunity structures.

A model that I propose for moving forward in the coming years on fair housing is opportunity-based housing. It is driven by the reality that ensuring housing throughout a metropolitan area results in improvements in other life areas. This model suggests that the creation and preservation of affordable housing must be deliberately and intelligently connected on a regional scale to high-performing schools, meaningful employment opportunities, transportation, child care, and institutions that facilitate civic and political activity. This means pursuing housing policies that create the potential for low-income people to live near existing opportunity as well as policies that tie creation of opportunity in other areas to existing and potential affordable housing. Simply put, recognizing that opportunity is not evenly distributed, opportunity-based housing deliberately connects housing with the other opportunities throughout a metropolitan region.

I want to be clear that by articulating the need for affordable housing throughout metropolitan regions, I am not merely advocating a housing dispersal strategy that requires families to relocate to new neighborhoods or cities. There are significant costs to forcing people to move, and these costs are extremely high when people have inadequate opportunity to find housing elsewhere. When a community is disrupted, the resulting costs can include the loss of political power and sense of place. This does not mean that we simply accept the status quo and endorse the current residential models based on individual choice. Prioritizing this notion of "choice" can obscure the legacy and persistence of racial discrimination in housing and falsely suggest that there is now a "level playing field" in the housing market rather than one that actually coerces impoverished people of color. Thus, the defining principle of a regional housing strategy should not be choice, but rather racial and economic justice.

EXPLAINING OPPORTUNITY-BASED HOUSING

The central principle of opportunity-based housing is that residents of metropolitan regions are situated within a complex, interconnected web of opportunity structures (or lack thereof) that significantly shape their quality of life.

The term "opportunity structures" refers to resources and services that contribute to individual and family stability and advancement. Conceived narrowly, opportunity structures are those minimum requirements or supports needed for people to achieve an acceptable level of health and stability. For example, shelter is a minimum requirement for stability. More expansively, opportunity structures are the vehicles for racial and economic fairness for all residents of the region. If all children had access to an education that prepares them for full participation in society, for example, ours would be a more participatory and racially just nation.

A second principle of opportunity-based housing is that opportunity structures are tied to metropolitan space. That is, the geographical distribution of these structures within a metropolitan region is strongly linked to the degree to which residents have access to them.

An analysis of opportunities must therefore recognize the reality of economic and racial segregation. Segregation functions differently for different communities of color. Latinos and other groups do not experience the severity of residential segregation that blacks do, although they are still segregated in the nation's metropolitan regions.

Blacks are also more likely to live in public housing than other racial groups. It is important to note, however, that access to opportunity is determined not only by physical proximity to sources of opportunity, but also by the interconnection of the unique characteristics of the residents of any one region. Given this reality, general trends of regional well-being must be evaluated in light of the particular needs, capabilities, and limitations of different populations.

As an adjunct to these principles, I assert that the reforms derived from an opportunity-based housing analysis must be responsive to more than housing concerns. Creating opportunity-based housing means extending the campaign beyond improvements in the affordable housing sphere and advocating reform of the full set of structures that create impediments to opportunity. One example would be to seek affordable, high-quality child care so that children who have stable housing are able to develop important learning and social skills.

In sum, the analysis and the creation of a model for opportunity-based housing should involve creating, connecting, and distributing opportunity structures throughout a metropolitan region. Importantly, this task is not static, but must be assessed and tracked over time. But before I describe other strategies needed to make opportunity-based housing a reality, I will review the current forces that constrain the attainment of opportunity-based housing and consider more closely the dynamics of other opportunity structures related to housing.

CONSTRAINTS ON OPPORTUNITY-BASED HOUSING

AFFORDABLE HOUSING CRISIS AND INEFFECTIVE HOUSING POLICIES

At present, the nation faces a growing shortage of affordable housing.[2] As of the mid-1990s, according to the Center on Budget and Policy Priorities, there were nearly two low-income renters for the number of affordable rental units in the United States for every low-cost unit.[3] Family units with a sufficient number of bedrooms are also greatly lacking.[4] This deficit, along with federal policies that favor owning over renting,[5] profoundly hampers the access of low-income families to housing and other opportunity structures.

To illustrate this crisis, one need only examine the national "housing wage"—the amount a full-time worker has to earn to be able to obtain affordable housing. For 2002, this wage increased to $14.66 an hour, 5 percent greater than the previous year.[6] For over 2.24 million Americans, 60 percent of whom are family heads or their spouses, the gap between housing costs and income renders housing almost completely out of reach.[7] And although 15 million households qualify for federal housing assistance, only 4.5 million actually receive aid, many after a wait of over two years.[8] Meanwhile, other forms of federal housing assistance, two-thirds of which benefit families with incomes over $75,000, flourish.[9]

HOPE VI,[10] the federal housing policy that replaces public housing developments with mixed-income communities of apartments and town houses, is partly responsible for this affordable housing crisis. Although its goals are admirable, its methods are the cause of considerable debate and legitimate concern. HOPE VI developments destroy far more units than they create. As a result, many displaced families cannot afford other housing even with federal "section 8" housing vouchers. Furthermore, displacement disadvantages impoverished persons of color more than those with greater economic means.

Moreover, vouchers have proven to be an insufficient substitute for public housing.[11] At a time when emphasis is being placed on subsidizing the private rental market rather than on creating new housing, voucher users face low vacancy rates and escalating rents in a "tight" housing market.[12] For example, New York City lost more than half of its low-rent apartments, or 500,000 units, in the 1990s.[13] Private developers of subsidized housing also seek tenants with the highest eligible income levels, squeezing out those who are impoverished.[14] Thus, assisted housing programs neither bridge the affordable housing gap nor give low-income families access to opportunity-rich areas. Moving forward on opportunity-based housing requires that we contend with these shifts in public and subsidized housing policy.[15]

RACIAL DISCRIMINATION AND CONCENTRATED POVERTY

While a tight housing market constrains access to housing opportunity for all residents of a region, it has a particularly pernicious effect on residents of color where it intersects with racist practices and with concentrated poverty. Since people of color are over-represented in the public housing and voucher populations, racial discrimination is particularly persistent.[16] Nationally, people of color comprise 68 percent of public housing residents and 58 percent of section 8 voucher and certificate users,[17] though they represent only 23 percent of the total population.[18] Research also shows that housing units available to participants in housing assistance programs are located in predominantly black areas. In fact, 80 percent of section 8 recipients reside in census tracts that are at least 50 percent black and have a median income of under $15,000. Even families who relocate from public housing to private rental housing live in areas that are 90 percent black.[19]

And people of color tend to be disproportionately cost-burdened. In a recent analysis, 27 and 28 percent of African American and Hispanic households respectively were found to experience severe housing problems, compared with only 19 percent of whites. When housing costs are high, low-income families are forced to make cuts in other areas of need, such as food and health care, which negatively affects their well-being. Nationally, as of the late 1990s, 40 percent of all renters had high housing cost burdens, and 20 percent had severe burdens, meaning that they were paying over 50 percent of their income on rent.[20] High housing costs can even result in families losing their housing altogether.

JURISDICTIONAL FRAGMENTATION AND GENTRIFICATION

Isolation from opportunity structures is also created by the concentration of existing affordable housing in the central city and inner-ring suburbs.[21] The relocation of opportunities to the outer-ring suburbs, subsidized largely by tax breaks and grant programs,[22] exacerbates this spatial divide. The resulting jurisdictional fragmentation has very negative implications for the creation and siting of affordable housing. *Fragmentation* is a term that refers to the proliferation in a metropolitan region of separate political jurisdictions, with autonomous control over zoning and planning, among other issues. In fragmented regions, jurisdictions often reduce the overall affordable housing supply and limit the access of low-income residents to other important opportunity structures.[23] One study found that higher levels of political fragmentation result in less collaboration between municipalities on public housing and community social services as well.[24] The result of fragmentation and exclusionary policies is that regions with higher degrees of fragmentation have higher levels of racial and economic segregation.[25] This suggests that any one jurisdiction alone cannot respond to the housing needs of the metropolitan region and that a regional approach to fair housing is necessary.

Gentrification is another force that constrains the development of opportunity-based housing by reinscribing fragmentation of another sort. Though the meaning of the term is contested and it is interchanged with the term *revitalization,* gentrification in reality is a process by which low-income families of color are priced and pushed out of their housing, typically by higher-income whites.[26] This pricing-out can take the form of rapidly increased rents, evictions, and rising property taxes that make homes unaffordable for low-income residents. Gentrification often destroys affordable housing without adequately replacing it.

As a result, neighborhoods that are gentrifying are not on the pathway to being stable, mixed-income, and multiracial. Rather, they are ones in which racial and economic changes occur rapidly, often fueled by various governmental policies and actions. In addition to the demolition of existing low-income and public housing, these policies can include tax incentives offered for middle-class home buyers and exclusionary zoning that limits the quantity and location of affordable housing in an area.[27] As a result, gentrification limits efforts to achieve opportunity-based housing by driving low-income residents away from emerging opportunities and relocating them to isolated areas.[28] Revitalization of a community, on the other hand, means that residents are able to experience the benefits of these new opportunities.

HOUSING AND OTHER KEY OPPORTUNITY STRUCTURES

As just suggested, housing plays a key role in determining access to other opportunity structures, including self-sustaining employment, a high level of educational attainment, good health, and the capacity to engage in political and civic structures.

HOUSING AND WEALTH ACCUMULATION

The link between housing and wealth accumulation is well documented. In addition to education, occupation, and income, accumulated assets affect a family's well-being and its children's life chances.[29] Home ownership is the primary source of wealth for most Americans and can enhance economic opportunity.[30] Access to other opportunity structures, such as employment and education, can affect the ability of individuals to purchase homes and gain home equity. Home ownership and home equity, in turn, can open the door to other opportunities by providing access to capital. Lack of housing assets, on the other hand, may produce (or may act as a proxy for) "neighborhood effects" such as inferior schools, inequalities between school districts, lack of economic resources of a wealthier neighborhood, and environmental hazards such as violence, drug abuse, and pollution.[31]

The link between housing, wealth accumulation, and race is also well documented. According to one study, in 1994 the median white family held assets worth more than seven times those of the median nonwhite family.[32] In the case of blacks, in the nineteenth century, lack of land redistribution, constraints on capital, and laws against black business ownership (not to mention lynchings) limited asset accumulation.[33] The virtual exclusion of blacks from Social Security in 1935, combined with redlining, Home Owner Loan Corporation (HOLC) discrimination, and the channeling of Federal Housing Administration and Veterans Administration home loans to the suburbs also limited asset accumulation in the twentieth century.[34]

Today's racial dynamics perpetuate these historical inequalities. For wealth to be created, and home ownership to be a means of access to other opportunity structures, homes must be located in economically vibrant areas. Not only is it less likely that blacks will own their homes, but white flight and residential segregation render their properties less valuable than those in nonblack neighborhoods.[35] This is true in Gary, Detroit, Chicago, and other highly segregated regions. In contrast, in the least segregated metropolitan regions, black home values are much closer to those of whites. As a result of these dynamics, more whites own homes, and own homes of greater value, than blacks. When these advantages are combined with mortgage payment[36] and local property tax[37] deductions, whites are able to accumulate wealth faster and gain access to other opportunities with greater ease.[38]

HOUSING, EMPLOYMENT, TRANSPORTATION, AND CHILD CARE

The lack of affordable housing in a community affects its economic development. Businesses do not locate where workers cannot live. In fact, housing is a proven economic stimulus.[39] Research also shows that over the past several decades there has been a movement of jobs away from the central city. Consequently, where people live in the metropolitan region plays a significant role in their employment prospects as well. Because long distances and traveling time restrain the ability of people to gain and keep jobs, people tend to choose housing or to relocate close to employment sites. This is true when there is a choice in housing, but when affordable housing is not present near job growth, this choice dissolves.

A growing body of evidence supports the theory that this "spatial mismatch" affects the employment and earnings of residents of central cities.[40] Barriers to affordable housing in areas where employment is growing, and the resultant distance between city residents and jobs, limits what should be a strong relationship between housing and employment.

Increased competition for jobs relocated in developing areas also results in longer terms of unemployment among blacks and lower wages among city or inner-ring suburban employees.[41] This reduction in income, in turn, limits the access of blacks to housing. And although many jobs remain in central business districts that are spatially accessible to both blacks and Latinos, these jobs are out of reach to many because of a skills mismatch.[42]

Opportunity-based housing also requires assessing the ways in which proximity to, cost of, and quality of transportation affects access to employment and other opportunities. The overemphasis on funding highway construction has reduced access to job opportunities for low-income households.[43] It has also benefited suburbs, encouraged longer commutes from auto-dependent communities, and provided hidden subsidies to motorists. Nationally, people of color tend to rely on public transportation far more than whites, and the distances they must travel to new jobs under a fragmented metropolitan scheme can hurt their employment prospects.[44]

Similarly, child care is an essential opportunity structure related to both housing and employment. Child care demands have greatly increased throughout the past two decades.[45] Between 1972 and 1999, the percentage of working mothers with children under six doubled, and the percentage of working mothers with children over six increased by over 25 percent.[46]

Despite these demands, many low-income families are unable to afford high-quality child care. Agencies' costs, locations, and hours often do not match parents' needs and ability to pay. Consequently, low-income families may find their housing and employment opportunities significantly limited when they attempt to meet their child care needs. Studies have also shown that the children of low-income families are more vulnerable to low-quality care and react more positively to high-quality care.[47] This suggests that an analysis of opportunity-based housing must incorporate an accounting of the cost, location, availability, and quality of child care in a metropolitan region.

HOUSING AND EDUCATION

The availability and condition of housing affect the quality of children's education as well. Access to educational opportunity is most limited by homelessness. Among homeless children under the age of five, 75 percent have at least one major developmental deviation or delay, usually in the areas of impulsivity or speech. Homeless children are four times more likely than other children to score at or below the tenth percentile in reading and vocabulary.[48] And because low-income families often have to move as rental rates change, the lack of affordable housing can result in increases in student transfers.[49] These increases make it significantly more likely that students will fail grades and have behavioral problems in school.[50] Finally, substandard housing can reduce student outcomes. For example, lead poisoning can delay development and decrease IQ points.[51]

A wealth of research also shows that students educated in economically and racially segregated schools receive substandard educations.

When a large number of students in a school face these challenges, it has a cumulative effect that significantly impedes the ability of the school to provide a high-quality education. William Trent has found that, as a result, "high concentrations of school poverty have strong negative consequences for the educational attainment of both African American and white students."[52] It is the poverty of the school, far more than the poverty of the individual, that determines educational outcomes. In fact, impoverished students do better if they live in middle-class neighborhoods or attend more affluent schools.[53]

Moreover, students of color are far more likely than whites to attend schools with larger populations of students in poverty.[54] Given these inequalities, it is inevitable that racial segregation in the public schools has devastating implications for the educational environment. Racially segregated schools more often rely upon transitory teachers and have curricula with greater emphasis on remedial courses, higher rates of tardiness and unexcused absence, and lower rates of extracurricular involvement.[55] As a result, educational achievement is highly racialized.[56]

By contrast, a wealth of research also shows that students of color who attend more integrated schools enjoy increased academic achievement levels and higher test scores, especially if they begin at an early age.[57] In fact, the desegregation era (roughly the 1960s through the mid-1980s) is largely credited for reducing the achievement gap, despite the fact that poverty, single-parent families, and unemployment worsened during the same period.

Intergenerational gains also ensue for students of color who attended desegregated schools.[58] Attending a more desegregated school also translates into higher goals for future educational attainment and occupational choices[59] and improved social networks.[60] Indeed, a 2000 study by the Harvard Civil Rights Project explicitly shows that the "diversity" of a desegregated school greatly benefits students of *all races,* not just whites.[61] Both blacks and whites who attend desegregated schools are more likely to attend a desegregated college, live in a desegregated neighborhood, work in a desegregated environment, and possess higher career aspirations.[62]

HOUSING AND HEALTH

The location of affordable housing and the opportunity to live a healthy life are related in multiple ways. To begin with, environmental hazards abound in segregated areas of concentrated poverty. The more blacks and Latinos living in a community, the more likely it is to have commercial hazardous waste facilities, sewer treatment centers, and chemical plants.[63] Toxic eyesores disfigure black neighborhoods, degrade property values, discourage public and private investment, and harm the health of residents. In fact, the Centers for Disease Control and Prevention has repeatedly found that blacks are more likely than whites to live in neighborhoods with higher air pollution levels and to suffer higher rates of respiratory and blood ailments.

Other spatial, racial, and economic factors influence a broad array of opportunities, exposures, decisions, and behaviors that threaten the health of these same neighborhoods.[64] For example, the presence of liquor stores, fast-food restaurants, and corner markets that sell cheap, unhealthy food at marked-up prices compromise dietary health. And increased levels of isolation, chronic stress, crime, and drug, alcohol, and domestic abuse compromise mental health. Discrimination also compromises availability and quality of standard medical care.

HOUSING AND DEMOCRATIC PARTICIPATION

Safe, stable, opportunity-based housing not only can lead to healthier living, but also can increase the capacity to partake in democratic structures. Full and meaningful participation in our society is the essential goal of civil rights, to which all other efforts—in employment, housing, and other opportunity areas—correspond and relate. According to *More Than Bricks and Mortar: Housing That Builds Community,* a report on efforts to increase home ownership in Santa Fe:

> An effective housing strategy does more than build buildings. If it is developed thoughtfully and implemented creatively, a housing strategy can have deeper implications, transforming both citizens and communities and the ties that bind each to the other. . . . Home ownership strengthens a democracy by giving people a stake in their community. When the number of stakeholders decreases rather than increases, the civic connections that create and sustain community are weakened.[65]

The web of opportunities associated with housing affects voting rights in particular. The voices excluded from the 2000 presidential election, for example, are the same voices excluded from our Constitution, wealth, and, ultimately, participatory citizenship. While the Voting Rights Act of 1965[66] and its subsequent amendments have remedied many of the most egregious forms of disenfranchisement such as literacy tests, poll taxes, and voter registration barriers, more subtle forms remain. Certainly, persistent economic inequality negatively affects political participation. More than two-thirds of people in the United States with incomes greater than $50,000 vote, compared with one-third of those with incomes under $10,000. This differential turnout is far greater than in Europe.[67] Political fragmentation and urban sprawl also limit participation and are particularly harmful. Persons of color, concentrated in pockets of poverty within a fragmented metropolitan region, do not have the resources to build the political clout necessary to participate meaningfully in the democratic process.

CREATING OPPORTUNITY—BASED HOUSING
VIA REGIONALISM

In attempting to meet the need for affordable housing, it is important to consider strategies that will both increase its supply and improve upon its connection to opportunity structures. If attention to location is absent, the potential for exacerbating concentrated poverty and further limiting opportunity is heightened. Rather, strategies must account for the unique experiences of the various racial and ethnic groups that stem from economic status, language or cultural issues, current residential patterns, and so on. I begin my discussion of how to create opportunity-based housing with the essential unifying approach called regionalism.

Most metropolitan areas across the nation contain an urban core that is growing increasingly poor and segregated. This concentration negatively affects the education, economics, and quality of life of the area. Meanwhile, at the outer rings, developing, largely white communities maintain their advantage through restrictive, low-density patterns of land use. In between these two areas lie the inner-ring suburbs, which suffer from both the exclusive development of the outer rings and the increased isolation of the urban core.

While current strategies of reinvestment in inner cities are meritorious, a regional approach to policy making is required in order to reduce polarization, stabilize the urban core and its immediate surroundings, and equalize the web of opportunities linked to housing.[68]

Regionalism offers policy makers a way to reconceptualize metropolitan areas for the common good of all residents. Instead of calling upon each jurisdiction within a region to take responsibility for itself, regionalism views the entire region as an organic system of interdependent parts. The whole will prosper only if all jurisdictions are able to. The surest way to equalize opportunities throughout the total metropolitan area is to create effective, visionary metropolitan governments or, if the region is too large, to require that all local governments pursue common policies.[69]

A regionalist approach traditionally fosters land-use reform that stems urban sprawl and provides adequate funding to older areas; "fair share" housing policies that encourage or, better yet, *require* the construction and maintenance of low- and moderate-income housing in all jurisdictions; housing assistance policies to disperse low-income families to small-unit, scattered-site housing projects and to rent-subsidized private rental housing throughout a diversified metro housing market; fair employment and housing policies that give persons of color full access to the job and housing markets; tax-base sharing arrangements between the central city and its suburbs;[70] welfare reform focusing on job creation and readiness; and, until affordable housing is available regionwide, lawsuits calling for adequate education in the inner-ring schools and metropolitan-wide desegregation.

Federal and state government can also foster regionalism,[71] but effective local regional bodies require the building of enduring political coalitions between the urban core and the inner-ring suburbs. They also require the active participation of communities of color. Yet regionalism often meets resistance from these very communities, who fear that dispersal of their members throughout an area will weaken their political and cultural power and do little to disrupt the existing white suburban opportunity structures.[72] Proponents of regionalism must present metropolitan efforts not as competition for resources and power, but as complementary to them. They must also convince these communities that regional opportunity-based housing strategies do not force minority communities to disperse but allow individuals a *real* choice to remain and find increased opportunities or to seek opportunities elsewhere.[73]

Adopting this frame of analysis and applying political pressure can result in policies and laws that promote opportunity-based housing throughout a metropolitan area. In the Twin Cities, for example, jurisdictions that receive Community Development Block Grant funding from the Department of Housing and Urban Development (HUD) came together in 2001 to produce a regional analysis of the impediments to fair housing choice. In the past, each jurisdiction receiving these funds prepared a separate assessment. By coordinating their efforts and seeking community input, individual jurisdictions are beginning to think of fair housing from a regional perspective.

Moreover, when a new development or policy is proposed, a regional impact assessment can also be made of the racial and economic status of the area. The particular needs and priorities of existing community members can be gathered through data analyses and qualitative methods, such as in-depth interviews with focus groups and public hearings. A nuanced determination, informed by affected communities, can then be made of the "match" or disconnect between projected outcomes of the proposal and the unique needs of community members. For example, if a mixed-income development made up of a certain number of units affordable at 50 percent of the median income is proposed, whether this level of affordability will genuinely be accessible to the existing residents can be determined. Whether it is linked to, or will lead to, the creation of other life opportunities can also be assessed. Alternative proposals must be allowed, along with discussion of the direct and indirect effects of each option throughout the region.

Because the location of opportunity structures, or the lack thereof, is geographical and socially situated in different ways throughout a metropolitan area, taking space into account is critical to this assessment process. That is, different racial, ethnic, and income groups experience opportunities differently and should be given the chance to determine which opportunities are critical to them and whether there is any growth in these areas over time. One way for these communities to assess and track these relationships is to map the location of affordable housing in relation to multiple opportunities across the metropolitan landscape.[74] "Opportunity maps" can also capture the unique characteristics and experiences of residents both within individual jurisdictions and in relation to entire regions, which can improve long-term regional planning. Finally, these maps can empower impoverished communities of color by providing them with convincing visual indicators of whether progress is being made.

California provides one example of an assessment process currently in use. State law provides that a "regional housing needs assessment" conducted by the state department of housing identify each locality's share of the regional housing need.[75] Localities are then required to respond to that allocation by developing appropriate plans for housing, including "land use plans and regulatory systems, which provide opportunities for, and do not unduly constrain, housing development."[76]

While regional analysis is essential, efforts must not stop there. Once stakeholders and community members are given the chance to assess housing needs, all levels of government should then employ tools to link opportunity structures to the affordable housing in meaningful ways. Several traditional strategies include fair-share housing mandates that require each municipality to account for its "fair share" of the regional affordable housing need; inclusionary zoning mandates that require new developments, particularly those with larger numbers of housing units, to set aside a portion of units for low-income tenants; or density bonuses that encourage the same result; linkage fees that are assessed on commercial or market rate residential developments to fund the creation of affordable housing;[77] and housing trust funds.

CREATIVELY LINKING HOUSING TO OTHER OPPORTUNITY STRUCTURES

It is not enough to increase affordable housing without considering where it is located within a region in relation to opportunity structures and to the particular needs of the various communities it serves. No one jurisdiction can provide the affordable housing needs of the region alone and survive (in terms of maintaining the necessary tax base, providing high-quality education, and ensuring employment of residents). Instead, housing must be created across the landscape and be deliberately tied to other opportunities.

MANAGING GENTRIFICATION AND SMART GROWTH

In order to facilitate equalizing of opportunities throughout a metropolitan region, it is necessary to mitigate gentrification and refine smart-growth policies. I argue that this must be done in an integrated fashion if it is to have meaning and coherence.

To begin with, regional policies that mitigate gentrification and prevent isolation from opportunity structures need to be developed and coordinated with fair housing policies.

I have proposed that different regions experience gentrification differently depending on whether they are rich or poor or somewhere in between. Gentrification in rich cities, with their corresponding lack of developable land, harms the impoverished residents more than gentrification in poor cities, with their many brownfields and abandoned housing units, and so the responses to these trends must differ.[78]

Smart-growth policies can be refined to lure investment into the communities most affected by the sprawl they attempt to control.[79] The benefits from luring development back to abandoned urban cores have been dubbed the "urban competitive" advantage.[80] As one scholar puts it, "The effects of current inequitable practices and policies could be reversed by smart growth policies that direct resources back to underutilized infrastructure, avert greenfield redevelopment, clean up abandoned industrial properties and redevelop poorly-maintained properties."[81] Through greater transit and housing choice, and fair and cost-effective development decisions, smart growth can be a useful tool in the achievement of opportunity-based housing.[82]

Maryland's Smart Growth and Neighborhood Conservation Initiative[83] has been recognized as the nation's first statewide, incentive-based program to reduce the impact of urban sprawl. It attempts to encourage economic growth while at the same time channeling it to those areas of the state where infrastructure and services are already in place to support it. In the end, the goal of the initiative is to foster inclusion and economically and racially diverse communities, not perpetuate gentrification and segregation.[84]

MAKING RACE-CONSCIOUS PLANS

However much we mitigate gentrification or refine smart growth, we will be unable to achieve regional equity without making race-conscious plans to integrate both housing and opportunities. Cara Hendrickson effectively argues this point by demonstrating how HUD's race-neutral Rule to Deconcentrate Poverty and Promote Integration in Public Housing[85] neither promotes fair housing nor addresses segregation.[86] The rule attempts to deconcentrate poverty by assigning higher-income tenants to lower-income buildings and lower-income tenants to higher-income buildings.[87] Like HOPE VI, however, this type of deconcentration effort is inadequate because of the dearth of moderate-income residents interested in the program and the plethora of low-income residents excluded from it.[88] Furthermore, the desired "rub-off" effect of higher-income neighbors remains unproven. Hendrickson argues that mixing income within a building alters neither the segregated, resource-depleted nature of the neighborhood nor the disparities between urban and suburban opportunity. A race-conscious, metropolitan-wide approach would be more effective.

LINKING AFFORDABLE HOUSING TO ACCESSIBLE EMPLOYMENT, TRANSPORTATION, AND CHILD CARE

To create the type of opportunity-based housing Hendrickson describes, it is essential to link it directly to accessible employment. One

way to do this is to target low-income tax credits to private developers willing to locate housing near employment and within transit-
oriented areas. States could enact a new policy to direct the incentives
available under the Low-Income Housing Tax Credit[89] program to
support an improved housing-to-jobs balance and provide greater ef-
ficiencies for businesses that need an available, proximate labor pool.
Just such an approach is being piloted in Chicago and two of its suburban counties.[90] The goal of the Regional Housing Initiative (RHI)
is to support the development or rehabilitation of well-managed,
well-designed, safe mixed-income housing located near jobs and
transit. Specifically, it attempts to meet the need for affordable housing for very-low-income households in areas of high job growth by
providing subsidies and tax credits to apartments that rent to these
households within a broader mixed-income community. In its pilot
phase, resources have been committed to finance 328 apartments
within mixed-income or supportive housing developments.[91]

An alternative way of increasing employment opportunity for
low-income households is to create jobs where affordable housing
currently exists. Smart-growth efforts to lure businesses back into the
inner cities can be accompanied by assessment, cleanup, and reuse of
contaminated brownfields. According the U.S. Conference of Mayors,
over half a million jobs could be created, and up to $2.4 billion in ad-
ditional tax revenues could be generated, through redevelopment.[92]

Another mechanism that merits consideration is employer-
assisted housing. Whether voluntary or provided for under municipal law, employer-assisted housing involves expanding the role of the
employer in helping lower-income households find affordable housing close to the job site. Typically, an employer may provide financial
assistance to employees purchasing homes nearby or directly provide
affordable housing to employees. In Minnesota, one employer that
recognized a lack of affordable housing near one of its job sites provided a construction loan to a developer to build a forty-eight-unit
structure accessible to company employees.[93] In the Chicago region,

participants in the Regional Employer-Assisted Collaboration for Housing provide a grant to employees toward a down payment on a home located near job sites, and organizations supporting this collaboration provide home-ownership counseling.[94] It is unclear what impact voluntary employer-assisted housing can have on the regional affordable housing need, but these efforts should be supported and strengthened by laws that require each sector of the region to provide its share of the regional affordable housing need. Importantly, employer-assisted housing should be guided by government and the civil rights community to reach the housing needs of all workers, and not exclusively moderate- and high-income workers, if opportunity-based housing is to be achieved.

Further assistance to purchase homes can be provided with federal subsidies that give priority to "location-efficient mortgages." Under such mortgages, the amount available to be loaned is a function of the degree to which the home is located in a transit-oriented location and not dependent on cars. This leaves owners with more disposable income and a greater capacity to make mortgage payments.[95] Increasing the minimum wage to make it a "livable wage" would also greatly improve the ability of families to secure safe, affordable housing.

Strategies that deal specifically with transportation could include allocating federal funding for inner-city light rail systems, trolleys, and streetcars instead of interstate highways[96] and instituting a grant program to enable community transit agencies to prepare for higher density and more mixed-use developments around transit stations.[97] The availability and quality of child care must also be addressed in attempting to link housing to employment and transportation.

LINKING EDUCATION OPPORTUNITIES

Increasing economic investment requires not only adequate housing but adequate schools as well. Because school desegregation between 1968 and 1973 doubled the rate of housing integration in twenty-five central cities with a black population of at least 100,000, school desegregation efforts should remain a priority. And because states generally have an obligation under their constitutions to provide all students with an adequate education, regional governments should attempt to achieve integration in the schools through mandatory metropolitan-wide efforts. State lawsuits could also be brought to ensure that this obligation is met.[98] Combined with smart growth and other regional efforts to locate housing near opportunity structures, these strategies could alleviate homelessness and inadequate schools and foster true integration.

IMPROVING HEALTH OPPORTUNITIES

Good health enables us to lead productive, fulfilling lives. While a comprehensive model for achieving good health is beyond the scope of this paper, we can identify strategies that attempt to address the social, spatial, and economic factors that affect health (income, housing, education, isolation, and transportation, for example). Indeed, the National Institutes of Health has declared the relationship among social status, race, and health to be one of its top goals. Responding to this, the Minnesota Department of Health constituted a Social Conditions and Health Action Team to identify the ways in which settings and systems outside the health sector affect health.[99]

Recognizing the impact of inequalities throughout various regions, the Minnesota team developed several action steps that are highly replicable. The first step is to conduct "health impact assessments" of policies, programs, and projects that potentially affect health, including community revitalization, public transportation, resource allocation, capital investment, and community participation.[100] Other recommended action steps link economic and community development to health improvement: fostering civic engagement and social capital; increasing the availability of safe and convenient parks to encourage recreation and neighborhood connections; improving family leave and high-quality child care efforts; reorienting funding to support innovative, long-term collaborative efforts; training more representative, culturally competent health care workforces. The team also calls for measures to remedy the discrimination and racism that limit access to unbiased medical care. This holistic approach to improving health could make great strides in increasing opportunity-based housing and full participation in society.

INCREASING DEMOCRATIC OPPORTUNITIES

To increase democratic opportunities even further, we need to reform our election system. West Germany and New Zealand have adopted proportional representation, whereby candidates win legislative seats in proportion to their share of the vote. Another approach, cumulative voting, gives each voter as many votes as there are seats to be filled. Voters are not limited to casting only one vote for the candidate of their choice, but can "plump" or cast all of their votes for one candidate if they have an intense preference for that candidate. This allows minority groups greater opportunity to win representation— even without being geographically districted together.[101] Instead, voters "district" themselves by the way they cast their votes.[102] Either system would open up the U.S. political process not just to impoverished racial minorities, but also to women, environmentalists, and all those with common interests who could then vote strategically. Either system would also preserve the political power of minority groups no matter where they chose to live.

In addition to voting reforms, increasing access to housing opportunity can have meaningful results for democratic participation. For example, a collaborative effort in the Santa Fe region to create affordable housing, increase home-ownership rates, and improve the physical condition of homes owned by low-income households resulted not only in enhanced assets for participants but also, according

to a survey of participants, in increased participation in neighborhood and civic structures.

COMMUNITY INVOLVEMENT AND ALLIANCE BUILDING

Community members have vital input to offer in assessing and planning any of the strategies described here. In the past, communities of
color did not have the opportunity to inform decisions on development and land use, and the result was that their interests were often
undermined. Certainly, the urban renewal policies implemented in
cities across the nation beginning in the 1950s are glaring examples
of this type of exclusion and its devastating effects on the lives and
neighborhoods of communities of color. Thinking regionally about
housing opportunity also requires forging alliances with other
constituencies—such as environmental groups—that have complementary interests in sound regional planning. The forces of fragmentation, segregation, and economic isolation are of such a scale in
the region that addressing opportunity concerns requires not only
combining forces but also building on and expanding beyond the
existing power base of advocates, communities, intermediaries and
academics, other sectors of civil society, and local government.

CONCLUSION

I have attempted to show that the interests of a broad base of stakeholders are affected by housing policy and that these players can be
engaged in and become resources for a movement toward opportunity-based housing. Because housing as an opportunity structure
interrelates with the structures of education, employment, transportation, and child care, among others, policy makers, advocates, and
community organizations working in these areas can be brought into
the discussion and made allies in the movement. In order to make

the necessary connections between these structures and to improve life chances for all residents of a region, we must build bridges beyond the housing sphere. No single jurisdiction can solve the housing problems, and no single organization can halt the forces of segregation, concentration of poverty, fragmentation, and gentrification. Instead we must work together on a regional level to achieve racial and economic equality in the form of opportunity-based housing.

NOTES

1. For a discussion of the ways in which governmental policies have produced segregation, see, generally, Douglas Massey and Nancy Denton, *American Apartheid: Segregation and the Making of the Underclass* (Cambridge, Mass.: Harvard University Press, 1993).
2. According to the U.S. Department of Housing and Urban Development (HUD), housing is affordable when all housing costs (rent or mortgage, utilities, property taxes, and insurance) do not exceed 30 percent of total household income. This standard applies to any person or household regardless of source or level of income. See U.S. Department of Housing and Urban Development, *Fiscal Year 1990 HUD Four-Person Very Low & Lower Income Limits and Area Median Family Income* (Sept. 15, 2000), available at www.huduser.org.
3. See National Low-Income Housing Coalition, *2000 Advocate's Guide to Housing and Community Development Policy,* available at www.nlihc.org.
4. See, for example, Susan J. Popkin and Mary J. Cunningham, *CHAC Section 8 Program: Barriers to Leasing Up* (April 1999), available at www.urban.org. See also Lynn E. Cunningham, "Managing Assets/Managing Families: Reconceptualizing Affordable Housing Solutions for Extended Families," *Journal of Affordable Housing & Community Development Law* 11 (2002), p. 390.
5. One-third of America's households are renters, yet our commitment to ensuring decent, safe, and affordable housing for every family has waned. National Low Income Housing Coalition, *Out of Reach 2002* (2002), p. 4, available at www.nlihc.org.
6. National Low Income Housing Coalition, *Out of Reach 2002: Press Release* (Sept. 18, 2002). The least affordable Metropolitan Statistical Areas and their housing wages are San Francisco, $37.31; San Jose, Calif., $33.85; Stamford-Norwalk, Conn., $27.62; Oakland, Calif., $26.42; Boston, $25.83. For a complete report for every jurisdiction, see www.nlihc.org.
7. *Id.*
8. Cara Hendrickson, "Racial Desegregation and Income Deconcentration in Public Housing," *Georgetown Journal on Poverty Law & Policy* 9 (2002), pp. 35, 55.
9. *Id.,* p. 56. For example, the government spends four times as much on mortgage interest and property tax deductions as it does on low-income housing.
10. See U.S. Department of Housing and Urban Development, *Homeownership and Opportunity for People Everywhere, Quality Housing and Work Responsibility Act of 1998,* Pub. L. No. 105–276, _ 35,112 Stat. 2641 (1998) (authorizing HUD to carry out HOPE VI).

11. See W. Pitcoff, "New Hope for Public Housing?" *Shelterforce Online* (March/April 1999), available at www.nhi.org.
12. HUD's threshold for a tight market is 6 percent.
13. Jonathan L. Hafetz, "Almost Homeless," *Legal Affairs,* July/Aug. 2002, p. 11.
14. Peter W. Salsich Jr., "Will the 'Free Market' Solve the Affordable Housing Crisis?" *Clearinghouse Review* 35 (2002), pp. 573, 577.
15. In Chicago, for example, the need for housing is increasing (there is a current gap of 113,000 units) even as the number of units is falling (over 13,000 Chicago Housing Authority units are slated for reduction in the next decade). It is predicted that 300,000 new units will be required to accommodate the growth in workers anticipated by the year 2020. See Michael Leachman et al., *Black, White, and Shades of Brown: Fair Housing and Economic Opportunity in the Chicago Region* (1998), p. 25; Metropolitan Planning Council, *For Rent: Housing Options in the Chicago Region* (Nov. 1999), p. 7; Chicago Metropolis 2020, *Regional Realities: Measuring Progress toward Shared Regional Goals* (2001), p. 32, available at www.chicagometropolis2020.org.
16. See Stacie Young, "Proxy for Discrimination: Vouchers in the Section 8 Housing Program," *Chicago Policy Review* 2 (1998), pp. 47–61 (for example, in the Chicago area, voucher holders of color have been found to experience discrimination at higher rates than whites who have vouchers, which raises serious concerns).
17. See U.S. Department of Housing and Urban Development, *1997 Picture of Subsidized Households,* available at www.huduser.org.
18. See U.S. Census Bureau, *Profile of General Demographic Characteristics for the United States* (2000), available at www.census.gov.
19. See Paul Fischer, *Section 8 and the Public Housing Revolution: Where Will the Families Go?* (July 1999), p. 2, available at www.metroplanning.org.
20. See *id.*
21. See *id.*
22. For example, a recent estimate put combined federal, state, and local investments in mainly new water and sewer facilities at $250 billion since 1970, which influences private real-estate markets toward exurban development. Daniel J. Hutch, "The Rationale for Including Disadvantaged Communities in the Smart Growth Metropolitan Development Framework," *Yale Law and Policy Review* 20 (2002), pp. 353, 359.
23. See Cameron Y. Yee et al., *There Goes the Neighborhood: A Regional Analysis of Gentrification and Community Stability in the San Francisco Bay Area* (1999), p. 17, available at www.urbanhabitat.org.
24. See Stephanie Shirley Post, "Metropolitan Area Governance Structure and Intergovernmental Cooperation: Can Local Governments in Fragmented Metropolitan Areas Cooperate?" (a paper delivered at the American Political Science Association annual meeting, Aug. 31–Sept. 1, 2000, Washington, D.C.), p. 13.
25. See, generally, David Rusk, *Cities without Suburbs* (Washington, D.C.: Woodrow Wilson Center Press, 1993); Alan Altshuler et al., eds., *Governance and Opportunity in Metropolitan America* (Washington, D.C.: National Academy Press, 1999), p. 31.
26. See john a. powell, "Sprawl, Fragmentation and the Persistence of Racial Inequality: Limiting Civil Rights by Fragmenting Space," in *Urban Sprawl: Causes, Consequences, and Policy,* ed. Gregory Squires (Washington, D.C.: Urban Institute Press, 2002).
27. Maureen Kennedy and Paul Leonard, *Dealing with Neighborhood Change: A Primer on Gentrification and Policy Choices* (April 2001), available at www.brookings.edu.

28. See *id.*
29. Dalton Conley, *Being Black, Living in the Red: Race, Wealth, and Social Policy in America* (Los Angeles: University of California Press, 1999), p. 17.
30. See, for example, George C. Galster, "Polarization, Place, and Race," *North Carolina Law Review* 71 (June 1993), p. 1421.
31. Conley, *supra* note 29, p. 61.
32. *Id.* For example, in the less than $15,000/year income bracket, blacks held no assets, while whites held $10,000.
33. *Id.,* p. 35.
34. *Id.,* p. 36.
35. *Id.,* p. 41.
36. See I.R.C. _ 163 (a) (1994).
37. See I.R.C. _ 25(a)-(b) (1994).
38. See U.S. Census Bureau, *Housing in Metropolitan Areas: Black Housing* (1995).
39. The National Housing Trust Fund Campaign, *2000–2002: About the Trust Fund Campaign,* available at www.communitychange.org.
40. See, for example, Richard Price and Edwin S. Mills, "Race and Residence in Earnings Determination," *Journal of Urban Economics* 17 (1985), pp. 1–18; and J. F. Kain, "The Spatial Mismatch Hypothesis: Three Decades Later," *Housing Policy Debate* 3(1992), p. 371.
41. See *id.*
42. These jobs require college degrees more than in any other submetropolitan area. See Michael Stoll et al., *Within Cities and Suburbs: Racial Residential Concentration and the Spatial Distribution of Employment Opportunities across Submetropolitan Areas* (1999), available at ideas.repec.org/PaperSeries.html.
43. Hutch, *supra* note 22, p. 358.
44. "[T]he time spent traveling per mile for black central city residents is twice that of suburban whites, partly because more whites use their own car to get to work than do blacks (69 percent for whites versus 43 percent for blacks) who are more dependent on public transportation." See *The Technological Reshaping of Metropolitan America* (1995), pp. 221–22, available at www.smartgrowth.org.
45. See J. Lee Kreader et al., *Scant Increases after Welfare Reform: Regulated Childcare Supply in Illinois and Maryland, 1996–1998* (2000), available at www.nccp.org/.
46. In 1999, 60 percent of working women had children under six. See National Council of Jewish Women, *Campaign for Quality, Affordable Childcare,* available at www.ncjw.org.
47. See M. Whitebook et al., *Who Cares? Childcare Teachers and the Quality of Care in America* 8 (1989), available at www.childcarecanada.org/index.html.
48. See Ellen Hart-Shegos, *Homelessness and Its Effect on Children* (1999), available at www.fhfund.org/index.
49. See Megan Sandel et al., *There's No Place Like Home: How America's Housing Crisis Threatens Our Children* (1997), available at www.housingamerica.net/.
50. See *id.*
51. See Sandel et al., *supra* note 49.
52. See William T. Trent, "Outcomes of School Desegregation: Findings from Longitudinal Research," *Journal of Negro Education* 66 (1997), p. 256.
53. Stephen J. Schellenberg, "Concentration of Poverty and the Ongoing Need for Title I," in *Hard Work for Good Schools: Facts Not Fads in Title I Reform,* ed. Gary Orfield & Elizabeth H. DeBray (Washington, D.C.: Brookings Institution, 1999).

54. See Gary Orfield, *Schools More Separate: Consequence of a Decade of Resegregation* (Cambridge, Mass.: Harvard Civil Rights Project, July 2001).
55. See *What Matters Most: Teaching for America's Future: Summary Report* (Spring 1996), available at www.nctaf.org/.
56. See Kati Haycock et al., "Closing the Gap: Done in a Decade," *Thinking K-16* 2 (Spring 2001), pp. 3–22.
57. See Michal Kurlaender and John T. Yun, "Is Diversity a Compelling Educational Interest? Evidence from Louisville," in *Diversity Challenged: Evidence on the Impact of Affirmative Action,* ed. Gary Orfield and Michal Kurleander (Cambridge, Mass.: Harvard Education Publishing Group, 2001).
58. See William T. Trent, "Outcomes of School Desegregation: Findings from Longitudinal Research," *Journal of Negro Education* 66 (1997), pp. 255–57.
59. See Kurlaender and Yun, *supra* note 57.
60. Amy Stuart Wells, "The 'Consequences' of School Desegregation: The Mismatch between the Research and the Rationale," *Hastings Constitutional Law Quarterly* 28 (2001), pp. 771, 773.
61. *Id.*
62. Robert Crain and Amy Stuart Wells, "Perpetuation Theory and the Long-Term Effects of Schools Desegregation," *Review of Educational Research* 531 (Winter 1994); M. Dawkins and J. H. Braddock, "The Continuing Significance of Desegregation: School Racial Composition and African American Inclusion in American Society," *Journal of Negro Education* 53 (1994), p. 394.
63. Juanita Marie Holland, "Touring Cancer Alley," *Africana* (June 21, 2001), available at www.africana.com.
64. Minnesota Department of Health, *Social Conditions and Health Action Team, A Call to Action: Advancing Health for All through Social and Economic Change, Executive Summary* (2001), p. 3, available at www.health.state.mn.us.
65. See Pew Partnership, *More Than Bricks and Mortar: Housing That Builds Community,* available at www.pew-partnership.org.
66. 43 U.S.C.A. _ 1973 et. seq.
67. Lani Guinier, "Making Every Vote Count," *The Nation,* Dec. 4, 2000.
68. See Myron Orfield and David Rusk, *Metropolitics* (New York: Brookings Institution, 1997).
69. Myron Orfield, a Minnesota legislator, calls this process of achieving regionalism "metropolitics." See, generally, Orfield and Rusk, *supra* note 68, pp. 104–55. Numerous metropolitan regions across the country acknowledge the regional nature of the housing market and the affordable housing need.
70. See Orfield and Rusk, *supra* note 68, pp. 11, 87–90; Rusk, *supra* note 25, pp. 85–87, 123.
71. Rusk, *supra* note 25, pp. 90–115.
72. Cornel West, *Keeping Faith: Philosophy and Race in America* (1993), p. 282; Orfield, *supra* note 68, p. 169; Lani Guinier, "More Democracy," *University of Chicago Legal Forum* 1, 6 (1995).
73. Orfield and Rusk, *supra* note 68, p. 169.
74. For a more detailed explanation of "opportunity mapping," visit www.umn.edu/irp.
75. See Brian Augusta, "Building Affordable Housing from the Ground Up: Strengthening California Law to Ensure Adequate Locations for Affordable Housing," *Santa Clara Law Review* 39 (1999), pp. 503, 509.
76. See California Department of Housing and Community Development, Housing Elements, available at www.hcd.ca.gov.

77. See Jaimie Ross, *Affordable Housing Production: Don't Just Think Money—Think Land Use* (2000), available at www.1000friendsofflorida.org.
78. See powell, *supra* note 26.
79. Hutch, *supra* note 22, pp. 362–70.
80. For example, one study found that inner-city communities have an unmet market potential of $85 billion. *Id.* p. 363.
81. *Id.*
82. For a more detailed account of the use of current federal statutes and executive orders to implement this type of smart growth, See *id.,* p. 363.
83. The 1997 smart-growth legislation included the following bills: Brownfields— Voluntary Cleanup and Revitalization Programs, 1997 Md. Laws 1; Job Creation Tax Credit Act, 1997 Md. Laws 756; Smart Growth and Neighborhood Conservation—Rural Legacy Program, 1997 Md. Laws 758; Smart Growth and Neighborhood Conservation-Smart Growth Areas, 1997 Md. Laws 759.
84. Parris Glendening, "Maryland's Smart Growth Initiative: The Next Steps," *Fordham Urban Law Journal* 29 (2002), pp. 1493, 1503–4.
85. 24 C.F.R. _ 903 (2001).
86. Hendrickson, *supra* note 8, p. 36.
87. 24 C.F.R. _ 903.2 (a)-(c). (2001).
88. Hendrickson, *supra* note 8, p. 76.
89. First created by the Tax Reform Act of 1986, Pub. L. 98–369, Title IV, Subtitle B, July 18, 1984, 98 Stat. 793, LIHTC credits were increased by 40 percent in 2001.
90. Cook and Lake Counties. Mary Sue Barrett, president, Metropolitan Planning Council (MPC), Peter Dwars, executive director, Illinois Housing Development Authority, *Letter to Colleagues,* 2002.
91. *Id.*
92. Hutch, *supra* note 22, p. 364.
93. See Greater Minnesota Housing Fund, *Employer Assisted Housing: Minnesota Examples,* available at www.gmhf.com.
94. See Metropolitan Planning Council, *The Regional Employer-Assisted Collaboration for Housing,* available at www.metroplanning.org.
95. Hutch, *supra* note 22, p. 365.
96. "Portland Cited as Model for Regional Planning, Smart Growth," *HDR Current Developments* 30: 6 (July 2002), p. 9.
97. *Id.*
98. It is important to note that desegregation efforts, which are assimilative, do not always lead to true integration, which is transformative. Additional efforts must be taken to alter regional, local, and school-level structures that perpetuate assimilation.
99. *Call to Action, supra* note 64, pp. 1–3.
100. *Id.,* pp. 3–8.
101. Richard L. Engstrom and Robert R. Brischetto, "Is Cumulative Voting Too Complex? Evidence from Exit Polls," *Stetson Law Review* 27 (1998), pp. 813, 815. The authors conclude in this article that cumulative voting is actually easier than other forms of election.
102. Lani Guinier and Stephen Carter, *The Tyranny of the Majority: Fundamental Fairness in Representative Democracy* (New York: Free Press, 1994), p. 15.

PROFESSOR POWELL is a nationally recognized authority in the areas of civil rights, civil liberties, and issues relating to race, poverty, and the law. He holds the Gregory H. Williams Chair in Civil Rights and Civil Liberties and is executive director of Ohio State University's Institute for Race and Ethnicity in the Americas. Prior to joining the faculty at Ohio State University in 2002, Professor powell held the Earl R. Larson Chair of Civil Rights and Civil Liberties at the University of Minnesota and was executive director of the Institute on Race and Poverty. He has taught at Columbia University School of Law, Harvard Law School, University of Miami School of Law, American University, and the University of San Francisco School of Law. Professor powell teaches civil rights, poverty law, and jurisprudence.

A BURDEN, A BLESSING

TONY HISS

Author and urban scholar Tony Hiss recounts his travels with Dan Burden, a city and town-center revivalist who tirelessly crisscrosses the United States helping citizens reclaim their communities by making physical changes that rebalance the spirit and the hopes of a place.

The spring night was dark; sudden rain lashed the windshield of the rented car; dense fog came and went, swirling trickily up from nowhere; and for almost an hour it was hard to see if the slick, twisty mountain road ahead had any plan to its wanderings, any destination at all. Inside, at the wheel, Dan Burden—who's been called, by one of his hundreds of recent clients, "the Johnny Appleseed of livable communities"—drove forward as confidently as if he were entering his own driveway and talked buoyantly about his work and his vision of the slowly emerging postsprawl American future.

Dan Burden's enthusiasm for the bright twenty-first-century landscape he sees looming ahead is strong and steadfast; he seems already a resident of a future that, for many, still only occasionally flickers into sight. People's optimism about sprawl, I find, often wavers when they talk about the evidence their senses bring—the clutter, confusion, and congestion they see twice a day or more through their own windshields. It falters again when they reach inside themselves to describe the absences sprawl imposes on our lives. Sprawl steals from us time, choice, and closeness, not just space.

We are not only farther away from schools and shops, from friends and neighbors, from fields and woods than many of our parents and grandparents were; more and more of each day is given over to a tense, effortful, unnourishing, and for now unavoidable in-betweenness. This townless, countryless, roadbound running around stretches us thin; our bodies are in motion—but what is there around us, out there on the highways, to anchor our hearts and minds?

In the Atlanta area, for instance—cited in a recent study by urban planners at Wayne State University in Detroit as the most grievously sprawled corner of the country—many suburban commuters now spend more than three hours on weekdays in traffic. Once they're home, these office commuters can't stop, except to switch hats, becoming family taxi drivers, fetching children and running errands. The average American family, in Atlanta and nationally—as Dan Burden often reminds people—makes fourteen car trips a day.

More and more time in the car, which at first seemed a small price to pay for pleasant suburban homes, becomes an almost intolerable burden when it occupies twenty to thirty hours and requires eighty to ninety drives each week. Under these circumstances, people are no longer driving, they're driven. U.S. gas consumption increased 25 percent in the 1990s. More farmland and woods—16 million acres—got converted to urban uses between 1993 and 1997 than in the entire decade of the 1980s.

Under these circumstances, the most common experience of sprawl is, not surprisingly, of a "worsening" in America. It is harder to stay focused on the genuine awakening that has paralleled it. In the 1990s, a number of new, and newly rediscovered, ways of building nonsprawl neighborhoods began to be more widely talked about and, here and there, put into practice. They go by many names: smart growth, sustainable development, community building, town building, place-based conservation, community-based planning, livable communities, the New Urbanism.

Burden himself seems to be part of a suddenly arrived, brand-new profession. Perhaps half a dozen groups of itinerant designers and facilitators—almost enough to constitute a brand-new profession—are now crisscrossing the country conducting workshops with residents to explore the possibilities of changing local streets and buildings in ways that would add pleasure and reassurance to their towns, making it easier for people to meet up with one another and stay in touch with each other's lives.

For the past few years, I've been hearing an increasing number of glowing reports about how Burden's rapid-fire and unorthodox interventions have been helping communities regain their confidence to work cooperatively and draw up plans for their own place in a postsprawl America. In 1996 he set up a nonprofit called Walkable Communities, Inc., with his wife, Lys, who answers the phones at their home in Florida. Since then he's worked with almost a thousand communities—some urban, some suburban—across forty-one states. Burden's goal is to transform communities and strengthen existing towns so they can fight sprawl from within.

Does a town become more lovable as it becomes more livable? Can we find a balance between cars and people? What about the even trickier balance between land and cars and people? Can developers and local officials move from blueprints to "greenprints," so that a town's growth plans add green space to people's lives, instead of taking it away? These are only a few of the many questions that Burden tackles with his clients, who range from small towns like Stevensville, Montana, with about a thousand inhabitants, to University Place, in Tacoma, Washington—a neighborhood of 30,000 people. He's also worked in Raleigh, North Carolina, a state capital with more than 200,000 residents, and in Phoenix, Honolulu, Detroit, Chicago, Orlando, Dallas, and twenty separate communities within Los Angeles.

In 1999, Burden spent all of eight days in his own neighborhood. Clearly, he's a man in demand. Burden, who is fifty-seven, has only one inviolable rule: he's in bed every night, wherever he is, on the dot of 9:30 local time. In every community he visits, Burden instantly and unobtrusively sets up a nonauthoritarian atmosphere: he comes off like a man of average height, for instance, though he's six feet, three inches, by making a point of wearing disarmingly colorful shirts and bold, goofy ties; he also sports a jaunty, Captain Kangaroo–sized mustache. It's more than mood-making—it's a point that gets across without words. Burden doesn't say, "Stop looking for experts and leaders, and listen to yourselves." Still, in the whirlwind conversations he convenes, towns redesign themselves.

When I got in touch with Burden, he said he'd be delighted to have me follow him around on his travels. His only stipulation was that I couldn't simply watch; I had to participate, like everyone else. He'd been invited to spend five days in Watsonville, a predominantly Latino California community in the middle of a strikingly beautiful farming valley near Monterey Bay, talking to its citizens—all of them, if possible—about their town's future. So in March 1999 I became the junior member of his Watsonville team, which also included a frequent collaborator, Ramon Trias, a thirty-three-year-old Spanish-born architect and planner, who's director of development for Fort Pierce, a Watsonville-sized city on the Atlantic coast of Florida. Some of the meetings would be bilingual.

On the winding drive to Watsonville, Burden said Watsonville was worth special attention because people there were taking on some deep and lasting American concerns about how to find balance and fairness in a community. Watsonville, a historic, struggling, and largely working-class city surrounded by prosperous farms, has for generations been one of the few places in Santa Cruz County where successive waves of immigrant farmworkers and packing plant workers—first Chinese and Japanese, then Portuguese, and now largely Mexican and Salvadorean—could find affordable housing.

Many small Watsonville bungalows and cottages are homes for up to twenty-five people apiece, and the city has a growing middle class as well. If the city expands, it would, like so many other American communities, displace prime farmland. The Watsonville area's ocean-cradled cool climate is another spectacular asset: farm fields can produce three crops a year, and, as residents like to say, "Drive ten miles east of here in summer, and you'll turn your air conditioner on; and then keep it on all the rest of the way across America."

What makes Watsonville unusual is that it's one of the few places in the country where nearby farming interests—in this case farmers who depend on labor that comes from the city—have for many years been strong enough to hold the forces of urbanization at bay. Traditionally, Watsonville administrations have been strongly progrowth. Now some people were wondering if the city could begin to reach out to its neighbors' needs by doing what it could to live more comfortably within its de facto growth boundaries.

Burden said that Watsonville clearly proved that smart-growth thinking was in no way merely a white, landed, middle-class movement. If all went well during his time in town, Watsonville's citizens would begin to redesign two pieces of the place: a hard-pressed, densely settled stretch of lower downtown, and a still-empty tract at the city's eastern outskirts that previously had been talked about as the site for a conventional kind of subdivision (a form of in-town sprawl), and might instead become a newly formed neighborhood with shops, parks, and a mix of larger and smaller homes.

The road these days is probably the only place where it's possible to have a long, contemplative chat with Burden. In the car we spoke about the increasing urgency of his work, but also about the excitement he finds in people who are ready to work together for change. Burden thinks the United States, in putting down roots for a new flowering, finds itself in the midst of a historic transition period that will occupy the first ten or fifteen years of the twenty-first century. At the end of that time, many of us—perhaps most of us, Burden seems confident—will open our front doors to dramatically more sustainable and more pleasurable communities.

"Take one step back from the 'worsening' people are seeing," Burden said. "What's new, and still largely invisible, is the dismay so many people now experience when they see something going badly wrong in their communities. It can hit so sharply they simply can't walk away from it. I'd call this a ripening, as well as a worsening— a new readiness to take charge of a town's future."

And the process of change, he thinks, necessarily takes quite a while. We're tied, for instance, to only slowly altered sets of regulations about zoning, and to the long-term cycles of investment decisions that take at least ten years to modify and redirect. The good and the bad, as Burden sees it, are both signs that the same great undertaking is moving forward. "Whenever change is going on," Burden continued, "some things are dipping to new lows, while others are rising to incredible heights. I tell my audiences that Schopenhauer long ago defined the three stages all new ideas go through: ridicule, violent opposition, and acceptance. I've never yet seen a single step skipped in any community."

Peering through the fog as he drove toward Watsonville, Burden said that if he had to adopt a colorful nickname, Johnny Applebloom would come closer than Appleseed. "What you're going to see," he went on, "is only the middle of something. Seeds and sprouting—all that precedes me. The fruit and the harvest will arrive some time after I've left town." Burden said there's no point in his entering any town until it's already worked hard by itself for a year or more. "That kind of effort," he told me, "is completely invisible to outsiders. And then it's ready for a week or so of clean thinking about its own future."

Towns on the rebound, Burden said, often have to go through several local elections to find new city managers who believe in better days ahead. They also need what he calls a "spark plug," someone either in or out of government for whom recapturing the community has become a full-time passion. "Decay is very visible," Burden said reflectively. "It's time to see the strong forces that will help move us beyond it."

▶ ▶ ▶

Our first day in Watsonville, we had an early breakfast with Martin Carver, an entrepreneurial young city planner who had been the "spark plug" to energize the community and bring Burden to town. When it turned out the city budget was already stretched and had no leftover funds for a week of talking about the future, Carver had snagged both a regional air quality grant and a federal energy efficiency grant to make it all happen.

Carver had a big smile on his face at breakfast. "We were ready for Dan's arrival," he told me later, "because a creative kind of frustration has been building for some time. After almost thirty years of stalemate between progrowth forces, who see the need for decent housing for local people, and the antigrowth forces, who see the importance of protecting farmland and who've been trying to prevent spillover from the still explosive sprawl growth in Silicon Valley just north of us, it was getting clear that both sides were right. And when people are beginning to reach out to each other, Dan's bounce and pep and lack of guile can be like sun on a seedling."

Carver said he'd had a couple of hopes that morning: "Short term, I was eager to see a couple of demonstration projects launched, one downtown, one out on the outskirts of town; and longer term, I wanted to see the vocabulary of smart growth become the common, and bilingual, language for all future local discussions." Right after breakfast, Burden put us all to work: we held three informal hour-and-a-half meetings, all well attended, in the big, barn-roofed downtown community center. We listened, first, to policemen and social service providers from a downtown "problem-solving partnership" that in the past few years had helped defuse what had become a serious gang problem.

In another meeting, we heard from city council members and other policy makers; the third was with people from the public works and fire departments. Burden, I could see, is an extraordinary listener, leaning forward, smiling encouragingly, hearing both words and voice tones, and carefully studying body language. Most of the few comments he made were requests for further information about what mattered most to people in their town. (He had told us before-hand that we were students, and the townspeople our instructors, so for the moment I participated by staying quiet, watching people become eloquent as Burden listened to them.)

Burden's idea is that once people start talking more candidly with outsiders in small peer groups they can then talk more easily with each other in public. Some of the things we were hearing in these nonconfrontational warm-up meetings, as Burden told me afterward, come up in almost every town he's ever worked with. Nationally, for example, several generations of firefighters have grown up thinking they can't get to fires on time except over forty-foot-wide, suburban-style streets (Burden's laptop has a video of fire engines racing to a fire through eighteen-foot streets).

Other things we heard were wholly unexpected—for instance, an insight the town's social service providers had gained from working with the Salvadorean community clustered around Front Street in the lower downtown area, most of them refugees from 1980s cold war violence in their country (Watsonville's current mayor is himself Salvadorean). Many immigrant communities, of course, are naturally suspicious of authorities, but in this case the social workers, rather than responding just with typical American optimism and energy, had learned to reach out to their clients by honoring and respecting their fears. "Fear," we were told, "had been a survival tool—in El Salvador, during the troubles, it was often the only force that could keep a family close together, and off the streets and away from gunfire."

From what was said both at the meetings and, even more infor-mally, out in the hallways between the meetings, it became apparent that what Watsonville residents were most vocal about—more and better housing, whether on open land or as redevelopment downtown—was part of a larger effort to heal a whole succession of wounds and create a town that could work for everyone. In 1986, three years before the Loma Prieta earthquake physically rearranged much of the town, a frozen-food packagers' strike by Latino broccoli and cauliflower packers had organized the town's mostly poorer Latino majority for the first time; this led, not long afterward, to redistricting that brought the first Latino representatives to the city council. After that, the old Anglo elite had felt distanced from downtown and started spending and investing its money elsewhere.

The strike also had economic consequences. Green Giant, a major employer, left town. Then came the earthquake, and then the prolonged business downturn that gripped most of California in the early 1990s. The adjacent lower downtown area around Front Street, which in the past year had been confronted (and almost dissected) by a new high-speed, state-built bridge across the Pajaro River at the southern edge of Watsonville that was far longer and taller than the bridge it replaced, was itself only very slowly recovering from its World War II days as a red-light district for servicemen from nearby Fort Ord, when fifty-seven bars had been crowded into three short blocks. (It had gotten as far as demolishing many of the most notorious bars, but so far, except for a Burger King and a few convenience stores, not too many new businesses had moved in.)

After all the meetings, I persuaded a man from public works to take us up onto the ten-foot-high levee along the Pajaro River (a small ridge that in such flat land confers sweeping vistas). It was there that I began to get my own ideas about how Watsonville could shape its future. The levee system—it also runs along a tributary river that serves as the eastern edge of town—forms a human-made network of high ground that holds the town in its embrace and also extends into the open land just beyond the city: the fields to the east and protected, wild wetland sloughs that run west down to the ocean.

The most densely settled parts of town are desperate for new parkland and recreational space. The levee, parts of which have already been opened as a bike path, is the only place anywhere around from which you can instantly see the interconnectedness of everything. Shouldn't that perspective start nourishing everyone's lives?

That evening, in a fully bilingual meeting, Burden presented a slide show for Front Street residents about what other turn-around American cities have been accomplishing and then opened the floor for a general discussion of Front Street issues. He ended the session with one of his favorite quotes, from the Australian transportation reformer David Engwicht: "Cities are an invention to maximize exchange—goods, culture, friendship, ideas, and knowledge—and to minimize travel." The turnout was high and, I noticed, included a number of families who came as full groups—grandparents who chatted with each other, parents who quietly offered suggestions, and small children who sat still, staring at the slides. Perhaps fear was still an organizing force, but no longer an immobilizing one.

The next day we had a second go-round with the firemen and public works folks. In meetings that followed, we touched base with high school students who lived downtown (they wanted to see a wider levee as a park for downtown, and bike paths throughout the town, and a final end to bars and liquor stores); with property owners and developers (they were worried about whether sustainable housing would sell; this was also the first group where cell phones kept ringing); and with a mixed group of farmers and environmentalists (who kept asking how it would be possible to build houses, create jobs, and save the land, all at the same time). I had to chair the last meeting, with the enviros, and nervously did exactly what I'd watched Burden doing: make sure everyone present both spoke and was heard.

Throughout both days, despite the seriousness of the issues, we saw a bubbling-up of energy and enthusiasm for tackling a couple of pressing city problems. The downtown bridge emerged as one big issue. People spoke their minds, listened to each other without rancor, and scribbled down suggestions: Couldn't the traffic somehow be slowed on the bridge? The bridge was so low-slung—wasn't there some way to dig out a new river's-edge pathway underneath it, so people on both sides could be reconnected along the riverside levee?

Open land also surfaced as an important issue. If open land had to be built on, couldn't it be constructed as a new neighborhood organized around a new park for active recreation? And couldn't the new homes also, at their back, have community walkways along the fingers of the sloughs that stretch up into the city? In decades past, many sloughs had been ploughed and planted, but they're now protected and fully recovered wetlands teeming with ducks and otters. (The fields beyond the sloughs have also changed character; when the big packers left town after the 1986 strike, fresh produce, like lettuce and strawberries, began to replace fruit and vegetables planted for canning or juice. Ancient orchards—Martinelli's cider has been produced in town since 1868—disappear every year.)

Some initially resisted the talk of neighborhood building, insisting that the only new housing that either lenders or buyers were interested in was standard subdivision large-lot single-family homes. City engineers began by saying that, whatever houses might get built, the central feature of the new development should be an all-new, four-lane, fifty-two-foot-wide highway. With so much potential contentiousness, what was it that encouraged cooperation to blossom in these meetings? I began to see that change can begin when a town starts to ask why it has been doing things to harm itself. It's the kind of simple question that changes the destiny of a town, melting decades of unexamined assumptions. But getting from dissatisfaction to action seems to depend on an awareness of both what to do differently and how to get started.

Dan Burden's presentations are mostly a matter of the *whats* people hadn't known existed. He explains traffic-calming treatments that Americans are importing from successful efforts in Europe and

Australia. These include the "boulevarding" of busy streets—adding landscaped medians and street trees that slow traffic by reminding drivers they have entered a place that people care about. Another topic is "road dieting," which means shrinking a four-lane road back down to two-lane size; and also "bulbouts," which are intersections you can walk across more easily, because the sidewalks get wider as they approach the corner.

Much of this *what* stuff is truly eye-opening. For instance, using the physics of traffic movements to explain why a small roundabout can work more smoothly than a standard, four-way intersection: in a roundabout, there are only eight "conflict points" where cars moving in different directions might potentially collide with one another; a four-way intersection has thirty-two conflict points. Or the finding that even intense police ticketing blitzes can't reduce speeds on roads whose wide-lane straightaways have already announced to drivers that it's okay to go fast. Burden cited a case in point: two similar, nondescript roads he worked on in University Place, in Tacoma, Washington, where people routinely drove forty-four miles an hour, despite posted speed limits of thirty-five. When local police wrote 300 traffic tickets in two weeks on one of the roads, speeds there dropped to forty—but only temporarily. When the neighborhood rebuilt the other road with narrower lanes and added bike lanes, sidewalks, and trees, speeds immediately dropped to thirty-one miles an hour, and, without police work, have stayed that way.

When you hear these stories there's an unusual kind of "aha! moment"—because what you're feeling is the "Oh, of course!" drivers sense when roads remind them that, like everyone else, they're just people moving through a community, in the same dance with the folks on foot or on bikes or standing still at a street corner. (Burden sometimes says a car is the only machine that can let a mouse pretend that it's a rhinoceros.)

But these stories are only the quantifiable half of what Burden passes along every time he starts talking with and listening to a town.

Working with Ramon Trias, Burden has been quietly reinventing a critical piece of democracy, creating a twenty-first-century version of the nineteenth-century town meeting. Without calling attention to it, he sets up a new forum of public decision making that moves people away from the poisoned, argumentative, frustrating debates so common at most public hearings—where people almost always are merely responding to someone else's predetermined ideas for change.

Echoing a famous old children's story, Burden sometimes calls his new kind of town get-together "stone soup." In the story, three hungry soldiers, returning empty-handed from a devastating war, genially trick a group of suspicious villagers into acting with generosity, cooperation, and compassion. Pleading poverty, the villagers refuse to feed the soldiers, whereupon the soldiers reply that in that case they will, all by themselves, feast the entire village on a dish fit for a king: stone soup. All they need is an enormous kettle filled with water, and a fire. When the villagers bring these, the soldiers ceremoniously drop in a carefully selected, round field stone.

The villagers, agog, watch the soldiers taste the broth. "Excellent," says the leader. "Of course, it would taste much better with some carrots—that way it would surpass even the soup we served the king. Too bad you don't have any. Oh, well."

A villager scurries off and returns with some extra-sweet carrots he's been hoarding. Small generous gestures start to add up. The soldiers then coax potatoes, beef, and all sorts of other good food from the excited villagers, who proclaim the banquet that follows the best meal they've ever eaten. "And to think," they say, still marveling, "that all this bounty came only from a stone!"

In the story, the soldiers evoke more than greed. And Burden's altruistic brand of sneakiness brings forward the same generosity, cooperation, and compassion. His trick is to offer such an enticing smorgasbord of chances to join in that everyone feels personally invited and responsible for the outcome. For people who talk more candidly in private, he convenes "focus groups," such as the sessions we held with the developers and property owners. For those who like lectures, he puts on a slide show—and adds a town vote on priorities. People walk to the front of the room armed with old-fashioned colored dots, which they stick on lists they've just generated.

In addition to dots, Burden cagily uses the latest high-tech gadgets. A former *National Geographic* photographer, he carries a digital camera on his walking tours of the cities he's been invited to. Since his slide shows are now computerized PowerPoint presentations, he can easily slide in photos of things he's seen around town that very afternoon. And he includes same-day shots of people who have turned up for just-barely-adjourned focus groups.

Burden's strategy also includes "walking audits," guided tours of a neighborhood that let people see for themselves how pleasant or arduous it is to make their way around town; and, at the heart of everything, a "design workshop," stone soup on the simmer, an afternoon-long session on the second or third day of a Burden visit at which groups of seven or eight people sit around tables and rethink and redraw the shape of their town. The sum of all these activities constitutes a process Burden calls a "charrette," or sometimes a "vision charrette."

Charrette, which means "little cart" in French, is an old architectural term that originally was a joking way of talking about students working feverishly up to the last moment, even inside the small wagons carting them off to their final exams. By extension, it's become a word for a concentrated team approach to a design project; and in recent years New Urbanist architects have used the charrette as a vehicle for bringing their new design concepts to larger audiences.

Burden and Trias have given the charrette a new twist: the professionals on hand have climbed down off the podium to become conversation starters and interested friends, not authorities. This mental jujitsu outwits the pessimism that Burden says is often lodged in many communities, even after they've started bouncing back from despair.

Years of watching things go sour, accompanied by years of not being able to talk productively about the situation, have left behind fears, suspiciousness, and a widespread set of assumptions, including: people can't agree; they don't know what to do; they have to rely solely on experts for ideas on how to improve town life.

The charrette gives a community a taste of what it's like to nourish itself again. It's an extended, four- or five-day-long moment that's one part revitalization, one part revivalism. As people pool their energies and resourcefulness, there's no time to stop and think about how the group they're in never existed before, at least not for the past generation. "It's always a lot of the fun," says Burden, "when people work in concert toward a dream and suddenly realize they actually like all those rotten people they've been arguing with for the past ten years."

The nudge that led Burden to his insight about community pessimism traces back forty years. Immediately before founding Walkable Communities, he served for sixteen years as Florida's first bicycle and pedestrian coordinator. But long ago, in high school, in Columbus, Ohio, he sat in study hall daydreaming of traveling around the world by bike. After college and four years in the Navy, Burden, along with Lys (who'd been his high school sweetheart) and another couple, lived a north-south half of this dream by spending the next three years bicycling from Alaska to Argentina.

"The long trip south was when I first began to feel connected to life, and life processes," Burden says. "The big surprise was that, in every place we passed through, danger was always perceived as being elsewhere. Close by, but elsewhere. No matter what kind of community or what part of the countryside we landed in for the night—it could be prosperous and smiling, or desperately impoverished—kindly people, always aghast, invariably asked us the same two questions about where we'd come from and where we were headed: 'You came through *there*? You're going *there*?'"

You could tell where *here* ended and *there* began by mapping where the fear line fell between what people felt they could trust and what they had no sympathy for. Burden thinks there's probably a similar sprawl line in many of us: the faster that communities change, the more that many people, deep inside, start pulling back into a safe zone that sometimes shrinks down till it's no larger than the few streets they know best, or maybe only as big as their own house and yard. Almost everything else becomes a *there,* or at best an *in-between*—a compromised, diminished, untrustworthy, no-longer-cherished landscape.

▶ ▶ ▶

Dan Burden's charrette in Watsonville helped recover and expand the *heres.* When I got home to New York City, I looked over the vision statements that Watsonville residents had constructed for their two problem areas: the disrupting bridge and the huge greenfield site on the edge of town. Reading them, I was struck by how quickly and generously people had moved beyond thinking up narrow solutions and had started caring about, and taking on responsibility for, some big, tough, remarkably complex *heres.*

The bridge report, for instance, transforms the bisecting span into a ceremonial gateway to town by adding a landscaped median that slows traffic and alerts drivers that they are entering a place where people live and not just cruising through space. And it incorporates the Front Street residents' idea of excavating land under the bridge to restore an old riverbank path that had been inadvertently cut in two. Then the report talks about building new and affordable housing on the site of a trailer park, and converting an old vinegar factory into more new housing. A few questions were also asked in the report: Why don't we, before anything else, build some temporary housing so people can immediately have a decent place to live? And while we're at it, why can't we tackle Main Street with beautification and traffic-calming projects, and build a few "pocket parks" that neighborhood residents themselves will design?

The report on the outlying site suggested that it should be developed, but not as originally planned. It would not be a standard series of isolated suburban tract-home developments interspersed with conventional big-box retail shopping centers, with a fast, four-lane highway right smack through the middle of it. In the report it re-emerged as a new kind of country-threaded city neighborhood, with a mix of housing and shopping and a large plaza at its center, echoing the beautiful historic plaza that anchors downtown. It would be tied to Main Street and downtown through a two-lane road (no four-laners), and a neighborhood greenway network would take residents out into and along two still-wild wetland sloughs; no wetlands would be lost in the deal.

Martin Carver, the city planner who had initiated the charrette process, still seems pleased by the outcome. He's moved on from Watsonville, at least officially—he runs Coastplans.com, a private planning firm in nearby Santa Cruz, and now acts as a spark plug for a much larger area up and down the coast—but he stays in close touch with Watsonville events. "Bringing Dan in was a very positive experience," he told me. "Nothing's harder than growing up in your thinking about growth, and I can see Dan's presence even in his absence—meaning that the process of rethinking the town, after so many years of stalemate, has been getting both shorter and less painful. I can't say wrangling has vanished—the idea of building a twenty-four-foot wide, two-lane street, for instance, is still being vigorously contested. But there's a thaw, a warmth. Everyone loves the Front Street ideas, and they're moving forward rapidly. The language of smart growth is now in the everyday speech of people who administer the city. And the city's being listened to more carefully by the rest of the county. No question, Dan's visit was an important event."

I told Carver I thought his encouraging news wasn't so surprising. Looking through the notes I'd made in Watsonville, I found I had been trying to describe what happens when people, by talking with Burden, learn to listen again to themselves and to each other. At the beginning of the afternoon design workshop, I'd written that thought-fulness, once evoked, can lead to healing. Later there was a note about everyone starting to sense common purposes and exchanging friendship, ideas, and knowledge. That was closer to it. Finally, as people presented their new designs to each other, I could see exactly what had been happening: the town had needed, and found a way, to hear its own heart beat.

TONY HISS is an independent author, lecturer, and consultant on the topic of restoring America's cities and landscapes. In 2002 he became a fellow of the CUNY Institute of Urban Systems. He is the author of twelve books, most recently *The State of the H2O Region—2003* (with Christopher Meier) and *The View from Alger's Window: A Son's Memoir* (a *New York Times* Notable Book). Other books include the award-winning *The Experience of Place* and *A Region at Risk: The Third Regional Plan for the New York–New Jersey–Connecticut Metropolitan Area.*

▶ THERE ARE MORE THAN EIGHTY DECORATIVE
MANHOLE COVERS ALONG THE PEDESTRIAN MALL
OF NICOLLET AVENUE IN DOWNTOWN MINNEAPOLIS.
DESIGNED BY KATE BURKE.

HOW TO FALL IN LOVE
WITH YOUR HOMETOWN

*Why do European cities seem so much more charming, interesting, and
vital than American cities? Editor and journalist Jay Walljasper points
out that the conventional wisdom is that they are older, but closer exami-
nation showed him that the vitality of European urban centers is not an
accident of history but the product of an ongoing process. Americans can
learn a lot about how to make our towns more livable and lovable by
looking at Scandinavian, German, and Dutch cities. Planning decisions
about transportation, traffic, economic development, and the environment
make an immense difference in how it feels to live in a city.*

My infatuation with cities began on a college-vacation visit to
Montreal, where I was enchanted by picturesque squares, sleek
subway trains, and the intoxicating urbaneness all around. Sitting up
most of the night in sidewalk cafés along rue St. Denis, I marveled at
how different this city felt from the cities I had known growing up
in downstate Illinois. Street life, in the experience of my childhood,
was what happened in the few steps between a parking lot and your
destination. Montreal showed me that a city could be a place to enjoy
in itself, not merely anonymous space that you travel through between home and work or school.

But it was later—appropriately enough, on my honeymoon—that I fell in love with cities. My wife, Julie, and I toured Paris, Venice, and Milan along with lesser-known delights like Luxembourg City and Freiburg, Germany, and we came home wondering why American cities didn't instill us with the same sense of wonder. At first, we accepted the conventional wisdom that it was because European cities are so much older, with street plans locked in place before the arrival of the automobile. Yet on subsequent trips abroad, we came to realize that there was something more at work. What explains the fact that most European cities gracefully end at some point, giving way to green countryside at their edges, unlike the endless miles of sprawl in America? How is it that public life and street culture feel so much richer in France and Austria? Why do you seldom see slums there?

Intrigued by these questions, I have returned to Europe over a number of years seeking answers. In scores of interviews with urban planners, transportation authorities, politicians, activists, and everyday citizens, I learned that a clear set of public policies accounts for the different spirit of European metropolitan centers. It's not just the antiquity of the towns, but also the way people there think about urban life.

In fact, many of the Europeans I talked to worried about the impact of increasing auto traffic and creeping suburbanization on the health of their cities. But rather than accepting these changes as the inevitable march of progress, as many Americans do, they were taking action to maintain the vitality of their hometowns. Urban decay was being reversed, historic neighborhoods protected, transit systems improved, pedestrian zones expanded, green spaces preserved, bike lanes added, pedestrian amenities installed, and development guidelines enacted to head off ugly outbreaks of sprawl.

▶ ▶ ▶

Throughout my travels, I was frequently thunderstruck at some sight (a beautiful plaza, comfortable public buses, a street crowded with bicycles) that was amazing to an American, but to Europeans simply a part of day-to-day life. These moments would depress me at first—why can't we do this at home?—and then rouse me. Of course we can! Americans are an enterprising people, restless in pursuit of improving their lives. If Europe's successes in making cities more livable and lovable were more widely known, people would insist on doing something similar here. Maybe even better.

This notion first hit me when I entered the central train station in the Dutch city of The Hague. In America, I marveled, this building would qualify as one of the world's wonders. Not for its ultramodern architecture; we have suburban office parks from Tampa to Tacoma that can match it for glitz. It was the building's basic function that startled me: the large-scale movement of human beings by means other than the automobile. Streetcars wheeled right into the station, unloading and loading throngs of commuters while an underground parking facility accommodated 3,000 bicycles. I consulted the electronic schedule board and counted more than twenty trains an hour departing for destinations all over the Netherlands and Europe—this in a city about the size of Chattanooga, Tennessee. Making my way from a day of meetings in The Hague to a hotel in the heart of Amsterdam, thirty-five miles away, was no more effort than my usual ride home on the Number 4 bus in Minneapolis.

A transportation network like Holland's would be beyond the wildest dreams of commuters, environmentalists, and city lovers across North America. In Amsterdam, for instance, only 20 percent of people's trips around the city are in a car; 36 percent are made on foot, another 31 percent on bikes, and 11 percent on transit. In the Dutch city of Groningen, 47 percent of all urban trips are on bikes, 26 percent on foot, and 23 percent by car. But that's not good enough for the Dutch. Alarmed by studies showing sizable increases in traffic in the years to come, government officials have worked to boost alternative transportation. Voters in Amsterdam approved an ambitious plan to eliminate most automobiles in a three-square-mile section of the center city, an idea later adopted in a number of other Dutch towns. Increased public funding has been invested in railroads and light rail, and major employers are now required to locate new facilities near transit stops. New housing and commercial developments are not approved without close scrutiny of their impact on traffic congestion. And with studies showing that people are much more willing to walk or take transit when the pedestrian environment is attractive, attention is being given to sprucing up train stations and making nearby neighborhoods more pleasant places to walk. Forward-looking transportation planners advocate expanded home delivery of goods and increased availability of public storage lockers, recognizing that some people stick with their cars because it's difficult to carry and stow belongings when they're biking, walking, or riding transit.

▶ ▶ ▶

On a trip to Germany, I sat in the ornate town hall of Heidelberg—a small city known widely as the setting of the beer-garden romance *The Student Prince*—while Bert-Olaf Rieck pointed out the window to a public square so picturesque it might have been used as a set for the famous operetta. He explained that it was where he parked his car while he was a linguistics student at the university. Now that he is a city official, it's his job to help clear cars out of the central city and make Heidelberg known for bike riding just as much as beer drinking and dueling.

Rieck recently had been appointed Heidelberg's bicycle commissioner, a new position arising out of the city's determination to reduce auto traffic in its historic streets. That's why Rieck was plucked out of the ranks of a bicycle activist group and installed at city hall. He was busy working on ways to make bicycles the vehicle of choice for at least one-third of all trips (up from 20 percent) around the city—an ambitious goal already achieved by Copenhagen and the German city of Munster. In the Dutch cities of Groningen, Harderwijk, Houten, Veenendaal, and Zwolle, bicyclists account for 40 percent or more of urban trips.

To put bikes on a par with cars, Rieck planned a major expansion of the city's twenty-five miles of separated bike paths. He had already succeeded in adding 1,500 new parking spots for bikes outside the main train station and snatched a lane of traffic from cars on Bismarckstrasse, Heidelberg's main thoroughfare. He proudly led Julie and me down this street on bicycles the city had recently purchased for its employees to use on trips around town. For a frequent bike commuter like me, it was nothing short of euphoric to pedal down a busy avenue in the safety of my own lane.

▶ ▶ ▶

Heidelberg has a way to go to match the accomplishments of another German university town, Freiburg, a city of 200,000 in the Black Forest. Freiburg showed the way for many European cities with its early efforts to incorporate environmental and quality-of-life concerns into its transportation planning. In the early 1970s it made the radical moves of not scrapping its streetcars, as most cities across the continent had been doing, and establishing one of Germany's first pedestrian zones. The pedestrian district is now the bustling heart of the city, filled with folks strolling between department stores, an open-air market, and numerous sidewalk cafés. The city has also built a new network of bicycle lanes and overhauled its streetcars into a modern light rail system. While people hopped into their autos for 60 percent of all vehicle trips around the city in the 1970s, cars accounted for less than half of those trips twenty years later—with bikes increasing from 18 to 27 percent of all trips, and light rail moving ahead from 22 to 26 percent.

Freiburg's success provides a firm answer to American naysayers who contend that people will never leave their cars at home and that what happens in densely populated Old World cities is not applicable to our own spread-out metropolitan areas. Freiburg is one of Germany's fastest-growing cities with new development stretching across a wide valley. You see packs of bicyclists waiting at red lights in its expanding suburbs and light rail trains gliding past single-family homes on ample lots.

Freiburg also has promoted many other environmental initiatives. It banned pesticides for urban uses and built a biochemical plant to recycle organic wastes from the city's garbage. The city established a hot line to answer citizens' questions about environmental matters, and it now subjects all new development projects to an in-depth environmental review.

What makes this small city so eager to buck business as usual in favor of environmental innovation? The presence of 30,000 university students helps, but most observers point to the citizens' deep regional pride. People cherish the city's historical charm (the center city was painstakingly rebuilt after suffering substantial damage in World War II) and the natural beauty of the Black Forest, which itself is under assault by pollution. Freiburgers celebrate their local wines, local cuisine, and local scenery, and they revel in the belief that they do things a little better than people in other cities.

▶ ▶ ▶

The Danish capital of Copenhagen is, as Danny Kaye sang in an old movie about Hans Christian Andersen, "wonderful, wonderful." It rivals Paris and Amsterdam for charm, with lively streets, tidy parks, vibrant neighborhoods, cosmopolitan culture, relaxed cafés, and cheerful citizens. But Copenhagen's wonderfulness stems not from some happily-ever-after magic but from inspired thinking and hard work in response to real-world urban conditions.

One of the first things a visitor notices about Copenhagen is the bicycles. They're everywhere, and everyone is riding them. You see prim, briefcase-toting business executives on bikes. Fashionable women in formidable high heels on bikes. Old people, schoolkids, and parents with toddlers on bikes. Half of all people who work in the central city arrive by bicycle in the summertime, and, despite Copenhagen's chilly, rainy, and sometimes icy weather, almost a third do in the winter.

All these bicycles, on top of a good train system and an extensive network of pedestrian streets, explain why Copenhagen feels like such a pleasant, relaxing, comfortable place. This is not just the luck of an ancient city unsuited for modern roadways. (Indeed, Copenhagen is no older than most East Coast American cities, having been completely rebuilt after 1807 when the British navy burned it to the ground.) It is the happy result of sensible urban planning with a strong emphasis on making the town attractive to pedestrians. Ever since a street in the heart of town was first closed off to traffic in 1962, planners have added additional blocks to the lively pedestrian zone each year, eliminated parking spots, and turned traffic lanes into bike lanes. Slowly, central Copenhagen has been transformed from a noisy, dirty, exhaust-choked downtown into a pleasant spot where you just naturally want to hang out. Jan Gehl, head of the urban design department at the Royal Danish Academy of Fine Arts, pointed to extensive studies showing that social and recreational use of the city center has tripled over the past thirty years. And he noted that the streets are just as lively when the shops are closed in the evenings and on Sundays: "A good city is like a good party," Gehl explained. "People don't want to leave early."

Copenhagen's initial plans to create a pedestrian zone were met with just as much skepticism as we would hear about similar plans in America today. "We are Danes, not Italians," Gehl recalled the newspapers complaining. "We will not use public space. We will never leave our cars. The city will die if you take out any cars." But the pedestrian zone was popular from the first day, he noted, and downtown business leaders eventually took credit for a plan they once adamantly opposed. One key to the success of Copenhagen's efforts, Gehl said, is that they have been implemented gradually over forty years. Drastic changes all at once provoke overreactions, he said.

Copenhagen's efforts to put pedestrians, bicyclists, and transit riders on an equal footing with motorists has delivered not just aesthetic enhancement and environmental improvement, but also social and economic reinvigoration. The lively, pedestrian-friendly mood of central Copenhagen has played a significant role in revitalizing the whole city as many suburbanites move back into town. Ironically, this economic revival brings with it the threat of more cars and trucks. To its credit, Copenhagen opened a new subway system in 2002 and expanded the existing commuter rail system along with constructing new bikeways and pedestrian streets. On the national level, Denmark has worked to halt sprawl with legislation that requires nearly all new stores to be built within existing commercial centers of cities, towns, or villages. Additionally, most new workplaces must be within a short walk of a transit stop, while stores, offices, and factories must make accommodations for bicyclists and pedestrians.

▶ ▶ ▶

Strolling away from the charming pedestrian streets and wonderfully preserved buildings of central Copenhagen on my first visit, I stumbled upon a sight familiar to urban Americans: a district of rundown apartment buildings, immigrant families, hookers, and drug and alcohol casualties. Middle-class flight to the suburbs in the 1960s and 1970s combined with cutbacks in blue-collar jobs brought dramatic changes to an area known as Vesterbro, and to other inner-city Copenhagen neighborhoods.

In America, urban decline is generally attributed to people's overwhelming preference for suburban amenities, but Denmark's policy makers bring a broad regional perspective to issues of struggling city neighborhoods. According to Jan Engell, an official in Copenhagen's planning department, the inner city is seen as an incubator where young people and immigrants can live cheaply as they launch their careers. And if many of them choose to move to bigger homes in outlying areas as they prosper and raise families, this is interpreted not as the failure of city life, but as a sign of its success.

This view of the metropolitan region as a single, unified community in which people choose to live in various areas at different times in their lives has led to an enlightened policy in which local tax revenues are shared between wealthier and poorer municipalities. Responsibility for the higher proportion of low-income, immigrant, elderly, mentally ill, and chemically dependent people who live in the inner city and require more government services is borne not just by Copenhagen taxpayers but by everyone in the region. Imagine what a difference it would make if Westchester County or Chicago's North Shore suburbs chipped in some of their local tax proceeds to boost public schools or drug treatment programs in the Bronx or the South Side. This is a key reason, along with higher levels of social benefits in general, why even Copenhagen's shabbiest quarters don't feel nearly as dangerous or as desperate as American ghettos. Vesterbro, despite its sex shops and drug addicts, remained at the time of my first visit a popular place for students, artists, and others attracted to the gritty energy of city life.

On later visits to Copenhagen I have seen the effects of an ambitious revitalization effort that aims to improve Vesterbro without driving away the people who live there. The Danish parliament allotted an ample pot of money for the city, working with landlords and in some cases tenants to fix up blocks of century-old five- and six-story apartment buildings. The goal is to provide a toilet, bath, central heat, and new kitchen in each flat along with creating new lawns and playgrounds in the courtyards.

All these plans are being carried out in close cooperation with community groups, and tenants have the right to opt out of certain improvements they think will jack up their rents. "They can even veto if they do not want to have a bath," Jesper Storskov of the Copenhagen planning department noted with a frown. "This does not upgrade housing as much as we want to—but it is fair."

"This is a democracy experiment as much as a social one," added planning official Jan Engell, noting, for example, that the emphasis on installing sophisticated energy and water conservation systems in the buildings came from residents themselves more than from city hall.

The Vesterbro redevelopment is drawing on lessons learned from the nearby Nørrebro neighborhood, where the city's efforts to make Copenhagen more attractive to middle-class families touched off riots during the 1980s. "Residents felt they were being forced out of the neighborhood," Storskov explained. People were outraged when old buildings were bulldozed and nineteenth-century streets were reconfigured to meet modern specifications. The new apartment buildings are far less popular than the old ones left standing, Storskov admitted. "That is why we began to renew houses rather than tearing them down, even though it costs more."

What's happening in Vesterbro ought to remind Americans that urban revitalization does not have to mean gentrification—and indeed that low-income people often know best what works in their own neighborhoods. The refurbished blocks of Vesterbro, where residents participated in making decisions, show far more signs of vitality than the sterile, modernized sections of Nørrebro, where planners foolishly erected their own visions of what they thought an urban neighborhood should look like without bothering to consult the people who actually lived there.

Aalborg, a Danish city of 160,000 on the peninsula that juts out into the North Sea, also embarked on an ambitious urban renewal program emphasizing pedestrian zones, historical preservation, ecological restoration, improved public transportation, and attractive public spaces. Special attention was devoted to revitalizing Greenland Square, a housing project once notorious for drugs and crime. Erik Büchert, a community organizer working in Greenland Square, said the area's biggest problem was that no one living there had any particular loyalty to the place—they simply wound up there because the rent was cheap.

To turn things around, Büchert helped launch an ambitious campaign to get people talking about their community and its needs. "People have to make the solutions themselves. You can't tell them how to solve their problems," he said.

Out of these discussions came the creation of a neighborhood newspaper, a senior citizen center, a cooperative secondhand store, a fitness and bodybuilding gym, a community information center, and a series of community celebrations to mark each season of the year. These projects have boosted community pride and changed the mood of the area. Drug dealers no longer rule the streets while people stay scared inside their apartments.

"We can't say all the problems are solved," Büchert added, "because there is still much unemployment, which we can't control. But it is a better, safer place to live now."

▶ ▶ ▶

All across Northern Europe, cities are exploring ways to boost their vitality and livability. Most cities now have bustling pedestrian zones, and bikeways crisscross even the most crowded metropolises. The German cities of Lubeck and Bremen have designated certain streets especially for bicycles—an idea Heidelberg also adopted. The Norwegian cities of Oslo, Bergen, and Trondheim (borrowing an idea from Singapore) levy a toll on all cars entering the city. Oslo used some of this money to reroute a harborside highway through a new tunnel, which gave the city a waterfront pedestrian plaza that's become a favorite hangout for local residents. London recently adopted a similar traffic-pricing measure with surprising success.

"Until recently, American cities with their wide lanes and fast traffic were the model for us," said Joachim Schultis, an urban planning professor in Heidelberg. "But all that has now changed."

Being able to get around by strolling, biking, or taking a train without always dodging trucks and cars enhances urban life in ways that are hard to imagine until you've experienced them. The more I visited Europe, the more charged up I got about wanting to see innovations like these back home. There's no reason why our cities can't follow suit, transforming themselves from conduits for cars into places for people. But the first step, I instinctively understood, was finding new ways for Americans to look at the places they live. We need to fall in love with our hometowns.

▶ ▶ ▶

Americans have always harbored a bit of mistrust toward cities— these crowded and complex and creatively chaotic places. Going all the way back to Thomas Jefferson's exaltation of yeoman farmers as the backbone of democratic culture, country life has been seen as the American ideal. Generations of conservationists and environmentalists have reinforced these views. Tracing their roots back to Henry David Thoreau and John Muir, ecology activists have sought redemption from ecological devastation in the untrammeled lands. Blessed with far more wilderness than any European nation, Americans generally have viewed any landscape shaped by human hands as somehow tainted. That's why protecting wilderness and saving wetlands are more often the focus of environmental organizations than curbing sprawl or revitalizing inner-city neighborhoods.

Yet our unease about cities—we see them as unnatural, unhealthy, almost un-American settings—has spawned one of the most spectacular environmental disasters in history: the modern suburban lifestyle. Over the past sixty years, millions of Americans have forsaken compact urban neighborhoods for sprawling acreage outside town. Closer connection to nature among the green lawns may have been the dream, but the truth is that suburban living really means count-less hours in the car, cruising down endless miles of pavement, pass-ing ceaseless stretches of new developments, all of which depends on limitless supplies of land, fossil fuel, lumber, and other environmen-tally precious resources. The suburban lawn needs gobs of pesticides, chemical fertilizers, and water. And the suburban dream house, with its extra garages, bedrooms, and baths, calls for more energy, furni-ture, and everything else it takes to outfit a modern household. The environmental price tag is just as steep when urbanites build vacation or permanent homes in the countryside, which mean septic tanks, new demands for paved and widened roads, more strip malls along the highway, and long commutes back to the city—which in most cases is where people still work and shop.

In terms of the environment, cities clearly offer the most earth-friendly lifestyle. A resident of an inner-city neighborhood who takes public transit to work, walks to local businesses, and shares a modest home with family or friends imposes far less damage on the environment than most Americans do. Of course, an urban address does not automatically confer an enhanced ecological consciousness; indeed, city dwellers are capable of merrily plundering the planet the same as anyone else. But city life does at least offer the opportunity to walk, bike, or take the bus to your destinations, and to conserve resources by living in a compact neighborhood. Those things are impossible in most suburbs, where autos are the only way to get from point A to point B. Houses are cut off from stores by impassable swaths of pavement. Schools, day care centers, libraries, and workplaces all sit isolated amid a sea of roaring traffic. A person on foot looks as out of place as a polar bear in Palm Beach.

The environment is not the only victim of this all-for-the-auto way of designing our communities. Children can't wander down to the park or skip over to the candy store. Sometimes they can't even cross the street to see neighbor kids. To go anywhere, they have to wait for someone to chauffeur them. Old people and the disabled, many of whom can't drive or have trouble walking across wide busy streets, are similarly restricted. They're placed under a sort of house arrest.

Low- and middle-income people also suffer. According to town planner Andres Duany, it costs in the neighborhood of $7,000 a year to buy and maintain the cheapest auto now on sale in the United States. When a car (and probably two or three) becomes a necessity simply to get to work and buy groceries, many families struggle to make ends meet. Even comfortably upper-middle-class people pay a steep price. Duany estimates that spending two hours every day in your car commuting to work, taxiing the kids around town, or running errands (not unusual in suburban areas) adds up to more than four weeks a year away from the people and pastimes you love.

James Howard Kunstler, the eminently quotable author of *The Geography of Nowhere: The Rise and Decline of America's Man-Made Landscape,* insists that there is an even deeper way we pay for this folly of poor urban planning. "It matters that our cities are primarily auto storage depots," he says. "It matters that our junior high schools look like insecticide factories. It matters that our libraries look like beverage distribution warehouses." To live and work and walk among such surroundings is a form of spiritual degradation, he says. It's hard to feel good about yourself when so much of what you see on a typical day is so unrelentingly drab. It's hard to really care about these places. I have fallen in love with Paris, Stockholm, Oxford, Florence, and Havana, as well as New Orleans, San Francisco, and even Madison, Wisconsin, and Montpelier, Vermont, because they stir something in my soul. It's more than scenic charm; it's a feeling they inspire as I walk around them with my family or soak up their atmosphere just sitting at a café table or on a public bench.

It's been well over a decade since I began roaming European cities in search of ideas that we could take advantage of here in America, and I am happy to report that I'm not alone. Many people, it seems, have returned from Barcelona, Sydney, Buenos Aires, or Savannah fired up by what they've seen and wanting to do something like it at home. Historic preservation and sidewalk cafés, tapas bars and Irish pubs, bicycle lanes and farmers' markets all owe some of their popularity to inspiration from abroad. Indeed, drawing on ideas from cities around the world, a number of social movements have been launched across America advocating rail transit, traffic calming, pedestrian-friendly policies, and regional revitalization.

URBANISM RIDES AGAIN

A growing legion of architects, planners, developers, neighborhood activists, and municipal officials gathered under the banner of New Urbanism are slowly changing the face of America with the message that there are other ways to build our communities besides the all-too-familiar patterns of sprawl. Andres Duany and partner Elizabeth Plater-Zyberk got things rolling with Seaside, a resort development in Florida that captured a lot of what's best about classic Southern towns and gained attention throughout the world. New Urbanist developments—some brand-new subdivisions at the suburban fringes but most redevelopment projects within urban borders—have changed many Americans' minds that all new roads must be wider, all new buildings more sterile, and all new neighborhoods hostile to the simple act of walking.

Duany notes that the New Urbanism is merely the reclamation of great planning traditions that can still be seen in Europe, Latin America, and older communities across the United States. "Everything you build should be either a neighborhood or a village," he declares, pointing out that great cities are nothing more than a series of villages artfully stitched together. These traditional villages and neighborhoods, he says, provide the basics within walking distance—a grocery, cleaners, café, pharmacy, bakery, park, day care center, schools, and perhaps a bookshop, ice cream parlor, movie house, and other social amenities. They should also offer a mix of housing types that can accommodate people of all ages and incomes. Ideally, a transit stop sits in the middle of things, and it is never more than a five-minute walk from the center of the neighborhood to the edges.

This simple wisdom, which guided the building of towns and cities for all of human history, was forgotten in America during the post–World War II years. What went wrong, Duany says, is that the massive production strategies developed in wartime defense factories were applied to the creation of communities. Instead of paying careful attention to all the details that make a neighborhood a pleasant place to live, planners focused narrowly on churning out large numbers of houses on an assembly-line scale. They succeeded in creating modern housing for millions of middle-class Americans but sacrificed quality in favor of quantity. With the rise of automobile ownership, it was assumed that people would forsake all other means of transportation. Little thought was given to how children might get around, or what would happen to suburbanites when they were too old to drive, or people who still like to take a stroll after dinner and greet their neighbors.

"This is how we murdered our cities," Duany says. And the New Urbanism, based on respect and affection for the traditional ways cities work, is how we bring them back to life.

GETTING BACK ON THE TRAIN

Public transportation in America is often dismissed as a nostalgia trip. We are often told that several generations of Americans have voted with their foot pedals: cars are now the only sensible way to get around. Yet worsening traffic congestion is encouraging many commuters to give transit another try. Public transportation ridership jumped from 7.9 billion in 1996 to 9.5 billion in 2001, a 20 percent increase—which significantly outdistances the increase in automobile miles driven during the same period.

Public transportation in many places now means trains as well
as buses. Light rail, a technologically updated version of the streetcar,
has been introduced over the past twenty years in Denver, Dallas,
San Jose, St. Louis, Portland, Sacramento, Los Angeles, Salt Lake
City, San Diego, Buffalo, Baltimore, Ottawa, Edmonton, Calgary,
and, most recently, between Bergen and Hudson in northern New
Jersey. New commuter rail lines have opened in Seattle, Los Angeles,
San Diego, and Dallas–Fort Worth. In the same period, rail lines (including both light and heavy rail) have been significantly upgraded
or expanded in Cleveland, Pittsburgh, Chicago, Toronto, Montreal,
Newark, New Orleans, and Vancouver.

Meanwhile, Houston, Phoenix, Memphis, Minneapolis, Seattle,
Charlotte, North Carolina, and San Juan, Puerto Rico, are now constructing new light rail lines. Even Kenosha, Wisconsin (population
90,000), recently opened a new two-mile streetcar line.

Despite growing popularity coast to coast, rail transit remains
controversial. Conservatives continue to harp, as they have for the
past fifty years, that trains are antiquated technology and a waste of
money. Clearly, they have never paid attention to how trains function as the circulatory systems of all great global cities from Tokyo to
Vienna. A number of political progressives have begun to complain
that fancy rail projects siphon funds away from bus service in poor
and minority neighborhoods. This was certainly the case in Los
Angeles, where massive cost overruns on subway construction led
to cuts in bus service. But in most communities, the arrival of trains
boosts buses. Middle-class commuters who leave their cars at home
in favor of the train end up taking the bus more often, too, and they
press public officials for better service. Salt Lake City, for instance,
saw a 21 percent jump in bus ridership during the period when its
light rail line opened.

While critics on both right and left come armed with economic
studies showing buses to be more cost effective, commuters show
a marked preference for trains. The southwest rail line in Denver

carries six times as many passengers as express bus service that once covered the same route. Trains lure motorists out of their cars with a smoother ride, the absence of diesel fumes, and a separate right-of-way, which means rail cars don't get bogged down in traffic as buses do. It's telling that almost all cities that have built light rail lines—with the exception of economically strapped Buffalo and Baltimore and corruption-clouded Los Angeles—have new lines or extensions of existing ones on the drawing board.

Busways—light rail lines without tracks—have appeared in Pittsburgh, Los Angeles, Minneapolis–St. Paul, Ottawa, and other places. This idea, pioneered in Curitiba, Brazil, as a lower-cost alternative to subways, has been adopted in Guatemala City, Bogota, and other cities in the developing world. Scott Bogren of the national transit advocacy group Community Transportation Association of America, said that while busways make sense in some situations, they often don't save as much money as promised or spur the same kind of urban revitalization along their routes as light rail. While buses will remain the heart of public transportation in most American cities and busways show potential in some situations, it's clear that light rail has a growing record of success in transforming public transit into something more than just mobility of the last resort. As G. B. Arrington, a transit expert in Portland, Oregon, which is now building its third light rail line, said, "This is not just a transit system for the poor, the elderly, and people with DWIs."

PEDESTRIANS GET ACTIVE

For most of this century, traffic has been seen as an inevitable by-product of modern life. Americans might mourn the calm and quaintness of life before the automobile, but most seemed thrilled at the possibility of going more and more places in less and less time. Over the past fifty years, our federal, state, and local governments have been preoccupied with building new and faster roads. The interstate highway system is the largest and most staggeringly expensive public works project in human history, and we've spent billions and billions more to widen streets and highways in almost every urban neighborhood and rural township throughout America. Millions of trees have been chopped down, tens of thousands of houses torn down, and communities everywhere ripped apart, all to meet the needs of the ever-escalating volume and speed of traffic.

But now, in place after place across North America, citizens are speaking out, holding meetings, and fighting city hall (and in some cases working with city hall) on the issue of slowing down traffic. They are fed up that the time-honored tradition of taking a walk has become a frustrating, unpleasant, and dangerous pastime. They are tired of worrying about the safety of their children, their pets, and their elderly and disabled friends, all of whom are imperiled by speeding drivers. They are determined to restore a sense of peace and community to their neighborhoods by taking the streets back from the automobile.

Speeding traffic sets in motion a vicious cycle in which people who might prefer to walk or bike end up driving out of fear for their safety. Numerous studies have shown that the speed of traffic, much more than the volume, is what poses a threat to pedestrians. One study conducted by the British government in the 1990s found that pedestrians were killed 85 percent of time when they were hit by cars traveling forty miles an hour (not an uncommon speed on streets in many American communities) compared to only 5 percent of the time when vehicles were traveling at twenty miles an hour.

Children are probably the biggest losers in this system, says David Engwicht, who led a fight against the expansion of a road through his neighborhood in Brisbane, Australia, and then wrote a seminal book, *Reclaiming Our Cities and Towns: Better Living with Less Traffic,* about what he learned. He notes that kids cannot wander and play in the streets anymore and must stay inside when they're not supervised by an adult. Instead of frolicking through the neighborhood, they watch shows like *Sesame Street,* "a make-believe street where children play safely and go exploring."

For thousands of years, Engwicht writes, city streets were a place to socialize as well as a pathway for all forms of transportation— carriages, wagons, pack animals, and, most of all, people. But over the past century, they have been turned over to the exclusive use of automobiles. In their campaign to claim sole ownership of the streets, motorists have been greatly aided by several generations of transportation planners who single-mindedly focused on ensuring the smooth and speedy flow of vehicles no matter what the cost. Pedestrians and bicyclists rarely have figured in their plans, except as nuisances who impede traffic.

Lowering speed limits is one logical response. Most German cities have posted a thirty-kilometer-per-hour (nineteen miles an hour) limit on all residential streets. But many observers note that people pay less attention to speed limits than to the look of a street in determining how fast they drive. Wide, open streets encourage motorists to zoom ahead. Many people herald the new idea of traffic calming as a more effective way of keeping drivers from barreling too fast down your street, because it's enforced twenty-four hours a day, not just when a police car is on the scene. Traffic calming was born in the late 1960s in Delft, Netherlands, when a group of neighbors, frustrated with cars roaring in front of their homes, placed furniture and other large objects at strategic spots in the street, which forced motorists to slow down. City officials, called out to clear these illegal obstacles, knew a good thing when they saw one and began installing their own more sophisticated traffic-calming devices. The idea spread across Europe and Australia, and now has come to North America.

Traffic calming encompasses a whole set of street designs that increase safety and aesthetic satisfaction for pedestrians. The aim is twofold: to slow the speed of traffic and to give drivers a visual reminder that they must share the street with people—on foot, on bicycles, in wheelchairs and in baby strollers. Speed bumps, narrowed streets, four-way stop signs, brightly painted crosswalks, on-street parking, median strips down the middle of streets, bans on right turns at red lights, crosswalks raised a few inches above the roadway, and curbs that extend a ways into intersections all help make the streets safer and more pleasant for pedestrians.

Opponents claim that traffic calming simply shoves speeding traffic onto someone else's street. But numerous studies have shown that traffic calming measures not only reduce speeds but can actually decrease traffic in general as people make fewer auto trips, either by handling a number of errands on one outing or by sometimes switching to biking, walking, or taking public transit. When Greenwich Village's Washington Square Park was closed to cars in the early 1960s, transportation engineers' studies showed that traffic on nearby streets decreased—exactly the opposite of what opponents of the plan had warned. Transportation officials in Nuremberg, Germany, found the same thing in 1989 when they closed a major downtown street.

David Engwicht sees traffic calming as more than just a way to promote safer streets. Traffic calming, he declares, quoting Australian town planner Phil Day, "involves a fundamental rethinking of metropolitan planning and organization—and a revised emphasis on quality rather than quantity of life. Some may see the ultimate goal as the calming of society itself."

More and more people across the country are embracing this view. In Atlanta, a public event marked the fiftieth anniversary of the killing of *Gone with the Wind* author Margaret Mitchell by a speeding taxi driver. In Boston, city officials were forced to abandon plans for a ten-lane highway in favor of a landscaped four-lane boulevard. Californians are busy mapping safe ways for kids all over the state to walk to school. After seventy-five years as the pawns in America's transportation system, pedestrians are asserting their rights to enjoy the health, fun, and community-building qualities of a daily walk.

They are lobbying public officials for traffic calming and lower speed limits, and conducting transportation studies to counter traffic engineers' claims that wider roads and more parking lots are beneficial to society.

"It's easy to become a pedestrian advocate," notes Ellen Vanderslice, whose harrowing attempts to cross a busy street with two toddlers in her neighborhood in Portland, Oregon, turned her into an activist. "Find out who's making the decisions about traffic in your community, how the process works, and where you can make an impact. Find people who feel the same way and get a group together."

That's exactly what Vanderslice did, joining the newly formed Willamette Pedestrian Coalition, which lobbied the city for better walking conditions. Local officials not only listened, they brought Vanderslice into city hall to devise a long-range plan to make Portland more pedestrian-friendly. When that project was completed, she became president of America WALKs, a national coalition of pedestrian advocacy groups representing cities from Philadelphia to Honolulu.

The interest in traffic calming and the rise of pedestrian advocacy groups is all part of what influential urban observer and *Governing* magazine executive editor Alan Ehrenhalt calls "the asphalt rebellion." "The asphalt rebellion ignited in many different places at virtually the same time," he writes. "It has become a full-fledged protest movement . . . [concerned with the] broader subject of how streets and highways are designed and built in America and the way those decisions affect communities and individual lives. It has grown into a rebellion against an entire half-century of American engineering ideology, and against an obscure but immensely important book: *A Policy on Geometric Design of Highways and Streets.*"

This book, updated regularly by the American Association of State Highway and Transportation Officials (AASHTO), is the bible of the traffic engineering profession, and its guidelines are frequently invoked with Ten Commandments authority to wave aside citizen concerns about what street and highway projects might mean for a neighborhood. The growing ranks of asphalt rebels contend that aesthetics, property values, or a sense of community don't matter to most traffic engineers, only how much more pavement it will take to keep the cars moving quickly. Traffic engineers defend themselves by noting that safety guides their decisions. They cite numerous studies proving that wider lanes and four-lane roads prevent traffic accidents.

But the safety issue cuts several ways. Asphalt rebels point out that many street and highway expansions make travel far more danger-ous for bicyclists and pedestrians—especially children and old people who have trouble crossing wider streets with faster traffic. (In New York City, the second leading cause of death for children ages five to fourteen is being hit by a car.) And asphalt rebels question whether designing streets to accommodate drivers traveling well above the posted speed limit, as the AASHTO guidelines do, ultimately promotes motorists' safety. Indeed, one very comprehensive study shows that narrow streets are actually safer. The city of Longmont, Colorado—a booming Denver suburb—looked at 20,000 accidents on local streets over an eight-year period and found that "as street width widens, accidents per mile per year increase exponentially." These findings fly in the face of the conventional wisdom of the traffic engineering profession, which views narrow streets and traf-fic congestion as safety hazards. The most dangerous streets in the Colorado study were wide, lightly traveled thoroughfares where drivers were able to really zoom.

Many communities are rethinking traffic issues, prodded by the efforts of environmentalists, advocates of sustainable transportation, neighborhood groups, historical preservationists, parents, and other varieties of asphalt rebels. Eugene, Oregon, which used to require that all streets be at least twenty-eight-feet wide, now allows some to be as narrow as twenty feet. Wellesley, Massachusetts, faced with a plan to widen its congested main street, instead chose to narrow it and expand the sidewalks to encourage walking. Even in auto-happy Southern

California, the cities of San Bernandino, Riverside, and Beverly Hills have narrowed major commercial streets. And Vermont has enacted a law that allows local officials to relax AASHTO standards in nearly all cases.

The asphalt rebellion is even winning a few supporters from within the ranks of traffic engineers, who are beginning to question whether moving cars as quickly and conveniently as possible is the most important goal for a community. Walter Kulash, a traffic engineer from Orlando who has become a leading voice for rethinking how we design our streets, says, "The difference between real bleakness and a vibrant urban atmosphere is a matter of seconds. When you ask the public, 'Would you rather take twelve more seconds to get where you're going and have this be a tree-lined wonderful street?' the answer is always, 'We want it to be vibrant and beautiful, not fast and ugly.'"

REGIONAL REVITALIZATION

American cities have long been harmed by the outward flow of wealth to the suburbs encircling them. This is not how it works in most European countries, where it has long been agreed that cities and suburbs function together as a single community. Taxpayers in the wealthy northern suburbs of Copenhagen, for instance, accept the fact that they must help fund social programs and revitalization projects in the poorer inner city and southern suburbs. This idea of a unified metropolitan area is now being promoted here by the growing regional revitalization movement. One of the movement's chief strategists is Myron Orfield, who has gained national attention for his research on patterns of decline and prosperity in America's metropolitan areas.

After twelve years in the Minnesota legislature, Orfield stepped down to devote more attention to Ameregis, an urban affairs research firm he founded. He also travels widely promoting an ambitious political initiative to slow suburban sprawl and revive the fortunes of poor neighborhoods in both cities and suburbs. Working with a growing movement of social justice activists, environmentalists, and municipal officials, Orfield promotes the idea that problems like poverty, affordable housing, and inner-city decline are best solved on a regional basis.

Orfield maintains that everyone who lives in a metropolitan area benefits from regionalist revitalization measures. Even residents of affluent suburbs, some of whom vehemently attack such ideas because they would be required to share some of their local tax proceeds and accommodate affordable housing in their neighborhoods, end up ahead. He mentions that he hears from many residents in affluent suburbs who support the regionalist agenda as a way to preserve the quality of life in their communities—by preventing further sprawl, easing traffic congestion, protecting open space, and ensuring future vitality. If the bulk of new investment continually flows to the outer edges of a metropolitan region, it's only a matter of time until currently prosperous areas begin to show symptoms of decline. After all, many of the older suburbs around the country that are now experiencing urban decay were settled in the 1960s and 1970s by families seeking a haven from what were perceived as the problems of the city.

Orfield cites studies done by Richard Voith, an economist at the Federal Reserve Bank of Philadelphia, showing that suburbs enjoy higher income growth and higher land values in metropolitan areas where the central city is economically vital. "If you live in a middle-class suburb and your center city is not doing well," Voith notes, "it's a good bet that your suburb is not doing as well as a similar suburb where the center city is doing well."

Our present pattern of metropolitan development benefits a fortunate few while at the same time degrading the natural environment, aggravating conditions for poor people, and setting the stage for decline in many middle-class communities. The regional revitalization movement directly challenges these trends with a simple set of ideas—and the promise of a formidable new political coalition— that offers help and hope for a majority of people. As a moral call for justice, the regional revitalization movement probably won't go far in the present political climate. But as a pragmatic program to improve the communities where most Americans live, it could.

LEARNING FROM PORTLAND

Portland, Oregon, often comes up in discussions of urban innovations in the United States. It's the one place that can hold its own against European cities in terms of fostering vitality and livability. Once dismissed as a hopelessly dull backwater, it has over recent decades transformed itself into a place that anyone who loves cities should visit. Here are some of the surprising sights to be seen:

▸ Tom McCall Waterfront Park, a pleasant patch of green downtown—with kids ducking in and out of a splashing fountain and couples walking hand in hand along the Willamette River—in what was once the site of a freeway.

▸ Pioneer Courthouse Square, a cosmopolitan town common with art exhibits, street singers, brown-bagging office workers, and an outdoor café occupying what was once the site of a parking garage. Light rail trains frequently glide by, taking folks to points across the metropolitan area.

▸ Downtown Portland itself, which was nearly written off for dead thirty years ago and now features block after block of lively storefronts, coffeehouses, restaurants, hotels, parks, rehabbed warehouses, and office towers, plus a Chinatown, and Powell's, the largest new and used independent bookstore in America.

The number of jobs downtown has doubled since 1971 with only a small increase in parking spots, making the area look like the heart of a real city, not another suburban makeover of a central business district.

▸ Martin Luther King Boulevard, which sports new apartment buildings, new stores, and new jobs along with dropping crime rates in the center of what has long been Portland's African American ghetto.

▸ West Union Road, a two-lane blacktop thirteen miles from downtown, featuring clusters of houses and apartments, with swing sets and grills in cozy backyards, on one side. Across the road lie rolling pastures and orchards with only an occasional farmhouse. This marks Portland's urban growth boundary, a line beyond which suburban development cannot sprawl.

▸ Downtown Gresham, the center of a largely blue-collar suburb that sits just a few blocks from a light rail station. Once of little consequence even to the people of Gresham, the area now bustles with new shops, new town houses, and a farmers' market. At the other end of the light rail line in the western suburbs, passengers can step out into several newly constructed downtowns. Beaverton, once a standard-issue 1960s suburb, is building a town center with substantial housing, shopping, and services around the train station. "You no longer will be able to say that there's no there there," boasted mayor Rob Drake when the light rail line opened.

Instead of accepting ever-escalating levels of traffic, air pollution, sprawl, and inner-city decay as inevitable urban problems, Portland has made a commitment to public transit, environmental quality, New Urbanist development, and revitalization of poor neighborhoods.

It offers a different vision of what American cities could look like in the twenty-first century. Most other growing metropolitan regions from Orlando to Las Vegas still follow in the tire tracks of Los Angeles, the classic twentieth-century city founded on an unwavering commitment to freeways and new subdivisions spreading as far as the eye can see. Since the 1960s, however, Oregonians have looked south to the sprawling cities of California with a certain horror. They didn't want to see their beloved forests, farms, and foothills plowed under by spreading suburbia. Yet it was clear that Portland, with its scenic setting and mild temperatures, was going to grow. So discussion around town began to focus on how urban growth could be managed to prevent the environmental and social problems popping up in other regions.

In 1972 Portland mayor Neil Goldschmidt (who was later Jimmy Carter's secretary of transportation), working with a coalition of neighborhood groups, canceled construction of the Mount Hood freeway, which was eventually replaced by the light rail line leading to Gresham. At the same time, Republican governor Tom McCall initiated an ambitious statewide program of land-use planning that requires all cities, including Portland, to enact an urban growth boundary beyond which development cannot take place. In another innovative move, an elected regional government named Metro was established in 1979 for the entire Portland metropolitan area, and it has taken the lead in implementing policies aimed at managing new development. Efforts to limit sprawl in other regions around the nation have been hampered by the clashing self-interest of various municipal, county, and state authorities.

Decades later, the wisdom of the Oregon decisions is borne out by Portland's attractiveness as a place to live. It is a magnet for ambitious kids graduating from college around the country, and creative people in many fields have moved there. Since 1991 there have been only scant violations of clean air guidelines for carbon monoxide and ozone, whereas in the 1970s Portland missed the mark almost one day out of three. A freeway expansion on the west side was beat back by citizen groups who proved to state highway planners that light rail and smarter land use planning could meet future transportation needs. Portland ranks number one among medium-sized U.S. cities in transit use, and $850 million in new development has gone up along the light rail lines.

Portland has not eliminated sprawl—you still see plenty of strip malls and tract houses—but it has contained sprawl. Suburbia stops on all sides of the city between three and eighteen miles from downtown, giving way to green expanses of fields and forests. John Fregonese, an urban planner, notes that the municipality of Portland grants thousands of permits for new units of housing in a city that is already built up. This is happening on top of an explosion of refurbishing old homes and revitalizing neighborhood business districts. Some Portland neighborhoods are beginning to approach what residents of Paris or Montreal would consider a real city: a place where you can walk comfortably to grocery stores, drug stores, cafés, parks, flower shops, child care centers, and specialty stores of all stripes. "The urban growth boundary bounces investment back inward," notes Henry Richmond, a longtime activist against sprawl. "The older suburbs get more investment and so does the inner city. This kind of thing is standard operating procedure in the rest of the industrialized world. Europe's done this for a century. That's why their cities look the way they do."

HOME SWEET HOME

Not long after coming home from my first fact-finding visit to Portland, still wide-eyed about what I had seen was possible in an *American* city, city officials here in Minneapolis unveiled plans to widen Lyndale Avenue, just one block from my front door. They anticipated no public objections. This, after all, was progress—a sensible step toward greater safety and better movement of traffic. Inspired by what we had seen in travels abroad and shining examples from other North American cities, some neighbors and I moved swiftly into action. We penned a flyer disputing claims that the plan would promote public safety and tucked it into every door within four blocks of the affected stretch of street. Then we waited, wracked with anxiety, for the public meeting about the project. Would anyone care? Would anyone show up? Would people who had not recently visited Amsterdam or Toronto understand our message that there was another way to think about cities? As it turned out, more than 300 people packed a local community center and offered an emphatic collective *no* to plans to widen Lyndale. City officials, who once smugly dismissed our complaints about the speed and volume of auto traffic as well-meaning but uninformed, backed down from the project right then and there. At the end of the meeting, two and a half hours of heartfelt and angry opposition to their plans with only one man voicing the tiniest bit of support, the officials appeared grateful to be leaving the meeting all in one piece. With the help of a citizen task force, including some of my neighbors and me, plans were drafted and approved to narrow the street instead. (That the plan has not yet been implemented may show that our local traffic engineers have changed their rhetoric and strategies more than their actual beliefs.)

This was not an isolated incident. In neighborhood after neighborhood across the city, citizens have risen up with new ideas about how to make Minneapolis a better place to live. One of the most vocal supporters of our task force proposal to narrow Lyndale Avenue was later elected mayor, unseating an incumbent in large part because of his vigorous urban-livability platform. After years of work by a neighborhood group, another busy street near my home now features traffic-calming measures and a bike lane. Many other streets around town have been narrowed or now have speed bumps. A series of new bike paths wind around the city. A light rail line is set to open soon. A busway is operating, and plans are under way for a commuter rail line. New Urbanist developments, reflecting the best of classic Minneapolis architecture, are popping up all over the city

and suburbs. Independent and idiosyncratic coffee shops have blos-
somed on corners all over town, giving a village feel to many neighborhoods. New investment has flowed into once rundown parts of
the city, bringing a new sense of hope. Smart-growth strategies—the
antidote to sprawl—have been implemented by state officials.

But most important of all, the citizens of Minneapolis have a
new appreciation for their home. They understand that the city will
thrive if it nurtures its special urban qualities and will fall on its face
if it merely tries to imitate suburbia by widening streets, developing
strip malls, and adding parking lots. Minneapolis has become proud
to be a city once again. It is far different from the town Julie and I
came home to from our honeymoon. The Minneapolis of that time
seemed lacking in charm and confidence; it felt like a place with its
best years behind it. But now Minneapolis feels like a city whose residents care about it. We've fallen back in love with our hometown.

JAY WALLJASPER is editor and editorial director of *Utne* magazine, where
he writes frequently on urban and community issues. He has also written for
the *Nation, Preservation, Mother Jones,* the *Chicago Tribune* magazine, *Toronto
Star,* the *New Statesman* (London), *Courrier* (Paris), *Planeta Humano* (Madrid),
Integrale (Barcelona), and *New Woman* (Sydney). He is coauthor of *Visionaries:
People and Ideas to Change Your Life.* Walljasper is in the process of establishing
a think tank to research and promote the kind of urban innovations discussed
in his essay.

WHAT IF?

EVEN THOSE WHO CONCEDE THAT OUR CITIES AND
our suburbs are in sad shape express a guarded optimism
about the prognosis for the future. In his role of urban
Cassandra, author James Howard Kunstler postulates
a different reality for the future of our urban centers—
indeed for our entire society. *What if* everything we take
for granted about that society were to change and we
had to rethink what constitutes a livable city?

In the problematic scenarios that Kunstler projects for
the American future, the Charter of the New Urbanism
would continue to be a useful document in the restructuring of our cities. These commonsense recommendations
engender hope and recognition that working in a variety
of partnerships presents our greatest opportunity.

▶ A TILE–DECORATED SIDEWALK FROM HOWARD
FINSTER'S "PARADISE GARDEN" NEAR SUMMERVILLE,
GEORGIA. PHOTOGRAPH BY BILL SWISLOW.

CITIES OF THE FUTURE IN THE LONG EMERGENCY

JAMES HOWARD KUNSTLER

The future of American cities and towns will not be a seamless continuation of past practices, according to James Howard Kunstler, influential urban gadfly, who believes that we are in for an era of fractious politics and civil disorder. The suburban living arrangement that became the norm through the mid- to late-twentieth century will prove to be short-lived. Kunstler believes that its demise will be resisted, though futilely, and will cause great economic distress. He concludes that the cities of the industrial age "smokestack era" are destined to contract and develop a far different character, and that the tyranny of the automobile and the infrastructure required for it will necessarily end.

Kunstler predicts that we are going to have to live much more locally and redevelop the networks of local economic self-sufficiency and inter-dependency that we allowed to be destroyed in recent decades.

Historian Jim Flink once made the surpassingly cogent remark that in the future there will be two kinds of societies: those that are overdeveloped and those that will never develop.

Flink was speaking pretty strictly in terms of industrial development—and writing (in *The Automobile Age,* published in 1988) from a perspective at the heart of the industrial age—so he was thinking of a very specific kind of development. His remark implied a number of things that were either against the grain of conventional thinking in the late twentieth century or so far out in the intellectual asteroid belt that hardly anybody was thinking that way. One implication was that the industrial age was not a permanent condition of life but rather just another dramatic historical act in the human epic with a beginning, a middle, and an end, and that we were somewhere past the middle and perhaps nearing the end. The other implication was that life is tragic. Historical circumstance leaves a lot of wreckage and losers behind. Some things (including peoples and nations) are truly hopeless. This last idea really flew in the face of logical positivism and all its outgrowths that so defined "progressive" political thought in the century we have now left behind.

I introduce my own thoughts on cities of the future in this spirit because my ideas are not all "positive," in the sense usually meant by the cheerleaders of political therapy who insist on happy outcomes—so that you may also conclude that my views, like Flink's, tend toward the tragic. We are entering an extremely dicey period of history. Huge events and conditions are under way that are going to drastically change our world and alter the terms of daily life, and we are woefully unprepared. Therefore, what you're going to get here is pretty far from a glitzy General Motors World of Tomorrow fantasy. I believe the century ahead is going to be rather grim, and I will spell it out presently in a bill of particulars.

I also believe that the future is telling us pretty clearly that we will have to make other arrangements for daily life, especially in terms of the suburban fiasco that has been our model habitat in America for half a century. In a word, this will mean the *downscaling* of virtually all our regular activities, from commerce to schooling to agriculture to the way we organize and move about our daily environments, and I will get to that too, presently in terms of the built environment, our cities and towns.

To begin, though, I believe we are entering the twilight of the industrial age. In particular, we face the end of the oil age, or at least the *cheap* oil age, which has provided the motive power behind mature industrialism—and that is a terrifically momentous thing. The catch is that, contrary to expectations of a huge number of people, including educated folks who ought to know better, it is very unlikely that we will have a smooth transition from the end of cheap oil to whatever replaces it—assuming that some advanced alternative fuel technology will replace cheap oil, which, in my view, may be assuming way too much.

Right now, the aging Aquarians and enviro-greenies and techno-nerds are all awaiting the development of these putative alternative technologies like Sumatran cargo cultists watching the skies and waiting for a B-29 to return out of time to drop K rations on them. It is true, for instance, that we know how to make fuel cells that run on hydrogen. But we are nowhere near knowing how to apply that knowledge on a mass basis that would allow all the commuters in America to swap their gasoline-powered cars for hydrogen-powered fuel cell cars—and certainly not at a price that would allow democratic participation.

It is true, for another example, that we know how to make solar cells and hook them up to batteries and lights and motors—but not in a manner that would replicate the current advantages of the grid for the masses of people.

The fact is that none of the alternative fuels now known can match oil for versatility or ease of transport and storage. And at the very least, the end of the cheap-oil age portends severe changes in our social relations. What are today "normal" rations of power, light, home heat, and individual transport may soon be luxury items enjoyed only by an elite.

The end of cheap oil is predicated on the plain geological fact that we are approaching a condition known as global peak oil production. The best models based on the best information indicate that this will occur sometime in the current decade. It means that half of all the oil will have been extracted from all known world reserves and that the amount remaining will be the half that is either difficult to extract or so costly to extract that it might not be worth expending the energy needed to extract it. (A summary of these ideas can be found in *Hubbert's Peak,* by Kenneth Deffeyes, Princeton University Press, 2001.) This will certainly lead to destabilization of oil markets and of many current economic arrangements.

It also implies a political contest over the remaining reserves, more than half of which lie underneath the sands of the Middle East and Central Asia, some of the most unstable places in the world. It seems to me that post-9/11 terrorism is to a very great degree both a product of this condition and an ominous portent of more political mischief to come.

The end of the *cheap* oil age—and I emphasize the word *cheap* because we don't have to run completely out of oil to find ourselves in a heap of trouble—will at least have the effect of rendering the uniform suburban environment of America problematical, and at worst obsolete, and probably with startling speed. As suburbia proves rapidly dysfunctional in a post-cheap-oil world, it will lose its presumed value as real estate, and since we have invested so much money in the infrastructure and furnishings of suburbia—the "housing" subdivisions, the commercial strips, the office parks, and so on—we are going to see the evaporation of a vast amount of hallucinated wealth.

This change will lead to a fiesta of defaulted mortgages and leases, and repossession, with poor prospects of gainful resale, or else vacancy, and abandonment and disintegration of buildings that were not designed to endure beyond their tax depreciation period, anyway. It will amount to a fight over the table scraps of the twentieth century. A good deal of personal financial ruin will ensue, and hence social unrest, including the birth of a new *former middle class,* a large group cut off from their presumed entitlements to the *American Dream* who will be very pissed off about it. I believe that this large group will attempt desperately to preserve their entitlements by electing extremist politicians who will promise to restore the perquisites of suburbia by any means necessary. Since this will not be possible in the face of implacable world conditions and trends, this kind of politics is apt to lead to scapegoating, xenophobia, and probably violence, including war.

In any case, conditions will be such that we are going to have to recondense the life of our nation into coherent traditional human environments, namely, towns, cities, and neighborhoods. Fortunately, we have a whole nation full of towns and cities waiting to be reinhabited. They exist where they do because they occupy the best sites, many of them on strategic waterways of one kind or another. The great majority are in terrible condition today.

I do not believe that our largest cities will retain the supercolossal scale they achieved at mid-twentieth century. That was a very special consequence of the special circumstances of mature industrialism, which will not be recapitulated. For instance, Detroit will never be the size that it was in 1950, nor Cleveland, nor St. Louis—the list is long. Their downtowns may reacquire more people than they have now, but the cities will continue to shrink or implode at their suburban margins. Nor do I think we will be able to use many of the extremely large or tall buildings that became normative at the height of the cheap-oil age. Rather, in response to the fall-off of cheap energy, I believe we will return to a much more traditional human scale. To me, this is ironic insofar as so many visionary gurus of New Age architecture, such as Paolo Soleri of Arcosanti, have projected a future based on megastructures. Forget it. The dwellings and buildings of the age to come are going to be much more medieval in scale, if not in style.

The end of the cheap-oil era suggests that the presence of cars in our lives will be greatly reduced. I do not believe that any so-called alternative fuel technology currently in development would be able to replace the internal combustion engine. None of them have the versatility or the ease of transport and storage that is characteristic of oil. Anyway, it is not a matter of cars being totally eliminated, but

of the ownership and use of cars becoming increasingly a preroga-
tive of elites in a stringent new economy. This kind of elitism would
be deeply at odds with the democratic nature of car culture in our
nation for the past hundred years. In fact, I think it is safe to say that
the suburbanization of America—and the car dependency that went
with it—was possible only because virtually all social ranks could
enjoy the putative benefits of car ownership.

In the kind of austere economy I project, car ownership might
become an object of envy and grievance, especially on the part of
people who were formerly able to participate in mass motoring but
are now deprived. In such a society, it is also likely that the current
massive subsidies for highway maintenance would not be happily
borne by impoverished taxpayers unable to participate as motorists.

This is precisely why I believe the urban environments of the
future will be walkable in scale. Some kind of public transit will also
be requisite, whether this is supplied by municipal lines, either bus
or rail, or by the less formal kind of arrangements seen in the jitney
fleets of what we now call the "third world."

Even at the height of affluence, America had a passenger railway
system that the Bulgarians would have been ashamed of. This will
have to change. It is unlikely that the airline industry is going to
function quite the way it has—which suggests in particular that we
will need rail service between towns and cities five hundred miles
apart and less. The current absence of public discussion over the future of passenger rail service is a prime symptom of our narcoleptic
lack of preparedness for the changes bearing down on us.

There ought to be no question that Americans would benefit
from reduced car dependency and from a reduced presence of cars
in our daily lives. Nothing has been more responsible for damaging the public realm of our nation and degrading the civic life that
takes place in it than the despotic presence of cars, with all their
impositions, from vast parking lot storage areas to ugly signage and
signal equipment, to the constant danger they pose to pedestrians.

Even the most benign scenario, in which the numbers of cars in daily circulation are reduced, while leaving access to rental cars on a democratic basis for special trips and special needs, would be an improvement. But personally, I think the outlook will be more severe than that. Car use is now so deeply identified with the so-called American way of life that tremendous social friction will be generated as the entitlements to it systematically disappear. Americans may be dragged kicking and screaming (by events) into a world of reduced car ownership and use.

Without having to accommodate massive numbers of cars, the redevelopment of existing towns and cities can take place at a fine scale, based on a return to the historically constant quarter-mile-radius walkable neighborhood, the traditional hierarchy of the street-and-block systems, and the normative building lot. Megastructures and megadevelopments will be a thing of the past. In the much more austere economy of the twenty-first century, redevelopment will have to be done on much smaller increments of investment.

My own guess is that towns and smaller cities will be the more successful places in twenty-first-century America. In them there is less extant destruction to overcome. It will take less to turn them around. The shrinkage of our largest cities, which had for the previous half century proceeded from the center outward, will now physically reverse, from the fringe inward, and the consequent social friction may make life in them that much more difficult.

A big part of the trends ahead, as the world moves toward chronic military mischief and resource wars, will involve the disintegration of current global economic relations and the desperate need to rebuild local networks of economic interdependence and self-sufficiency. Those networks were devastated by the Wal-Mart–type economics of the late twentieth century—itself a prime manifestation of cheap oil. In the foolish rapture over "bargain shopping," Americans allowed untold local networks of employment and production to be destroyed and, along with them, countless occupational niches. All of these things combined to form the complex organisms that we call *com-munities,* and the damage is obvious to anyone who travels around the United States today. The much decried "lack of community" around America, even where large numbers of people live and work, is not a metaphysical matter. Its direct cause is the absence of local economic interdependence and the social relations and economic roles required to animate it.

The rebuilding of these networks is an enormous and daunting task, and it will go hand in hand with the downscaling, rescaling, and right-scaling of our physical daily environments. When big-box stores are no longer economically viable, the big boxes themselves will no longer be needed. Some of them may be retrofitted to other activities, but my hunch is that most of them will join the rest of our obsolescent suburban furnishings in a state of disutility, abandonment, and, ultimately, ruin. The prospects for thousands of strip malls and regular malls are equally dim. It is perhaps not an accident that so many of the buildings that compose suburbia were consciously designed to last only as long as their tax depreciation schedule. Perhaps there was a collective precognition that suburbia was not a living arrangement destined to endure.

The rebuilding of local commercial networks will require rich multilevel, hierarchical systems for the production and distribution of goods. In fact, this is exactly what existed prior to World War II in America—a system that included a lot of local and regional production, artisans, technicians ("mechanics" as they were called in the nineteenth century), middlemen, jobbers, wholesalers, distributors, and, finally, small retailers. These systems, by the way, remain intact in other parts of the industrialized world. Many European nations consciously chose to support these networks as a social good and used licensing restrictions, subsidies, and other means to sustain them, even while a certain amount of Wal-Mart–style commerce was allowed to operate at the margins.

In the austere economic conditions of the new century, it is very likely that our choices of goods will be reduced and that we will have to pay more for them. That will only underscore the abnormality of the cheap-oil age that we will have left behind. It is conceivable to me that in the decades and perhaps even the centuries ahead, humankind may lose much of the technical knowledge acquired over the past two hundred years of robust industrialism, just as the technics of ancient Rome were lost. If we really are unable to find a replacement for fossil fuels, then we may be facing a very long period of social darkness. I hesitate to use the term *Dark Age,* but it may not be inappropriate.

Other world conditions also loom ominously to promote that outcome, namely, the spread of epidemic disease (AIDS in particular) and global climate change. Both of these things are certain to worsen in the decades ahead. AIDS itself is capable of decimating whole continents. It has left sub-Saharan Africa in destitution and political anarchy, and the disease is now advancing at terrible speed across Russia, India, Indochina, and mainland China. As if that weren't enough, the world is already overdue for an influenza outbreak on a par with the so-called Spanish flu of 1918—which actually started on a Kansas hog farm. Factory farming of animals has grown exponentially in the past half century. A 1998 outbreak of avian influenza, which "jumped species" (that is, it mutated and became transmissible to humans), was averted only by the immediate slaughter of all the poultry in Hong Kong. Climate change is sending disease vectors from the tropics into what have been until recently temperate zones. Incidence of dengue fever, malaria, and west Nile virus are spreading each year up North America. SARS and monkey pox are two of the latest additions to the list.

Both climate change and the advance of disease will aggravate the movements of desperate populations around the world and armed contests over territory and resources, as well as contributing to political anarchy. The enormous amount of small arms loose in the world, including rapid-fire assault rifles, rocket-propelled grenades, shoulder-launched missiles, and plastic explosives, can turn even the most impoverished gang of bandits into a potently destructive force capable of frustrating the best-equipped armies, as illustrated by the U.S. Army's misfortunes in Somalia in 1993 and the aftermath of the 2003 Iraq War.

In this coming era of persistent emergency, not all regions of America will be affected equally. I believe that the Sun Belt is going to suffer disproportionately under the conditions I am describing (just as it benefited disproportionately during the cheap-oil era). Places like Atlanta and Houston grew tremendously over the past fifty years because of affordable air-conditioning and cheap gasoline. We are going to rediscover why there were very few cities of any consequence in the American Southeast (the "wet" Sun Belt) before the advent of affordable air-conditioning.

We are liable to see a different set of problems in the "dry" Sun Belt extending from Texas to California. Robert Kaplan has written extensively about the increasing political friction over the U.S.-Mexican border (*An Empire Wilderness,* 1998). As the U.S. economy declines in the face of unraveling globalism, the Mexican economy will suffer by another order of magnitude. If the past is any guide, then conditions of revolution, political anarchy, and impoverishment in Mexico may send huge numbers of Mexican nationals across the border into the United States (as did the long revolution from 1915 to 1940). A growing "Aztlan" or "Reconquesta" movement already in existence could turn this part of the Sun Belt into contested territory. Applications of political correctness will not avail to mitigate this as a possibility, distasteful as it may seem to even raise the subject of strife over massive illegal immigration.

Apart from this potential political problem, the "dry" Sun Belt is also subject to tremendous pressure over declining water supplies as the great aquifers of the West have been systematically drained and climate change has reduced the snowpack and rainfall that typically feed western rivers such as the Colorado, upon which so many western cities now depend.

My conclusion about the Sun Belt, both "wet" and "dry," is that in the decades ahead, both regions will experience intense and possibly disabling political problems that will both arise out of the harshness of their economic predicaments and significantly aggravate them in a vicious feedback loop. It may be the destiny of states like Georgia and South Carolina to become primarily agricultural again in the future under the conditions I am describing. I'm inclined to believe that the Southeast will be significantly depopulated and that parts of the American Southwest may be yielded to Mexican hegemony by sheer force of numbers—though in the longer view, Texas, New Mexico, and Arizona may not support current populations levels of any ethnic composition.

This perhaps comes as bad news to those of us who would like to think of the United States as a permanent bright constellation in the historical firmament. But borders change frequently in history, and it may be the next "manifest destiny" for the United States to become a smaller nation, or a collection of regional subnations. Even under the best circumstances, the Southwest may have little in common politically or economically with the Northeast in another fifty years. The trend worldwide in recent decades has been the steady breakdown of large political units into smaller ones—the former Soviet Union being Exhibit A—and America may not be immune to this process.

Readers who have followed me this far may find this a discouraging picture of the future. We have a lot to be concerned about. But there may be benefits in the new arrangements that circumstances will force upon us. A return to human-scaled towns and cities that support local economic networks and varied vocational roles will lead to the rebirth of real communities. Anyway, the state-of-the-art megasuburbs of recent decades have produced horrendous levels of alienation, loneliness, anxiety, and depression, and I believe we will be better off without them.

Finally, the times ahead are sure to produce a vastly different group mentality (zeitgeist or ethos) than the narcissistic transports that modernism produced in the century now gone. In the face of real hardship, I expect many species of cultural relativism to go out the window. The willingness to suspend value judgments was another sly luxury of the cheap-oil age among the intellectual elites who could indulge in moral noncommitment, fashion-mongering, phony political therapeutics, and plain licentiousness. In the face of economic hardship, political disorder, and organized violence, a firmer worldview is probably requisite. Ideas consigned for decades to the scrap heap, like virtue, heroism, and beauty, may play a larger role in determining what we make of our world.

If I had one succinct piece of advice to give to the young people who will spend many years of their lives in this long emergency of the twenty-first century, I would tell them to prepare to be good neighbors.

JAMES HOWARD KUNSTLER is the author of *The Geography of Nowhere, Home from Nowhere,* and *The City in Mind: Notes on the Urban Condition.* He has also written eight novels and is a regular contributor to the *New York Times Sunday Magazine* and op-ed page, where he writes on environmental and economic issues. He lives with his wife, Jennifer Armstrong, a children's book author, in Saratoga Springs in upstate New York.

CHARTER OF THE NEW URBANISM

The Congress for the New Urbanism (CNU) is a nonprofit organization aimed at stopping sprawl and reestablishing compact, walkable, and environmentally sustainable neighborhoods, cities, and towns. It is an international network of over 2,500 individual members from a diverse set of disciplines, including design, development, finance, environment, social equity, and elected office. In its short ten-year history, it has helped shape a national conversation about the consequences of growth and helped bring to life an alternative vision for community development and regional sustainability based on the Charter of the New Urbanism. CNU sponsors annual conferences, known as congresses, for sharing and discussion of best practices in New Urbanism. It also works with like-minded leaders and practitioners to remove barriers to building places that create lasting value and treasured community assets. The following is the organization's charter statement.

The Congress for the New Urbanism views disinvestment in central cities, the spread of placeless sprawl, increasing separation by race and income, environmental deterioration, loss of agricultural lands and wilderness, and the erosion of society's built heritage as one interrelated community-building challenge.

We stand for the restoration of existing urban centers and towns

within coherent metropolitan regions, the reconfiguration of sprawling suburbs into communities of real neighborhoods and diverse
districts, the conservation of natural environments, and the preservation of our built legacy.

We recognize that physical solutions by themselves will not solve
social and economic problems, but neither can economic vitality,
community stability, and environmental health be sustained without
a coherent and supportive physical framework.

We advocate the restructuring of public policy and development
practices to support the following principles: neighborhoods should
be diverse in use and population; communities should be designed for
the pedestrian and transit as well as the car; cities and towns should
be shaped by physically defined and universally accessible public
spaces and community institutions; urban places should be framed
by architecture and landscape design that celebrate local history,
climate, ecology, and building practice.

We represent a broad-based citizenry, composed of public and
private sector leaders, community activists, and multidisciplinary
professionals. We are committed to reestablishing the relationship
between the art of building and the making of community, through
citizen-based participatory planning and design.

We dedicate ourselves to reclaiming our homes, blocks, streets,
parks, neighborhoods, districts, towns, cities, regions, and environment.

We assert the following principles to guide public policy, development practice, urban planning, and design.

THE REGION: METROPOLIS, CITY, AND TOWN

1. Metropolitan regions are finite places with geographic boundaries derived from topography, watersheds, coastlines, farmlands,
   regional parks, and river basins. The metropolis is made of multiple centers that are cities, towns, and villages, each with its own
   identifiable center and edges.

2. The metropolitan region is a fundamental economic unit of the contemporary world. Governmental cooperation, public policy, physical planning, and economic strategies must reflect this new reality.

3. The metropolis has a necessary and fragile relationship to its agrarian hinterland and natural landscapes. The relationship is environmental, economic, and cultural. Farmland and nature are as important to the metropolis as the garden is to the house.

4. Development patterns should not blur or eradicate the edges of the metropolis. Infill development within existing urban areas conserves environmental resources, economic investment, and social fabric, while reclaiming marginal and abandoned areas. Metropolitan regions should develop strategies to encourage such infill development over peripheral expansion.

5. Where appropriate, new development contiguous to urban boundaries should be organized as neighborhoods and districts, and be integrated with the existing urban pattern. Noncontiguous development should be organized as towns and villages with their own urban edges, and planned for a jobs/housing balance, not as bedroom suburbs.

6. The development and redevelopment of towns and cities should respect historical patterns, precedents, and boundaries.

7. Cities and towns should bring into proximity a broad spectrum of public and private uses to support a regional economy that benefits people of all incomes. Affordable housing should be distributed throughout the region to match job opportunities and to avoid concentrations of poverty.

8. The physical organization of the region should be supported by a framework of transportation alternatives. Transit, pedestrian, and

bicycle systems should maximize access and mobility throughout the region while reducing dependence upon the automobile.

9. Revenues and resources can be shared more cooperatively among the municipalities and centers within regions to avoid destructive competition for tax base and to promote rational coordination of transportation, recreation, public services, housing, and community institutions.

THE NEIGHBORHOOD, THE DISTRICT, AND THE CORRIDOR

1. The neighborhood, the district, and the corridor are the essential elements of development and redevelopment in the metropolis. They form identifiable areas that encourage citizens to take responsibility for their maintenance and evolution.

2. Neighborhoods should be compact, pedestrian-friendly, and mixed-use. Districts generally emphasize a special single use and should follow the principles of neighborhood design when possible. Corridors are regional connectors of neighborhoods and districts; they range from boulevards and rail lines to rivers and parkways.

3. Many activities of daily living should occur within walking distance, allowing independence to those who do not drive, especially the elderly and the young. Interconnected networks of streets should be designed to encourage walking, reduce the number and length of automobile trips, and conserve energy.

4. Within neighborhoods, a broad range of housing types and price levels can bring people of diverse ages, races, and incomes into daily interaction, strengthening the personal and civic bonds essential to an authentic community.

5. Transit corridors, when properly planned and coordinated, can help organize metropolitan structure and revitalize urban centers. In contrast, highway corridors should not displace investment from existing centers.

6. Appropriate building densities and land uses should be within walking distance of transit stops, permitting public transit to become a viable alternative to the automobile.

7. Concentrations of civic, institutional, and commercial activity should be embedded in neighborhoods and districts, not isolated in remote, single-use complexes. Schools should be sized and located to enable children to walk or bicycle to them.

8. The economic health and harmonious evolution of neighborhoods, districts, and corridors can be improved through graphic urban design codes that serve as predictable guides for change.

9. A range of parks, from tot lots and village greens to ball fields and community gardens, should be distributed within neighborhoods. Conservation areas and open lands should be used to define and connect different neighborhoods and districts.

THE BLOCK, THE STREET, AND THE BUILDING

1. A primary task of all urban architecture and landscape design is the physical definition of streets and public spaces as places of shared use.

2. Individual architectural projects should be seamlessly linked to their surroundings. This issue transcends style.

3. The revitalization of urban places depends on safety and security. The design of streets and buildings should reinforce

safe environments, but not at the expense of accessibility and openness.

4. In the contemporary metropolis, development must adequately accommodate automobiles. It should do so in ways that respect the pedestrian and the form of public space.

5. Streets and squares should be safe, comfortable, and interesting to the pedestrian. Properly configured, they encourage walking and enable neighbors to know each other and protect their communities.

6. Architecture and landscape design should grow from local climate, topography, history, and building practice.

7. Civic buildings and public gathering places require important sites to reinforce community identity and the culture of democracy. They deserve distinctive form, because their role is different from that of other buildings and places that constitute the fabric of the city.

8. All buildings should provide their inhabitants with a clear sense of location, weather, and time. Natural methods of heating and cooling can be more resource-efficient than mechanical systems.

9. Preservation and renewal of historic buildings, districts, and landscapes affirm the continuity and evolution of urban society.

ADDITIONAL READING

Alexander, Christopher, et al. *A Pattern Language: Towns, Buildings, Construction.* New York: Oxford University Press, 1977.

Alexander, Christopher, et al. *The Timeless Way of Building.* New York: Oxford University Press, 1979.

Alexander, Christopher, et al. *A New Theory of Urban Design.* New York: Oxford University Press, 1987.

Alvord, Katie. *Divorce Your Car! Ending the Love Affair with the Automobile.* Gabriola Island, British Columbia: New Society Publishers, 2000.

Appleyard, Donald. *Livable Streets.* Berkeley: University of California Press, 1981.

Avidor, Ken. *Roadkill Bill.* Praha, Czech Republic: Carbusters, 2001.

Bacon, Edmund N. *Design of Cities.* New York: Penguin Books, 1974.

Beatley, Timothy. *Green Urbanism: Learning from European Cities.* Washington, D.C.: Island Press, 2000.

Berger, K. T. *Where the Road and the Sky Collide: America Through the Eyes of Its Drivers.* New York: Henry Holt and Company, 1993.

Callenbach, Ernest. *Ecotopia.* New York: Bantam Books, 1975, reissued 1990.

Calthorpe, Peter. *The Next American Metropolis: Ecology, Community, and the American Dream.* Princeton, N.J.: Princeton Architectural Press, 1993.

Calthorpe, Peter, William Fulton, and Robert Fishman. *The Regional City: Planning for the End of Sprawl.* Washington, D.C.: Island Press, 2001.

Crawford, J. H. *Carfree Cities.* Utrecht: International Books, 2000.

Dauncey, Guy, and Patrick Mazza. *Stormy Weather: 101 Solutions to Global Climate Change.* Gabriola Island, British Columbia: New Society Publishers, 2001.

Davis, Mike. *City of Quartz: Excavating the Future in Los Angeles.* New York: Vintage Books, 1992.

Davis, Mike. *Ecology of Fear: Los Angeles and the Imagination of Disaster.* New York: Metropolitan Books, Henry Holt and Company, 1998.

Duany, Andres, and Elizabeth Plater-Zyberk. *Smart Growth Manual.* New York: McGraw-Hill, 2003.

Duany, Andres, Elizabeth Plater-Zyberk, and Jeff Speck. *Suburban Nation: The Rise of Sprawl and the Decline of the American Dream.* New York: North Point Press, 2000.

Dixon, Terrell, ed. *City Wilds: Essays and Stories about Urban Nature.* Athens: University of Georgia Press, 2002.

Durning, Alan Thein. *The Car and the City.* Seattle: Northwest Environment Watch, 1996.

Engwicht, David. *Street Reclaiming: Creating Livable Streets and Vibrant Communities.* Gabriola Island, British Columbia: New Society Publishers, 1999.

Fishman, Robert. *Bourgeois Utopias: The Rise and Fall of Suburbia.* New York: Basic Books, 1989.

Fishman, Robert. *American Planning Tradition: Culture and Policy.* Baltimore: Johns Hopkins University Press, 2000.

Garreau, Joel. *Edge City: Life on the New Frontier.* New York: Anchor Books, 1991.

Gehl, Jan, and Lars Gemzøe. *Public Spaces—Public Life.* Copenhagen: Danish Architectural Press and Royal Danish Academy of Fine Arts, School of Architecture Publishers, 1996.

Gratz, Roberta Brandes. *The Living City: How America's Cities Are Being Revitalized by Thinking Big in a Small Way.* New York: John Wiley and Sons, 1994.

Gratz, Roberta Brandes, and Norman Mintz. *Cities Back from the Edge: New Life for Downtown.* New York: John Wiley and Sons, 1998.

Hall, Peter. *Cities of Tomorrow: An Intellectual History of Urban Planning and Design in the Twentieth Century.* Oxford: Blackwell, 1988.

Hart, Stanley, and Alan Spivak. *The Elephant in the Bedroom: Automobile Dependence and Denial: Impacts on the Economy and Environment.* Pasadena, Calif.: New Paradigm Books, 1993.

Hiss, Tony. *The Experience of Place.* New York: Alfred A. Knopf, 1990.

Howard, Ebenezer. *To-morrow: A Peaceful Path to Real Reform.* London: Swan Sonnenschein, 1898.

Jackson, Kenneth T. *Crabgrass Frontier: The Suburbanization of the United States.* New York: Oxford University Press, 1985.

Jacobs, Jane. *The Death and Life of Great American Cities.* New York: Random House, 1961.

Jacobs, Jane. *Cities and the Wealth of Nations: Principles of Economic Life.* New York: Vintage Books, 1984.

Katz, Peter. *The New Urbanism: Toward an Architecture of Community.* New York: McGraw-Hill, 1994.

Kay, Jane Holtz. *Asphalt Nation: How the Automobile Took Over America, and How We Can Take It Back.* Berkeley: University of California Press, reprint 1998.

Kemmis, Daniel. *The Good City and the Good Life: Renewing the Sense of Community.* New York: Houghton Mifflin, 1995.

Kunstler, James Howard. *The Geography of Nowhere: The Rise and Decline of America's Man-Made Landscape.* New York: Touchstone, 1993.

Kunstler, James Howard. *Home from Nowhere: Remaking Our Everyday World for the Twenty-First Century.* New York: Touchstone, 1996.

Kunstler, James Howard. *The City in Mind: Notes on the Urban Condition.* New York: Free Press, 2002.

Le Corbusier. *The Radiant City.* London: Faber and Faber, 1967.

Leopold, Aldo. *A Sand County Almanac.* New York: Ballantine Books, 1991, originally published in 1949.

Marshall, Alex. *How Cities Work: Suburbs, Sprawl, and the Roads Not Taken.* Austin: University of Texas Press, 2001.

McHarg, Ian L. *Design with Nature.* New York: John Wiley and Sons, 1995.

McKibben, Bill. *The End of Nature.* New York: Doubleday, 1989.

Moe, Richard, and Carter Wilkie. *Changing Places: Rebuilding Community in the Age of Sprawl.* New York: Henry Holt and Company, 1997.

Morrish, William R., and Catherine R. Brown. *Planning to Stay: Learning to See the Physical Features of Your Neighborhood.* Minneapolis: Milkweed Editions, 1994.

Mumford, Lewis. *The City in History: Its Origins, Its Transformations, and Its Prospects.* New York: Harvest Books, 1968.

Norquist, John. *The Wealth of Cities: Revitalizing the Centers of American Life.* New York: Perseus Books, 1999.

Orfield, Myron. *Metropolitics: A Regional Agenda for Community and Stability.* Washington, D.C.: Brookings Institution, 1997.

Register, Richard. *Ecocities: Building Cities in Balance with Nature.* Berkeley, Calif.: Berkeley Hills Books, 2001.

Rogers, Richard. *Cities for a Small Country.* London: Faber & Faber, 2000.

Rudofsky, Barnard. *Streets for People: A Primer for Americans.* New York: Doubleday, 1969.

Rue, Harrison Bright. *Real Towns: Making Your Neighborhood Work.* Charlottesville, Va.: Citizen Planner Institute, 2000.

Rybczynski, Witold. *City Life: Urban Expectations in a New World.* New York: Scribner, 1995.

Spirn, Ann Whiston. *The Granite Garden: Urban Nature and Human Design.* New York: Basic Books, 1985.

Whyte, William H. *City: Rediscovering the Center.* New York: Anchor Books, 1988.

Wolfe, Tom. *From Bauhaus to Our House.* New York: Farrar Straus Giroux, 1981.

Wright, Frank Lloyd. *Frank Lloyd Wright Collected Writings: 1939–1949.* New York: Rizzoli, 1994.

Zuckermann, Wolfgang. *End of the Road: From World Car Crisis to Sustainable Transportation.* White River Junction, Vt.: Chelsea Green Publishing Company, 1991.

PUBLIC INTEREST ORGANIZATIONS

Design Center for American Urban Landscape
www.cala.umn.edu/design_center/dcaul.html
The center's mission is to educate public and private decision makers, professionals, and citizens about the value of design as a strategic partner with economic and human interests in the making of community-based development strategies and sustainable urban landscapes. Recent projects have examined issues of urban redevelopment, suburban redesign, collaborative planning, urban place making, and metropolitan coordination, in cooperation with communities, public agencies, students, and the private sector.

Friends of the Mississippi River
www.fmr.org
Friends of the Mississippi River advocates a new vision for the Mississippi, especially the river and its watershed in the Twin Cities metropolitan area. Through active leadership and education, FMR seeks to preserve and restore the river's fish and wildlife, its vital floodplains and scenic bluffs, its natural and cultural treasures, its beauty and its romance.

Great River Greening
www.greatrivergreening.org
Great River Greening is a nonprofit, community-based organization that restores and maintains urban natural resources throughout the Twin Cities river valleys in partnership with public and private landowners and citizen volunteers.

Institute for Agriculture and Trade Policy
www.iatp.org
The Institute for Agriculture and Trade Policy promotes resilient family farms, rural communities, and ecosystems around the world through research and education, science and technology, and advocacy.

International Making Cities Livable Council
www.livablecities.org
The council is an interdisciplinary, international network of individuals and cities dedicated to making our cities and communities more livable. Council members are active in organizing and participating in conferences held twice a year, once in North America and once in Europe, and in publishing books, consulting, teaching, and improving the livability of their own cities.

Minnesota Center for Environmental Advocacy
www.mncenter.org
The center is a private, nonprofit organization working to protect and restore Minnesota's natural resources through sound science, public policy, and legal expertise. MCEA uses legal action and legislative advocacy, as well as research, communications, and collaborations, to improve Minnesota's environment.

Minnesota Department of Natural Resources Metro Greenways
www.dnr.state.mn.us/greenways
Metro Greenways helps local governments and citizens more effectively incorporate nature into their communities. By coordinating funding sources, providing technical assistance and grants, and identifying significant natural features, the program empowers communities to preserve the resources that are important to them in a way that earns local support.

Minnesota Land Trust
www.mnland.org
The trust permanently protects the lands and waters that define communities and enrich quality of life by establishing and monitoring conservation easements—legal agreements by which landowners voluntarily limit the development potential and use of their land. The trust is the only Minnesota-wide organization that extensively uses conservation easements as a preservation strategy.

Natural Resources Defense Council
www.nrdc.org/cities/smartgrowth
NRDC employs diverse strategies to make cities healthier and more livable. With offices in New York and Los Angeles, it is improving the environment of the two biggest U.S. cities—and proving it can be done in all urban areas.

The Priorities Institute
www.priorities.org
The institute is dedicated to sustainable land planning, car-free city design, holistic indexing, and twenty-first-century constitutions.

Sierra Club
www.sierraclub.org
The Sierra Club is a nonprofit, member-supported public-interest organization that promotes conservation of the natural environment by influencing public policy decisions: legislative, administrative, legal, and electoral. Hundreds of urban, suburban, and rural neighborhoods are choosing to manage sprawl with smart-growth solutions. The Sierra Club is calling attention to the problem of sprawl with yearly reports, providing resources for activists across the country, and exploring how transportation patterns can be improved to make neighborhoods safer and more convenient.

Smart Growth America
www.smartgrowthamerica.com
This nationwide coalition promotes a better way to grow: one that protects farmland and open space, revitalizes neighborhoods, keeps housing affordable, and provides more transportation choices. With more than 100 partner organizations across the nation, Smart Growth America is working to realize a shared vision of growth that protects the environment while developing the economy, advances social equity, promotes affordable housing and community development, and preserves farmland.

Smart Growth Network

www.smartgrowth.org

In 1996, the U.S. Environmental Protection Agency joined with several nonprofit and government organizations to form the Smart Growth Network in response to increasing community concerns about the need for new ways to grow that boost the economy, protect the environment, and enhance community vitality. The network's partners include environmental groups, historic preservation organizations, professional organizations, developers, real estate interests, and local and state government entities.

Sustainable Communities Network

www.sustainable.org

Around the country, citizens are coming together to create a vision of what their communities might be and to make these visions come true. These efforts to create "healthy," "livable," "sustainable" communities are integrative, inclusive, and participatory. In many communities—large and small, rural and urban—issues are being addressed in an interconnected manner, demonstrating how innovative strategies can produce communities that are more environmentally sound, economically prosperous, and socially equitable.

The Trust for Public land

www.tpl.org

Founded in 1972, the Trust for Public Land is the only national nonprofit working exclusively to protect land for human enjoyment and well-being. TPL helps conserve land for recreation and spiritual nourishment and to improve the health and quality of life of American communities. Its Green Cities Initiative helps create parks and protect greenspace in urban areas, where 80 percent of Americans live, work, and play. TPL has helped nearly twenty cities complete more than 250 park projects.

SUBJECT INDEX

Aalborg, Denmark, 240–41
Agricultural lands: urban growth and, 216, 218
AIDS, 273
Air pollution. *See* Pollution
Alternative fuels, 267–69
Ameregis, 254–55
America WALKS, 252
American Association of State Highway and Transportation Officials (AASHTO), 252–53
Amsterdam, Netherlands: bicycles and bicycle ways, 232
Ann Arbor (Mich.), 58
Aquapolis (periodical), 107–8
Arboretums, 69–70
Architecture: New Urbanism and, 281–82
Arctic National Wildlife Refuge, 64, 71–72
Army Corps of Engineers, 128, 133
Arrington, G. B., 248
Art, public, 230
Atlanta, Ga.: commuting, 213; oil dependence, future and, 274; sprawl, 213; traffic accidents, 251
Automobile industry, 57–58
Automobiles: cartoons, x, 41–52; costs, 39, 244; dependence on, 51, 243–44, 265; disadvantages of, 57–58; dominance of, 246, 250; environment and, 41–42, 50, 270; future of, 265; influence of, x; isolation and, 164–65; Kunstler on, x; monopoly, effect, 44–46; New Urbanism and, 282; oil dependence and, 49, 269–70; planning and, 250; pollution and, 43, 50, 58; psychological aspects, 41–42; public policy, 248–50; road rage, 43–47, 61; sprawl and, 43, 48, 50, 58. *See also* Commuting; Oil, dependence on
Avidor, Ken, x, 41, 52

Baltimore, Md.: Harbor Place, 124; light rail, 247–48
Bartholdi, Frédéric Auguste, 13
Bender, Richard, 108–9
Bennett, Edward, 122

Bergen, N.J.: light rail, 247
Bergen, Norway: traffic-pricing, 241
"Better Edge, A" (James Sanders), 113
Beverly Hills, Calif.: streets and roads, 254
Bicycles and bicycle ways: connectivity and, 226; environment and, 243; in Europe, 232, 234–37, 245; New Urbanism and, 280; public planning and, 250; safety issues, 253
Big Bend National Park, Tex., 71–72
"Big Dig." *See* Boston, Mass.
Birds, in urban areas, 65–70, 92
Bishop, Elizabeth, 147
Black persons: education, 192–93; employment, 190; housing, 172–73, 183–84, 186, 190; poverty, effects, 192–93; wealth accumulation, 189
Bogota, Columbia: busways, 248
Bogren, Scott, 248
Boston, Mass.: architecture, 12–14, 15, 16–17; Back Bay, 10, 12, 13; Beacon Hill, 10; "Big Dig," 105, 148–51; bridges, 155; buildings, scale, 11, 14, 16; change, 5–10, 12–13, 16–18; Chinatown, 11; churches, 12–14, 16; Combat Zone, 11; commuting, 33, 36–37; construction, economic aspects, 10; Copley Square, 14; cultural diversity, 3, 5–6, 13, 34–35, 155; Custom House Tower, 4, 150; Deer Island, 145–46, 148; dirt, 3; financial district, 15; Flour and Grain Exchange, 150; harbor, 146–48, 152–55; highways, 16, 148–49, 251; homeless persons, 18; hotels, 16; housing, 151; immigrants and immigration, 13; infrastructure, 145, 148–49, 154; James Hook Lobster Company, 150, 155; Ladder Blocks, 11; libraries, 14; museums, 32, 34; nature and natural areas, 147; New England Aquarium, 150; New Land, 13; noise, 3, 154; open space, 149–51; parking facilities, 18; parks and parklands, 17, 105, 147–56; pedestrian ways, 153, 155; pollution, 22, 147; public transit, 34–35, 149; Quincy Market, 124, 150; railroads, 148–49; recreational facilities, 155–56; redevelopment, 11–12, 124; restaurants, 11–12; South Boston, 11; South Station, 150; streets and

Transportation and Regional Growth, xi
Trent, William, 192
Trias, Ramon, 215, 224–25
Trinity Church (Boston, Mass.), 14, 16
Trolley systems, 202
Trondheim, Norway: traffic-pricing, 241
Twin Cities (Minn.): busways, 248; housing, regional cooperation, 196–97; land use, xi; livability, 93–95; public-private partnerships, xv; public transit, xii; riverfront development, xv; sprawl, xii; transportation, xi–xii. *See also* Minneapolis, Minn.

Unitarian-Universalist Arlington Street Church (Boston, Mass.), 13–14
University Place (Tacoma, Wash.): traffic-calming, 223; urban revitalization, 214
Urban revitalization: light rail and, 248; New Urbanism and, 281–82; public transit and, 248; regional revitalization and, 254; revenue sharing, 239–40, 254
U.S. Conference of Mayors, 201

Vancouver, Canada: railroads, 247
Vanderslice, Ellen, 252
Vaux, Calvert, 117
Veenendaal, Netherlands: bicycles and bicycle ways, 235
Venice, Italy: planning, 232
Ventura, Calif., 171–72
Veterans Administration, 189
Voith, Richard, 255
Voting: cumulative, 204; housing and, 194, 204; public participation, 204
Voting Rights Act (1965), 193–94

Wages: housing costs and, 185, 202; job accessibility and, 190
Walkable Communities, Inc., 214, 226
Walker Art Center (Minneapolis, Minn.), 126
Walking: advantages of, 60–61, 63; arboretums, 69–70; in cities, 33; community and, 59–60, 214, 225–26; disadvantages of, 61–62; environment and, 243; in Europe, 234; future and, 270–71; New Urbanism and, 245; sauntering, 64–65, 71, 75–76; social aspects, 59–60, 64; spiritual aspects,

71, 76; in suburbs, 29, 33; urban nature walks, 65–71
Walljasper, Jay, 231, 261
Wastewater treatment facilities, 143, 145–48
Water management: public policy, xii
Water pollution. *See* Pollution
Water rights, 145
Water supply, xii, 274–75
Waterfront Center, 107
Waterfronts: maritime industry and, 97–98, 107; redevelopment, x, 53, 107–10, 124. *See also* Minneapolis, Minn., riverfront, development; New York City waterfront, redevelopment
Watsonville, Calif.: bicycle ways, 221; bridges, 220–22, 227; business and community development, 215–22, 227–29; earthquakes, 220; employment, 220; farms and farmlands, 216, 218; firefighters, 219; highways, 220, 222; housing, 214–16, 220–22, 227; immigrants and immigration, 215–16, 219; levees, 220–21; neighborhoods, 216, 222, 225, 227–28; open space, 222, 227–28; parks and parklands, 221–22, 227; planning, 218; recreational facilities, 222; redistricting, 219; smart growth, 216, 218, 228–29; social services, 219; sprawl, 218; streets and roads, 227–28; traffic-calming, 222–23, 227; walking audits, 225; wetlands, 220, 222, 228
Wellesley, Mass.: streets and roads, 253
West Germany: elections, 204
Weston, Reiko, 128
Wetlands, 92, 242
Wilderness, 71–74, 77, 242
Wildlife: in urban areas, 67–68, 72
Willamette Pedestrian Coalition (Ore.), 252
World Trade Center (N.Y.), 111

Xavier, Valencio, 166–67

Zelle Family, 128
Zoning: change and, 217; gentrification and, 188; housing and, 188, 198; political aspects, xiii
Zwolle, Netherlands: bicycles and bicycle ways, 235

EMILIE BUCHWALD is publisher emeritus of Milkweed Editions, which she cofounded in 1979. Buchwald has edited more than 185 books and is the author of two award-winning children's books. She has taught English literature, poetry, and writing for children. Buchwald received a Ph.D. in English literature from the University of Minnesota, and in 2001 the university awarded her an honorary doctor of humane letters degree. She was named the McKnight Distinguished Artist for 2002.

Buchwald and her husband, Henry, live in a first-ring suburb of Minneapolis, from which it takes twenty minutes to get downtown, except during the lengthening number of hours misleadingly called "rush," when it seems to take forever.

MORE BOOKS ON

The World As Home

FROM

MILKWEED ⬯ EDITIONS

To order books or for more information,
contact Milkweed at (800) 520-6455
or visit our website (www.worldashome.org).

The Credo Series

THE WORLD AS HOME, the nonfiction publishing program of Milkweed Editions, is dedicated to exploring our relationship to the natural world. Not espousing any particular environmentalist or political agenda, these books are a forum for distinctive literary writing that not only alerts the reader to vital issues but offers personal testimonies to living harmoniously with other species in urban, rural, and wilderness communities.

MILKWEED EDITIONS publishes with the intention of making a humane impact on society, in the belief that literature is a transformative art uniquely able to convey the essential experiences of the human heart and spirit. To that end, Milkweed publishes distinctive voices of literary merit in handsomely designed, visually dynamic books, exploring the ethical, cultural, and esthetic issues that free societies need continually to address. Milkweed Editions is a not-for-profit press.

JOIN US

Since its genesis as *Milkweed Chronicle* in 1979, Milkweed has helped hundreds of emerging writers reach their readers. Thanks to the generosity of foundations and of individuals like you, Milkweed Editions is able to continue its nonprofit mission of publishing books chosen on the basis of literary merit—the effect they have on the human heart and spirit—rather than on the basis of how they impact the bottom line. That's a miracle that our readers have made possible.

In addition to purchasing Milkweed books, you can join the growing community of Milkweed supporters. Individual contributions of any amount are both meaningful and welcome. Contact us for a Milkweed catalog or log on to www.milkweed.org and click on "About Milkweed," then "Supporting Milkweed," to find out about our donor program, or simply call (800) 520-6455 and ask about becoming one of Milkweed's contributors. As a nonprofit press, Milkweed belongs to you, the community. Milkweed's board, its staff, and especially the authors whose careers you help launch thank you for reading our books and supporting our mission in any way you can.

Interior design by Christian Fünfhausen.
Typeset in EricSans 28/15 and Granjon 11.5/15
by Stanton Publication Services on the
Pagewing Digital Publishing System.
Printed on acid-free 50# Perfection Antique Recycled paper
by Maple-Vail Book Manufacturing.